THE TEXAS BANKER

THE TEXAS BANKER
The Life and Times of
Fred Farrel Florence

H. Harold Wineburgh

Foreword by Willis M. Tate

Dallas, Texas

IN MEMORY
OF
FRED FARREL FLORENCE

THIS BOOK IS DEDICATED TO
HELEN, DAVID, AND CECILE
AND THE MULTITUDE OF MEN AND WOMEN
WHO HELPED FRED REALIZE HIS VISION
AND IN SO DOING
ENRICHED THEIR OWN LIVES

CONTENTS

W. 767

FOREWORD

Fred Florence is a legend. Fred Florence needed some time to become recognized as a legend, because so many of the wonderful things done by this man were accomplished in private or in confidence. Slowly the magnanimity of his legend takes form as more and more testimony confirms the greatness of his mind and spirit. His helpful, humanitarian concern and generosity take form as a dimension of the reputation of his integrity and business genius.

But if a legend is a story, it needs a teller, and here we have the right person to collect and tell of the human miracles and wonder of this fabulous man.

Only a person of unusual sensitivity could collect and organize the flood of rich anecdotes and experiences that came to light after the death of Fred Florence. Born in New York, a scion of a prominent New York family, and a graduate of Princeton University, the author was a contrast in background to Fred, who was the son of a Lithuanian immigrant who migrated to the piney woods of East Texas. Maybe the contrast of experiences in their youth gave Harold Wineburgh the sensitivity to the genius of Fred Florence. Certainly their value systems were attuned. Their common love of what was important, what was exciting, and what was beautiful and meaningful is abundantly apparent in the word portrait that we have of Fred.

The recorder of a legend must have a sense of the flow of factual history as well as the subtle meanings of actions and words. Only a man of letters, educated to literary discipline could be adequate for the telling of the legend.

The task of telling the Fred Florence story is complicated by the never ending revelation of material. Each day a new story about the humane influence Fred had on others came to light. Each time a chapter was finished, new exciting experiences that people and institutions had with Fred became known for the first time. Even when a legend has to be confined between the covers of a book, Harold lets us read between the lines to enhance our love and admiration of a man without resorting to sentimentality.

The whole legend was made possible by Helen Florence. This life partner of Fred became his security and the one who understood and encouraged him. This marvelous lady of strength and culture gave support and magnificence to the legend. How marvelous it is to have her wealth of experience and understanding to guide and verify the colorful life of Fred Florence through the trust and affectionate confidence that she has for the author.

Fred Florence was human. He made mistakes, and one can find decisions that turned out unhappily. He pressed hard and expected much from those around him. He knew that success depended on hard work and utilizing every resource. His simple, direct approach in problem solving was never understood completely by his peers. Nevertheless, Fred is remembered for his manifold instances of successful genius and humane concern.

Everyone who knew Fred has a story to tell. I am no exception. Once in a Board of Governor's meeting at Southern Methodist University a problem arose on how to return a scholarship fund of $10,000 to Kansas Methodists. The Methodist churches in that state provided the money to fund scholarships for theology students from that state who attended Perkins School of Theology at S.M.U.—In the meantime a new school of theology had been organized in Kansas City, and the S.M.U. Board wanted to return the scholarship fund to the new school. The S.M.U. lawyer maintained that the giving away of S.M.U. assets was illegal

ii

and could not be done. Finally Fred spoke up and asked if a $10,000 check from him to the new Methodist Seminary would solve the problem—a simple solution but remarkable since it came from a Jew, who didn't even know there was a Methodist Seminary in Kansas.

The legend of Fred Florence is important to Dallas, to Texas, to banking, to citizenship at its best, and to the many who called him friend. It is providential that those who come after him will have a record of his achievement and a suitable telling of the legend.

WILLIS M. TATE

INTRODUCTION

Volumes have been written about the world's Hannibals, Caesars, and Aga Khans, about Casanova, the Rothschilds, Livermore, and many other legendary giants. We know of our great political leaders, our prophets and sages, our great writers and artists, the scientists, explorers, and humanitarians. My story about Fred Florence reaches into a simpler but, in a way, greater realm than that of the giants I mention. This is the story of a man who fits into a special niche of his own. Although he was a man of large talents who achieved considerable prominence and influence, he was not driven by the desire for personal power. Although he did become a success financially, he made no attempt to amass a truly great fortune for himself and his family. He never thought of himself as a Napoleon or a Baruch. Instead he was a gentle combination of a fine friend, a loving husband, a good citizen, and, above all, a *builder*, in the broadest sense of the word.

Though he never knew the full impact of his efforts, Fred Florence helped to build one of the greatest metropolitan areas in the world. In 1920, Dallas was a nice, small, residential city with a population of slightly over 150,000. Today Dallas is the financial center of the Southwest and, with its environs, has a population of over two million—the seventh largest city in our nation. The Republic National Bank, which Fred was associated with for forty years, is today the second largest bank in the United States outside of New York, Chicago, and the West Coast. The Republic of Texas Corporation, which owns the Republic National Bank, has assets of more than $14,000,000,000.

There were other banks in Dallas before Republic, and other bankers besides Fred Florence who helped make

Dallas what it is today, and I do not intend to take away any credit that rightfully belongs to them. But I do believe that Fred Florence provided the essential element of leadership for the entire banking and business communities of Dallas. He had a knack for finding ways for almost everyone involved in a given situation to come out a winner. With his keen perception, he was able to see common goals for seemingly diverse interest groups, and he inspired people to work together for their mutual benefit. Fred was a man of extraordinary imagination, vision, and determination: he dreamed big, and he made those dreams come true. He had confidence in people, and they had confidence in him. His foresight, guidance, and practical administrative assistance were instrumental in the building of many Dallas-based companies.

I met Fred in the early fall of 1923 and, over the years, had many personal experiences with him, but it was not until his death in 1960 that many of us came to realize his greatness. The Southland Life Insurance Company's Board of Directors (of which Fred was a member) passed a Memorial Resolution, shortly after his death, which I would like to quote here in part:

MEMORIAL RESOLUTION TO
FRED FARREL FLORENCE

Fred Farrel Florence, one of the master builders of Dallas, departed this life on December 25, 1960. In his death the City of Dallas, the State of Texas and the Nation suffered a great loss. Although he was an outstanding banker and businessman, he was first and foremost a great citizen and a great American. Rising from the humblest beginnings, he recorded truly outstanding achievements in his chosen field of banking, but his success in banking was exceeded by his deep and abiding compassion for service to his fellow men of all races and creeds.

During a long and fruitful life, he received honors and tributes too numerous to list in full, but notable among these were the first Dallas banker to be elected President of the American Bankers Association; the Linz Award in 1944; the Dallas Dintinguished Salesman Award for 1954; three Honorary Doctor of Law Degrees; the Benemerenti Award, the Roman Catholic Church's highest decoration for a nonmember; the 1959 Distinguished Civic Service Award of the Greater Dallas Planning Council; and a building on the campus of Southern Methodist University named in his honor. His personal philanthropies were legion. No worthy call for help was ever unheeded by him.

On February 21, 1928, Fred was married to Helen Lefkowitz, who is now my wife. We were married on March 1, 1964. Both Helen and I had previously enjoyed many years of matrimonial happiness. My deceased wife Hortense and I had been married for 37 years. Since our social activities were different, Helen knew Horty and me only casually. As you shall see, Fred Florence and I had been business friends, and our paths had crossed much more often than those of our spouses.

One evening in early 1971, the Mayor of Dallas, J. Erik Jonsson, appeared on television in a farewell interview. After six years of service, he was retiring, leaving behind a remarkable record of achievement. During his term as Mayor, Dallas had earned the title of "The All-American City." Mayor Jonsson, a director of the Republic National Bank of Dallas, had also been one of the founders of Texas Instruments. During the interview, he gave great credit to Fred Florence for helping start this great industrial company. Naturally, Mayor Jonsson's reference to Fred pleased Helen. A few days later the Mayor and I were waiting for our cars in the Republic garage, whereupon I thanked him for his kind words. He told me that Fred had made it

3

possible for many Dallas companies to become successful. He then suggested that someone should write Fred's biography. I told this to Helen, and her one-woman unanimous decision elected me. Because Helen and I had such mutual admiration for our former spouses, and even today have their pictures on our dressing table, this decision seemed quite natural. Jokingly, I told her that if I wrote it, I could entitle it *My Wife's First Husband*.

Most people, at some time, have a desire to write a book. In 1968, I privately published my autobiography, which I called *A Boy, A Man...An Era*. I liked it because I felt that some day some descendant would discover through it that the old portrait on the wall was that of a real human being and not just a meaningless character out of the past. Many of my friends enjoyed my story, and I am inclined to think that even some of my family read the book. This modicum of success encouraged me to a second endeavor in 1970 titled *Reflections*, in which I wrote a few additional things about myself and about some of my travels. This brought forth many compliments and only a few minor disagreements, so I decided to quit while I was ahead. However, the persistent urge for personal expression prompted me to write *Reflections II*, which has recently been released.

4   I am convinced that writing a biography is more difficult than any other form of literature because no two people see other people alike. My first three books were easier because I was part of the story and I wrote it as I saw it. No one knew the subject from my standpoint better than I, so there could be little disagreement. You can judge a scientific treatise by how well the author observes certain rules of scientific inquiry—or if you know nothing about the subject, you may just accept his word blindly. Fiction is fiction, and you either like it or you don't. Humor makes you

laugh, or you just don't find it funny. A biography relies totally on the ability of the author to capture the subject's image—a different image, reached by each individual who has known him. Often I have seen a portrait of a person that I felt was a great likeness, yet have heard it violently criticized by others who were also close friends.

I was aware of the enormity of the undertaking. As I began to write and found the research to be endless, I wondered whether my original apprehension should ever have let me start. Perhaps I saw the difficulty of the task even more clearly when I read Fred's obituary in the *Texas Bankers Record* of January, 1961, which I quote:

> Chronicling the obituary of even a financial genius, an amazing city builder, a business wizard with true story-book magic, a nationally admired and respected man, such as Mr. Florence was, is a rather easy task. Reporting the worth of such a man to his country, to his friends, to his loved ones left behind, is something else again—something to tax the reporter's skill.

Soon after I began this project, I realized that I could use some help from an experienced historian. I phoned Harry Ransom, then Chancellor of the University of Texas, who immediately agreed to give me whatever information and advice he could. Greatly encouraged to know that I would have professional help, I began working harder. Some months later, Harry was stricken with a fatal heart attack. After this tragedy I lost all interest in the book, and it was several years later before the Florence family persuaded me to go back to work.

In writing the story of Fred's life, I had what I thought was the best source of information right at hand. Many friends have told me that the task should be easy with Fred's devoted wife Helen readily available to supply infor-

5

mation not documented and an insight into the man's intimate feelings. In a way they were right. Helen certainly knew Fred better than anyone. However, sometimes it was much like the saying about not being able to see the forest for the trees. Her closeness to Fred made it difficult for her to see the total picture. Therefore, in addition to Helen's information, I will draw this picture from his accomplishments; from the voluminous and well-preserved family archives; from what hundreds have said or have written; and from my own experiences with him. Also, I found so many of Fred's friends who were enthusiastic about helping, that the fund of information made me wonder how one man, in the short span of life allotted to him, could have done everything he did. Each hour of research led into new fields, many of which will never be fully explored.

At first Helen seemed shy about working with me on the book, although always anxious to help. As time went by she became more a part of the project. This usually occurred when I would ask her to read a draft of something I had written. Sometimes I became a little controversial to provoke a discussion, and usually a slightly different angle of Fred's character would emerge.

Were it not that I was one of Fred's great admirers, I could not qualify in any way as his biographer. I know that many knew him far better and more intimately than I. I am aware that my history will miss much—there *was* so much. I shall err in a few facts because my informants erred. I may lay greater stress on one thing than another because to me it had more importance. That doesn't mean that my judgment was right. I have taken the liberty of injecting some of my own experiences with Fred, as I felt that these quite definitely throw light on his way of doing things. I have further been presumptuous by including my own comments and philosophy, which in most instances paralleled Fred's.

In my research, I have uncovered some of the deep-rooted jealousies that inevitably occur from time to time in personal relationships among business associates. Some may have expected an advancement and were passed over, or they may have made a suggestion which they thought deserved praise and action, and it was shelved. I have attempted to understand and to take from my interviews the true facts, eliminating any erroneous impressions not shared by others. In the final analysis, the following is what I have uncovered and written as I see it.

My only regret is that I did not know Fred better so that I could have learned of many more of his deeds and actions that should be recorded. I regret that I did not have the opportunity to observe him more closely and to learn more from his philosophy. Hopefully, these words will fittingly document the life story of this great man. Often while writing, I have wondered how Fred would have written his own story.

CHAPTER I
EARLY HISTORY

Life was hard for Jews in Czarist Russia in the latter part of the nineteenth century—a life of ghetto isolation, intolerable persecution, and constant fear. However, it still could not have been easy for Moses and Celia Fromowitz to decide to leave their native Lithuania and brave the uncertainties of the New World. To do so required the same kind of vision and determination that their son Fred Florence would exhibit many years later. Undoubtedly, one of the strongest motivations for Moses and Celia was the dream of a better life and greater opportunities for their children. In Fred's life—and the lives of his brothers and sisters as well—this dream was to be fulfilled to a degree they would not have thought possible.

Moses was born in Kretinga, Lithuania, on September 20, 1844, and Celia on September 18, 1863. Kretinga is in the southern part of Lithuania, then known as Memel, and is located about 20 miles inland from the Baltic Sea. Before he married Celia, Moses had been married to her sister, Marguerite, who I presume died young although there is no record of the date of her death. Apparently the two sisters were quite close, because Moses and Marguerite named their daughter, born June 6, 1875, Celia for her aunt, who would later become her stepmother. Helen tells me that Fred and his other brothers and sisters never thought of their half-sister Celia as a *half*-sister, but simply as their sister.

According to a newspaper account of Fred's mother's death in 1938, she and Moses Fromowitz were married in Lithuania in 1881. If this date is correct, she was 18 years old and Moses was 37 at the time of their marriage. Fred's brother Meyer, known as "Mike," was born in Lithuania on December 28, 1882. In 1883, the family came to this country and settled in New York City. During the years before they moved to Texas, three children were born: Jennie on March 15, 1884, Nathan on January 15, 1890, and Fred on November 5, 1891. Rebecca was born November 20, 1895, after the family had moved to Rusk, Texas. She became known as "Bobbie," and at this writing is the only survivor of that generation. Family records list another child, Charley, who was born on June 4, 1896, and died October 20, 1899. I am told that he was born prematurely and was a sickly child. However, it is obvious that there is some kind of discrepancy in the dates of his birth and Bobbie's. If these dates were correct, Charley would have been born—-and survived the birth—only six months and two weeks after Bobbie was born—and even for the Florence family, this seems a bit improbable.

In a memorandum dictated by Fred on December 1, 1927, he says that his parents moved from New York City to New Birmingham, Texas in 1892, and later moved to nearby Rusk in 1894. His living heirs put his age at becoming a Texan somewhere between four months and eight months old. It is safe to surmise that it was in the spring of 1892 that the Fromowitz family came to Texas, but there seems to be no positive record of the motivation. While no one can predict the future of a child, I venture to say that the move gave Fred an opportunity that he probably would not have had in New York. I want to think that the boom in New Birmingham, Texas was the inducement that caused the emigration. I could find no information as to where the family lived in New Birmingham or what Mr. Fromowitz did there for a living. I am inclined to think that they actually moved to Rusk in the very beginning. New Birmingham adjoined Rusk, which in 1890 had an official population of 1,383.

In October, 1891, the New Birmingham Development Company published a booklet in which the city was called the "Iron Queen of the Southwest." It had many pictures of the iron ore sitting on top of the ground and a picture of the Southern Hotel, a fantastic structure for a brand new town, having been built at a cost of $150,000 with seventy-five rooms and an eighty-foot long bar. The registers of this palatial hostelry include the names of Grover Cleveland, R. B. Roosevelt (uncle of Theodore Roosevelt), Jay Gould, and Texas Governor James S. Hogg. The booklet contained a considerable amount of advertising for the railroads, and even an advertisement for Eastman Kodak. The New Birmingham Building Company advertised shares of stock predicted to pay dividends of from 15% to 20%; the money was needed to build workmen's cottages.

The story, as written then, follows in full:

THE CITY OF NEW BIRMINGHAM

Is situated in Cherokee County, in the center of the iron ore deposits of East Texas, on the Tyler Southeastern Railroad, a part of the Cotton Belt System. This branch was purchased by the Cotton Belt with a view to giving them an outlet to the Gulf at Sabine Pass.

The Dallas Trunk Line, now in operation from Dallas to Cedar, and pointed for New Orleans, will pass through New Birmingham. This line has recently been acquired by the Southern Pacific interest and will, no doubt, be pushed with vigor.

The recently chartered road (the Rusk, New Birm-

11

ingham & Palestine) will give us another valuable connection with the International & Great Northern at the latter place.

Further, there is every inducement for new railroads to build to this city, in the fact that the freight from the three furnaces and two pipe plants, now in operation and building, together with the commercial business of Rusk and New Birmingham, will amount to from $350,000 to $400,000 per annum.

New Birmingham is midway between St. Louis and New Orleans, and is within a night's journey of the important cities of Texas, such as Galveston, Houston, Austin, San Antonio, Fort Worth, Dallas and Waco. It has no large city near enough to interfere with its trade. The nearest competitive iron producing point is more than 500 miles distant, and this fact gives New Birmingham undisputed possession of the great markets of Mexico, Texas, Louisiana, Mississippi, Arkansas, Kansas, Nebraska, Colorado, New Mexico, together with all the Central and South American countries.

On the 12th of November, 1888, New Birmingham had not a house completed. It was entirely in the woods. Today, with nearly 400 buildings completed and occupied, she claims, and justly so, a population of 1500. The streets are graded, and houses and streets lighted with electricity; the business houses are the best class of brick buildings; it boasts a street railway and a magnificent hotel, the Southern, with all modern improvements. The industries represented today are two blast furnaces, a pipe foundry, planing mill, sash and door factory, bottling works, ice factory, steam laundry, and steam bakery, and other industries being negotiated for.

New Birmingham, as a place to live, has no superior in Texas. It lies 590 feet above tide-water, with a residence plateau 160 feet more elevated, being the highest point between Tyler and the Gulf. It is above the fever line, and sickness is almost unknown.

Its proximity to the Gulf affords a Gulf breeze day and night, and this fact and its elevation makes it probably the coolest city in the South.

12

The water, which is freestone, is clear, cold, and plentiful, besides which are numerous sulphur and chalybeate springs.*

The city being built upon hills, the most beautiful views can be obtained from many points.

Taking into consideration these natural advantages, together with its valuable products, especially iron, and its being located in the center of the greatest market in the world, we see every reason why New Birmingham will soon have a large population and be one of the strongest and most profitable manufacturing cities in the Southwest.

New Birmingham enjoys postal, telegraph, express, banking, and insurance facilities for conducting business with all the world.

COME TO NEW BIRMINGHAM . . .
A WORD TO THE WISE IS SUFFICIENT . . .

The 46-page booklet, not counting the six pages of "ads," gives many interesting statistics and shows many enticing pictures. The Rusk Tourist Committee, which reproduced this booklet in 1968, comments:

The national panic of 1893, the passage of the Texas Alien Land Law (which discouraged foreign investment), and a disastrous fire at the largest furnace, the "Tassie Belle," combined to bring about insurmountable financial problems which sounded the death knell of New Birmingham.

By the end of the 19th Century, the "Iron Queen" was numbered among Texas ghost cities."

Even Rusk had suffered. The record shows that the 1890 population of 1,383 had dropped to only 846 by

* Actually the springs became popular in 1885 because of iron-rich mineral water—used for baths and drinking to improve the appetite.

1900. At the peak of the boom, New Birmingham had had more than 3,500 persons.

Some of my readers may never have been to East Texas. For that matter, many who live in the large metropolitan cities may believe that our great State is composed entirely of just three parts: a valley that grows citrus fruits and vegetables; a panhandle (God only knows how far away) that grows wheat; and a vast expanse of prairie and desert west of Fort Worth that supplies our markets with cattle, plus the oil which has made *everybody* rich!

There are many beautiful parts of Texas, but there are none that surpass the heavy foliage of the Piney Woods, the beautiful evergreen live oaks, the flowering dogwood, and the magnificent vistas from the hill tops of East Texas. These counties are enriched with lakes, truck farms that grow superb melons and world famous tomatoes, and the rose gardens of Tyler, the area's principal city, which is called "The City of Roses." It is easy to understand why this place in which Fred had his beginnings gave him a great loyalty to Texas and the tranquility that lay beneath his driving energy.

The Fromowitz house was at 206 Barron Street in Rusk, and it still stands in good condition. Fred's half-sister Celia, who was sixteen years older than he, married Ben Wolins, a successful salesman, and they lived in the house next door. Tragically, Ben died at an early age, killed in a flash flood. Fred's father operated a dry goods store, which was next to the bank. Both buildings still stand. All of Fred's brothers, who eventually moved to Dallas, became highly regarded business men. Jennie and Bobbie became housewives.

Only a few years after Moses came to Rusk, he applied for citizenship. When Fred was eighteen years old, clerk Alex Black of Cherokee County proclaimed M. E. Fromowitz (Fred's oldest brother, then twenty-seven years old)

14

and his family henceforth to have the name of Florence:

Cause No. 6013

Exparte M. E. Fromowitz *et al*

In the District Court of Cherokee County Texas, 1st day of January 1910. This day coming on to be heard the application of M. E. Fromowitz for himself and as next best friend for Fred F. Fromowitz, Nathan Fromowitz and Rebecca Fromowitz, wherein they pray that their names be changed to M. E. Florence, Fred F. Florence, Nathan Florence, and Rebecca Florence, and appearing to the court that the name of Fromowitz is a name that was adopted by the fathers of said petitioners in this cause because he desired to evade military service under the laws of Russia, and that said petitioners, *desired that they bear the name originally borne by their ancestors*; and the court having heard the evidence, and being convinced that good ground is set forth in the application filed herein, and that it is for the best interests of the applicants, is of the opinion that said application should be in all things granted by the court that the name of M. E. Fromowitz shall hereafter be M. E. Florence, that the name of Fred F. Fromowitz, shall hereafter be Fred F. Florence, and the name of Nathan Fromowitz, shall hereafter be Nathan Florence, that the name of Rebecca Fromowitz shall hereafter be Rebecca Florence.

The name change document is interesting because it gives an answer to the question of where they got the name Florence. However, it is unlikely that this was an ancestral name. Helen and I know that Florence is an English name and by no stretch of the imagination Russian. This statement in the proclamation was probably used to conform with a law requiring a reason.

Apparently, Fred had only a middle initial, but as time progressd, he was pressed for a middle name and took the name Farrel. Fred often said that he got this name from a

15

favorite baseball player. The National Baseball Library lists seven ball players who played in the major leagues at some period during the years 1882 to 1925 whose last names were Farrell. None had the name Fred, or even an F., in his first or middle name. At some time during Fred's life, he dropped the last L from Farrell, but as late as 1954, a newspaper article that mentioned his name twice spelled the middle name both ways. Fred's father never changed his name from Fromowitz. The parents moved to Dallas in 1915, and, after the father's death in 1926, Fred's mother used the name Florence.

CHAPTER II
GROWING UP IN EAST TEXAS

The precise sequence of events that led to Fred's permanent move to Dallas is no more important than exact dates in history. We all remember that the battle of Hastings was fought in 1066, but I have often wondered whether a pupil who forgets the exact date, yet knows the significance of the battle, may not turn out to be a greater scholar than one who is merely chronologically accurate without having any real understanding. For this story, I have been very fortunate in getting a great deal of factual background, in spite of the fact that my subject entered school over eighty years ago.

Fred lived in East texas during the first twenty-eight years of his life. For this reason, Helen and I began our search there. Fortunately, there were many people alive who remembered him and his family during all these years, and they made every effort to help me with his history. Helen and I drove to Rusk, Alto, and Jacksonville, Texas, to spend several days talking to those who remembered him. Fred had lived in both Rusk and Alto, and in both we obtained interesting information about the boy and young man whose life I shall trace.

When I began to investigate Fred's school days, I thought immediately of the success stories written by Horatio Alger and the "Rover Boy" series by Edward Stratemeyer. I think it would be correct to say that Fred was an ordinary schoolboy. However, he *was* intelligent, hard-working, and honest, and undoubtedly virtuous and patriotic as well. On the whole, I would say that Fred's life story definitely does qualify as a "rags-to-riches" story of the Horatio Alger genre.

Fred probably entered the Rusk public school in about 1898, and, there being only ten grades at that time, with a skip or two, we can put his graduation at about 1907. Fred was an excellent scholar, envied by his classmates for his good marks. One of his teachers, Miss Ella Baker, called him an outstanding student, and one classmate said that everyone knew how proud she was of him. Miss Baker told me that everyone is better in one field than in another—with Fred it was math. He was not active in athletics, and those who attended school with him say that he just didn't have time. Undoubtedly, he did many odd jobs to earn some money for his family. In Rusk I talked to Eldridge Gregg, who had only recently retired as President of the First National Bank of Rusk. Fred had his first job at this bank when Eldridge's father, E. L. Gregg, was its president. Eldridge knew Fred well, and told me, "You asked about Fred selling some papers. Well, he *did* sell some papers. I would think that he sold more copies of the *Dallas Morning News* than were ever sold in any other town this size in Texas!"

18   Old friends of Fred's gave me some background of his early years which, while not spectacular, indicates how even in his formative years, he showed unusual maturity. Eldridge Gregg said, "Yes, even while he was still in school, Fred was Treasurer of the Rusk City Band, and I think he played the baritone horn." Helen looked very surprised and said, "He couldn't carry a tune to save his life!" That may be true, but he undoubtedly made a good custodian of the money!

Eldridge also told me that Fred often championed the smaller boys who were bullied by the older ones. Eldridge, younger by a few years, said, "Fred was a big favorite of my age group. The older boys were not always too good to the younger ones, but Fred always was. He was always kind and considerate. I recall that he had a fight—right up close to the school—he and this other boy jawing at each other all the way down to the school; they finally squared off and got into a fight there, and, of course, we gathered around, and Fred was gettin' the worst of it; so we just separated them. That was just the way we felt about him." Eldridge continued, "If somebody doesn't write some of this history in the next few years, it will be almost impossible to get it all together because people, unfortunately, just pass away or they get to the point where they can't remember."

As a schoolboy, Fred had the thought of some day becoming a lawyer. He confided this to Helen and told her that there were times when he went into the woods where he could be alone and out of earshot, stood on a tree stump, and delivered speeches. I learned that the Rusk school at that time had no provision for debating or public speaking, so the urge for an outlet for self-expression was natural.

Virginia Cameron, whom I have known for many years, was born in Rusk; her brother, an attorney, was in partnership with Helen's brother, Lewis. Virginia has given me considerable help about Fred's early history. I obtained the names of several girls Fred dated, including Virginia's aunt Sammie Tittle. Virginia tells me that it was a real romance and that he was pretty ardent in his courtship. Helen confirms that Fred often referred to Sammie as his early girl friend.

All of those interviewed, including Virginia Cameron, spoke highly of Mr. Fromowitz. Virginia tells me that although her parents were teetotalers, Mr. Fromowitz would bring wine to them and candy to the kids when he visited them. Eldridge Gregg said that his mother had

19

described Mrs. Fromowitz as a very sweet, retiring person, busy at home with children of various ages. In this era in rural East Texas, family life was quite different from what it is today. There were fewer diversions, fewer reasons to leave home. As Eldridge Gregg told me, "Church was the main gathering place; then we'd all get together on picnics and all that kind of stuff, you know, but the group was always together. It was not like it is now . . . get in the car . . . well, we didn't have any amusements like that, movies or television. We had to make our own." The closeness of the Fromowitz family lasted throughout Fred's life.

Florrie Gregg Gee, Eldridge Gregg's sister, told me that she well remembered the day that Fred got his first job. She said that Fred appeared at their house on Sunday morning and asked her father for a job at his bank. Mr. Gregg told Fred, "Well, I'll tell you, it's Sunday, but if you'll be there tomorrow morning, I'll start you at work." She said Fred took off and ran all the way home to tell his mother. And so, on that Monday morning in 1907, a 15-year old boy became a banker. Those whose memory I trusted the most said that during his three years with the bank, Fred did everything from sweeping the floors to keeping books before becoming assistant cashier in 1911. It was in this year that he first went to Dallas to attend a business school.

20   After completing the business course, Fred took a job as a bookkeeper with the American Exchange Bank in Dallas, which was the forerunner of the present First National Bank in Dallas. Once when a goodwill delegation sponsored by the Dallas Chamber of Commerce stopped at Rusk, Fred helped to entertain the group, particularly Royal A. Ferris, who was President of the American Exchange Bank. Mr. Ferris was so impressed with young Fred Florence that, shortly thereafter, he offered him a job paying $50.00 a month. Then an opportunity arose for an advancement as cashier at the First State Bank of Ratcliff, a

small but thriving town about fifteen miles south of Alto which hardly exists today and has no bank. After a short time, Fred saw even greener pastures and resigned his position as cashier to accept the Vice Presidency of the Alto State Bank in Alto, Cherokee County, Texas. The Alto experience was important and spanned almost eleven years of his life, including nearly two years spent in the Air Corps.

Because the town of Alto was such a vital part of Fred's life, and to dispel the thoughts that Alto was just a wide place in the road, I quote its short history written and given to me by Emma B. Yowell, who at the time of my interview was a librarian in Alto. She was Fred's contemporary and knew him well.

HISTORY OF ALTO

Alto is situated on the El Camino Real, the King's Highway, one of the oldest roads in America. When La Salle visited this section in 1687 his historian noted in his diary: "Thirty well-mounted warriors took us by a well beaten road as good as from Paris to Orleans."

Some think St. Denis in 1715 was the first white man to go over this route, but long before his time, numbers of white men had tramped over the winding old trail. We read of DeGusman in 1527; De Soto in 1538; Coronado in 1543; DeMoscoso in 1543; Mendoso in 1648; La Salle in 1685-1687; La Harpe in 1717 and Captain Ramon, Espinosa and De Rios 1716; Don Pedro, De Rubie and many other notables who tramped this Old Spanish Trail. None has ever trod this road better loved than a Methodist Minister and a country Banker—Bishop A. Frank Smith* and Fred F. Florence.

Alto is situated on part of the Old Barr and Davenport land grant which was made to them in 1798. The

---

* Reverend Smith had his first church in Alto, and later became the Methodist Bishop of Houston.

town was named Alto because the site was the highest on the dividing ridge between the two rivers—Neches and Angelina. Alto is a form of the Latin word for HIGH. Historic sites in the vicinity of Alto are:

> Hinckley Bridge, Buckshot Crossing, Durst Crossing, Wolf Home and Stage Depot, Sam Houston's Spring, the Grave of Candice Bean, Home of Peter Ellis Bean, Old Palestine Church, Lockranzie, Forest Hill Plantation, Village of Hinai Indians, Bowles Village, Death Place of La Salle, La Salle's last Camp Site, Mission San Francisco De Los Neches, Indian Mounds, and also the site of Bishop Smith's first Church and site of F. F. Florence's first bank.

Emma B. Yowell, Historian

Only a year after joining the Alto State Bank, Fred became its President. Frank X. Tolbert, perhaps Texas' greatest living historian, wrote:

> Florence was offered the Presidency of the Alto Bank in 1915. W. T. Whiteman, one of the owners of the small bank, said, "Only trouble about giving you the Presidency, Fred, is that we only want to pay you $125.00 a month, but we will leave it to your judgement as to what your salary is to be." "Fine, now that we have that settled we can go to work," replied Fred, "my salary will be $150.00 a month."

Fred was active in this position until he resigned to enlist in the Signal Corps Aviation School of the United States Army with the rank of Corporal on February 15, 1918. He was first stationed at Love Field, Dallas, then was transferred to Brindley Field, New York, and went from there to Camp Gordon, Georgia. His job as an enlisted man (later commissioned to 2nd Lieutenant) was uncrating and assembling airplanes. "Flew in some of them, too," he once said, "I had faith in my work."

I also served for a short time in World War I, in the Navy and I became nostalgic when I read the following minutes of a meeting of the Alto bank at the time of Fred's resignation:

> This meeting was called by Director F. F. Florence, who feeling the patriotic spirit THROBBING in his soul could no longer resist the call to the colors of his Country, tendered his resignation as Director and President of this bank. After some reluctancy motion was duly made and seconded and his resignation was unanimously accepted. Mr. Parrish, Chairman, made a short but impressive talk, which was responded to in a very able manner by Mr. Florence.
>
> Mr. Florence had served the bank for several years in the above capacities, and under his administration the Institution had a very prosperous growth and the entire Board deeply regretted that conditions were such that such pleasant relationships had to be severed, and all joined in bidding him God's speed in the great and important task of assisting in bringing the GERMAN KAISER and DESPOT in humble submission to the will and wishes of a WORLD'S DEMOCRACY.

23

At the close of the war, Fred returned to Alto and assumed his former duties at this bank. He became an alderman of Alto, and, beginning in April 1919, he was its mayor for a year. During this period, he received the huge salary of $2.00 a month for his services. He signed his own checks (six in number), countersigned by the town secretary, W. F. Shattuck. The last check was for the three-month period ending April 24, 1920; so it was about then that he moved to Dallas permanently. The checks were never cashed, and Helen still has them.

I really pumped those who knew Fred during his East Texas days about his social life. They must have felt about me as a politician does about a TV interviewer who just won't quit. Apparently, in Alto as well as during his earlier school days in Rusk, Fred dated a few girls and went to picnics and other socials, many of which were church oriented. There was no synagogue or temple of Fred's faith in either Rusk or Alto, so Fred participated in many activities of the Methodist Church. The Reverend Frank Smith, referred to above by Emma Yowell, once said of his good friend Fred, "If Fred had stayed in Alto for another year, I probably could have made him a good Methodist!" The two men enjoyed a lifetime friendship. An Altoite told me that Fred had been Treasurer of Smith's First Methodist Church in their town.

The period from Fred's high school graduation in 1907 until his move to Dallas covered thirteen years, and my comments are inadequate because there were so few specific facts about anything, except that he was an outstanding young banker, greatly admired, and a civic leader in both Rusk and Alto. One thing that is positive is that he was very fortunate in having two fine men—both brilliant bankers and each a great guiding force in his own community—as his mentors, friends, sponsors, and inspiration. These two men were John S. Wightman, the cashier of the bank in Rusk, and H. H. Berryman, who had been the President of the Alto Bank before Fred. At one time, Fred and Berryman were partners in a real estate business, and I have been told that they were also once in the automobile business together. Both Wightman and Berryman were an important and fine influence on this young man who, at this point in life, had only boundless energy, high ambitions, and a burning desire to succeed.

CHAPTER III
THE NEW DALLAS BANK

Even today, the Bank of New York, founded in 1784, is spoken of as the Alexander Hamilton Bank; the first National Bank in New York, now the Citibank, is still thought of by old New Yorkers as the George F. Baker Bank; in Pittsburgh, the principal bank bears the name of the Mellon Family, its founders; and the largest bank in our country, the Bank of America, is still often referred to as the Gianini Bank. While Fred was beginning his banking career in East Texas, the Dallas bank that eventually would become almost synonymous with the name "Fred Florence" was also getting its start.

In the summer of 1919, Colonel Eugene DeBogory, a 1907 graduate of the University of Texas law school, had an idea for a new bank. World War I was over, and the number of wage earners in Dallas had vastly increased. After doing some research, the Colonel decided that if banking hours were expanded to be more convenient for working people, who were never free during conventional banking hours, many new potential customers would seek bank services otherwise unavailable to them. His idea was to have a "day and night" bank, which would not only offer service to the individual depositors but would encourage payroll accounts.

DeBogory solicted help from his friends, which he got, and with $40,000 that he had personally borrowed, the new bank applied for a charter on January 2, 1920, under the name Guaranty Bank and Trust Company. To get approval was difficult and, at one time, seemed hopeless. The State Banking Commissioners, who had always supported the Commissioner, George Waverly Briggs, in his decisions, were unwilling to issue the charter. About the hearing, DeBogory said:

> I thought it necessary to put the cold steel to Briggs, so in this open hearing I asked him what banking experience he had had, and he stated that that was no concern of the board. I then appealed to the board and made the statement that as the board was more or less governed by the opinions of the commissioner, it was of vital importance for the board that it know whether the commissioner was an experienced banker. The board voted that the commissioner be made to answer questions pertaining to his experience. Then I asked him the following question: whether or not his information pertaining to banking was gained solely from a six weeks' correspondence course in banking. He admitted that to be a fact. This somewhat riled the commissioner, who at that time had been given a job with the City National Bank of Dallas, which was strongly opposed to the charter application of the Guaranty Bank and Trust Company.

Opposition to the new bank was not confined to Board hearings. Colonel DeBogory has also told of the personal pressures put on him by Mr. E. M. Reardon, President of the American Exchange National Bank. He relates:

> Mr. Reardon, who was a close friend of mine, talked to me for hours and hours, and tried to persuade me not to organize the bank, saying that it was a foregone conclusion that it would fail, for at least a score of small banks in the downtown district had failed. He was particularly anxious that this bank not be opened because of the fact, I surmised, that the bank would secure payroll accounts from large firms, which I told

him was included in my plan, and I thought these accounts would ultimately mature into substantial deposits if they were given courteous and efficient service. At least, I think these reasons account for his opposition to the Guaranty Bank, but of course, he did not make mention of these facts as his grounds for objection. He merely said the bank could not survive. He and many other people were wrong: a small idea made a hell of a big bank.

Many other obstacles made the going hard, but a charter for the Guaranty Bank and Trust Company was finally granted, and the opening set for Saturday morning, February 14, 1920. The original capital was 1,000 shares of a $100 par value, or a total of $100,000. The first available minutes·were of a board meeting held on February 3, 1920. DeBogory, who was the vice president, presided. The organizational president, George S. McGhee, submitted his resignation at this meeting, as did several others. These minutes are signed by T. M. Dees and Eugene DeBogory, and the cashier, Rupert Eldridge. At this meeting Mr. Dees, who had just recently made a fortune in the new Texas oil fields, was made the President at a salary of $3000 a year. McGhee had objected to the long hours contemplated (9:00 A.M. to 8:00 P.M. daily and 9:00 A.M. to 10:00 P.M. on Saturday), but the idea of a day-and-night bank appealed to Dees. For a while some people did refer to it as "The Day and Night Bank." Dees was interested in working people because, as he said, "I am one myself." Also at this meeting the resolution was passed to rent the A. E. Boger Building for a period of ten years at $1,100 per month. This building was at 1305-07 Main Street. The building had been used previously for a banking function—early during the previous year, 1919, it had been remodeled for the First State Bank which later in the year merged with Security National Bank—so that its conversion for a new bank was

27

easy. At a meeting of Guaranty April 26, 1921, it was decided to buy the Boger Building for $225,000 in cash.

George F. Gibbons, a former Vice President of the Republic Bank, wrote a brief history from which I have learned many facts. Of the opening day, he says:

> This was a memorable day, when those in charge realized that their opening was a success. Everyone was surprised at the number of flowers received, and when the day's totals were counted, there were 659 accounts on the banks books, totaling $804,524.45, excluding those of officers and directors, believed to be a record for one day for a bank of only $100,000 capitalization.

On March 29, only seven weeks after the opening, the Board passed a resolution to increase the capital to $1,000,000 with $100,000 in surplus. The surplus was provided by assessing the original owners of the stock ten percent. This immense expansion was approved by the stockholders and the pattern was set for continued increases up to the present time.

Although Mr. Dees was vitally interested in the bank, he preferred to pursue his oil business, so his successor as President was sought. Mr. William Ott Connor took office as the chief executive in April of the same year. At this time he was sixty-eight years old, but his experience with Sanger Brothers, a retail department store of major importance in the Southwest, made him the ideal choice for the bank's presidency. Since "W. O.," as he was called, played a major role in the progress of the bank, it is important to know something of his background.

He was born in 1847 on a Tennessee farm and in early infancy moved with his family to Corinth, Mississippi, where his father became mayor. When he was six years old,

28

his family moved to Madison, Arkansas, and the next year came to Texas, first settling in Paris, then Jefferson, and finally in 1867 in Dallas. His formal education was limited to only a few months of schooling, but his avid general reading, his travels both in this country and abroad, and his participation in the commercial and financial life of the pioneer Southwest, produced an unusually comprehensive fund of knowledge. To W. O. is attributed a saying which throws a clear light on his outlook in life: "It isn't how little you can do for your community and your people, it is how much—and in as friendly a way as possible."

Connor's business career began when he was fourteen. At nineteen he operated his own dry goods business and at twenty he joined the firm of Connor and Walker which had been founded by one of his brothers. His extensive state-wide travels with this wholesale drug firm afforded him the opportunity of making life-long friends and qualified him for a salesman's job with Sanger Brothers. Three years later he was made manager of their wholesale department and general credit manager.

When Connor joined the bank, he had the undisputed reputation of being the best credit manager in the Southwest, and the fourteen years of his service to the bank proved this to be correct. He was known to his friends to be a man of great honor and integrity, and, though lacking in banking experience, he knew people. He had the further advantage of being unbound by tradition, permitting him to view the business objectively. He often quoted the late Mr. James Cash Penney in his statement: "Never turn your back on the front door, because that's where the customers come in." W. O. further stated to his fellow officers in his own succinct way, "When they stop coming, you and I are out of a job." Connor set a personal example, which he insisted the other employees follow, of spending as much

29

time as possible getting acquainted and talking with people in the lobby. He had the lobby designed to place his desk (and later Fred's also) where no one could enter the bank without being seen by both of them. His sales experience taught him the value of taking your product to your prospect, and he never allowed the members of his staff to fall into the attitude of some bankers, sitting at their desks to await business which might be brought to them. "I'd rather my men wore out the soles of their shoes than the seats of their pants" was an adage attributed to him.

All profit-making organizations need capable and experienced top personnel. Established businesses can not only draw from their own employees with good track records, but they can also attract people from their competitors. For a fledgling enterprise, the selection of a top management team is both more difficult and more important. For this reason, the founders of the new bank, themselves not bankers, sought a young, aggressive man with promise, with ambition, with a clean background, and the other required qualifications to be a part of the team.

CHAPTER IV
THE TWENTIES

I have heard several stories about how Fred Farrel Florence came to Dallas to become W. O. Connor's right-hand man. Although the method of selection really makes little difference, it is my belief that Colonel DeBogory had heard of him favorably. Fred had been in Dallas with east Texas bankers and at meetings of the Chamber of Commerce. In any event, Mr. Connor received excellent references from Fred's East Texas banker friends, H. H. Berryman and John S. Wightman, and a great number of other bankers and merchants, and thereupon hired him. As Frank Tolbert put it in the *Dallas Morning News,*

> The man he wanted was the $150 a month president of the Alto State Bank. This seems about like Dan Topping, owner of the New York Yankees, trying to talk one of the East Texas Baseball League skippers into becoming manager of the Yankees. But Banker Connor knew what he was after: "Fred Florence knows money."

It is pure speculation as to why "W. O." Connor selected Fred, because he must have weighed many factors in making his decision. The following story, related by Eugene Whitmore in an article about Fred in the April, 1953 issue of *American Business*, tells what may have been the clincher:

A customer of the Alto bank (Note: Fred was then its president) wanted to buy $50,000 worth of stock in the Guaranty Bank and Trust Company (later Republic), and asked Mr. Florence to arrange for the purchase of the stock.

Guaranty's president had already been making overtures to Mr. Florence. Then he received a letter from Mr. Florence, outlining the wishes of his customer to buy Guaranty stock. "Why not let us keep this money here in Alto, and we will send you a credit for the $50,000 for the stock?" wrote Mr. Florence.

Wow! That sealed the career of Fred Florence. Guaranty's President Connor wanted a man who would ask for such deposits. He made Mr. Florence an offer which was not easy to decline.

All big city banks need the country banks as customers, along with other large city banks. Readers who are not bankers may wonder why keeping an account in another bank is good business. In fact, the law requires that banks maintain deposits in other banks. The large banks want the money because lending money is the way they make their profit. The small banks need services which the larger banks can provide for them and their customers. A full-service bank can give advice on real estate, insurance, credits, investments, foreign exchange, etc. Since Fred was so well known in East Texas and had the confidence of bankers throughout the area, he was able to bring most of their accounts into Guaranty Bank and Trust Co. At the Director's meeting on May 6, 1920, Fred was elected First Vice President, and, at the same meeting, the bank was authorized to become a member of the Federal Reserve System.

The economic climate of the 1920's was not a healthy one. Financial history shows that as an aftermath of the war the country reached a point of reckless extravagance, indulgence in luxuries, and stock and commodities speculation which created a "fictitious prosperity," with abnormal profits, high wages, and high prices of all goods and services. This condition quickly drained off the dammed-up savings of 1917-18, and the true economic factors began to exert their pressures early in 1920, just after the new bank opened its doors. Economic catastrophe began to occur in agriculture, which was basic to the Southwest, and a drastic decline in merchandise prices that had started earlier in the year in other areas of the country reached the Southwest in August. Yet in spite of this unhealthy climate, the developing bank grew and progressed. Mr. Connor was well experienced in dealing with commercial and farm credit in the ups and downs of an agriculturally based economy. It may be surmised that the general economic pressures of the period worked to the advantage of men with credit experience who had new money to loan. Older banks were faced with the necessity of pressuring their customers for liquidation to meet required reserves to offset the decline in deposits. Many of these customers turned to new sources such as the Guaranty for relief, and new relationships were formed which lasted and grew through the years.

The bank published its first statement on November 15, 1920, nine months after starting operations. It showed deposits of $4,719,000. During the following month, the Board declared a cash dividend from earnings of five percent, transferred $10,000 to the Surplus account, and paid each employee an extra ten percent of his earnings from the time he was employed by the bank. This accomplishment, in the face of long odds against success during this first year, certainly augured well for Mr. Connor and Mr. Florence in the fast-growing and highly competitive Dallas financial commmunity.

The basic principles of success in any business are hard work, dedication to the job, honesty, and good common sense are necessities. The difference between mediocrity and superiority can be summed up in one word—management. Unless the enterprise is a one-man or one-woman job, the boss must seek the most qualified people available and then get the most out of them. This ability to select was the attribute that the team of Connor and Florence shared to its greatest degree. With Connor nearly 40 years older than Florence, the team had the experience of age and the exuberance of youth. Each had his own philosophy and his own particular skills and talents, and it was fortunate that they were different because what one lacked, the other had in great sufficiency. Each man had ability beyond the requisites, and each functioned in a way that brought customers to the bank and profits for the stockholders. In addition, they understood and respected each other.

The bank grew so quickly that W. O. and Fred were hard pressed to find competent personnel for the upper echelons. However, they were fortunate and smart enough to make excellent selections, many of whom remained with the bank until their retirement. Many of these employees contributed immeasurably to the success of the bank, as did the members of the Board of Directors. Most banks choose their Board of Directors for their ability to bring solid support from their own firms, or because of their personal wealth. Large deposits and loan requirements are the two vitally needed ingredients for a bank's success. Mr. Connor wanted this, but he also wanted his directors to be an active, working board. Fred was a great believer in the potential power of his board and his stockholders, and this belief became one of the most important reasons for his and the bank's success.

Even in the early days of the bank's existence, Mr. Connor had begun weighing the relative advantages of State and National charters. He was obviously already looking to

34

increase the scope of activity beyond local business, and State banks were faced with the liability of a recently enacted State Bank Guaranty Fund law, under which all State bank charters were assessed to cover losses of other banks in the system if necessary. The State Bank Guaranty Fund law was particularly detrimental to the Guaranty Bank and Trust Company because the fee was based on the amount of the deposits, and Guaranty had between $10 and $12 million, which at that time was a large amount for a State bank. This made the switch to a National Bank all the more desirable.

At a special meeting of the Board on April 3, 1922, the Board authorized the officers of the Guaranty Bank and Trust Company to apply for a National Bank charter with a new name for the bank. A director, George S. Wright, won a $100 prize for his suggestion of "Republic National Bank of Dallas." The National Bank Charter was granted quickly, and at a meeting held April 15, less than two weeks later, the Guaranty was dissolved and Republic was born.

The name seemed most appropriate because it stood for the Republic of Texas and the Republic of the United States. Today Republic uses a modification of the Lone Star of the Republic of Texas as their insignia. The exterior of the bank's headquarters today is emblazened with a four-pointed star in the decoration of its aluminum skin, and its basic theme of advertising is "Silver Star" service. Every employee of the bank is requested to wear a little pin in the shape of this star. No other American bank used the name "Republic" until the early 1960's, when a New York City bank began using this name.

It is interesting to note that the Board took necessary action in 1922 to authorize branches in Oak Cliff and near Fair Park. In all probability, the banking commissioner squelched this, and no other mention is ever made of the

35

proposal, but the authority was granted and recorded in the minutes of June 14, 1922. It does show how early Mr. Florence and Mr. Connor began thinking in terms of expanded services.

Because of the bank's phenomenal growth, they had outgrown the Boger Building which they had occupied from the beginning. On August 8, 1923, Connor and Florence were authorized by the Board to buy the adjoining Scollard Building, owned by Wirt and Percy Davis and Leslie Waggener. As soon as the transaction was completed, this building was razed and construction begun on a handsome new 20-story building which was completed in 1926. A few years after this building was completed and occupied, demoliltion of the Boger building was begun and on its site was built a new 20-story building with matching architecture and then known as the "Annex." This addition was completed in 1931, then making this office building the largest in Texas.

The purchase of the Scollard building involved a deal whereby the bank agreed to service the farm and ranch loan business of the Davises and Waggener. These men had represented the Travelers Insurance Company for many long years, going back to the turn of the century, and they wanted Republic to handle this business. However, during the early twenties, the national banks had restricted powers relating to loans on real estate. State banks had more liberal powers. Therefore, in order to handle this type of business, an entirely separate bank was built within the lobby of the Republic National Bank on Main Street, complete with its own teller windows and enclosed offices. Under the law a state bank headquarters had to be separate from a national bank. This new bank was called The Republic Trust and Savings Bank. In these quarters began the operations which the national bank was not permitted to engage in at that time. The stockholders of the Republic National Bank were given the right to subscribe to stock in The Republic Trust and Savings Bank.

When the law was changed to liberalize the rights of the national banks and this device was no longer necessary, Republic National Bank absorbed the state bank on June 26, 1928, and the name was changed to Republic National Bank and Trust Company. The shareholders were given stock in this bank for their stock in The Republic Trust and Savings Bank. Late in 1929, Republic absorbed the North Texas National Bank through consolidation. The name was changed back to Republic National Bank of Dallas on January 12, 1937.

Fred was elected President of the bank on January 8, 1929, continuing in this office until he relinquished this position to James W. Aston in 1957. From that time until his death on December 25, 1960, he served as Chairman of the Executive Committee and Chief Operating Officer.

Republic Bank's impressive growth is demonstrated by the following figures, which represent a year-end accounting of total assets at ten year intervals:

1920—	6.5 million
1930—	62.0 million
1940—	101.6 million
1950—	447.1 million
1960—	1.2 billion

37

Measured by total assets, Republic became a 100 million dollar bank in 1940. It passed the billion dollar mark in 1958, and by the end of 1960 had total assets of 1.2 billion and deposits of 1 billion.

In the twenty years since Fred died, the State of Texas has permitted the use of holding companies to own 100%

of the stock in other Texas banks. Because branch banking is not permitted, a new corporation was formed, "Republic of Texas Corporation." It came into being on June 11, 1974, is listed on the New York Sock Exchange, and in 1980 owns 23 banks including the Republic National Bank. Republic of Texas Corporation has assets of over $11 billion. There are now numerous bank holding companies in Texas. This new concept of banking has been beneficial to the banks as well as to their customers.

While great credit is due those who followed Fred, I am reminded of the old Chinese proverb, "When you plan a trip of 1,000 miles, remember—there is always that first mile." At this point in our story I believe it is time to take a closer look at the man who was so important in guiding the bank through that first mile and through so much of the long journey that followed.

CHAPTER V
THE FAMILY

When asked, "What was the biggest deal you ever pulled?" Fred would reply, "Marrying the Rabbi's beautiful daughter." He loved this remark, and it has been widely quoted by his friends.

Helen says that she met Fred about 1926. Her recollection is that she flirted with him in Temple Emanu-El, then on South Boulevard. This preceded an evening date several weeks later. The announcement of their engagement was made on New Year's Day, 1928, and they were married on February 21, 1928. The wedding was at the home of her parents, and only family and a few close business friends of Fred attended. Her father and an uncle, a Rabbi from Vicksburg, Mississippi, conducted the marriage ceremony.

Helen and Fred went to Europe after their wedding, the first trip for Helen and the second for Fred, an experience that would have been the greatest thrill of their lives but for the fact the Helen was sick for part of the trip, which very much delayed their return. The eastbound voyage was on the then pride of the French Line, the S. S. Paris. After visiting France, Italy, and Austria, they returned in early May on the S. S. Berengaria of the Cunard Line. The newlyweds lived at Maple Terrace, Dallas' first nice apartment, then moved to a house on Lakewood Boulevard, and, a short time later, to a house on Lorraine, before they bought the magnificent mansion at 6525 Turtle

Creek. This two-story brick home occupied nearly two acres in the finest residential district of University Park, which, with the adjacent City of Highland Park, forms an island known as the Park Cities, entirely surrounded by the City of Dallas. The house, then only a few years old, had been built by Dr. R. B. McBride, and the Florence family occupied it from the early fall of 1931 until five years after Fred's death. This house was a fitting residence for a man who was to have a major role in all civic and business activities. With its gorgeous chandeliers, its dignified and tasteful furniture, the house was in perfect harmony with its owners. Neither Fred nor Helen was a gardener—neither had a "green thumb"—but both had a feeling for elegance that enabled them to give the landscape people good instructions; so even the grounds were perfect. Yet, while stately and elegant, their house was always a home.

From the day Helen's father joined Helen and Fred in holy matrimony, she stood firmly at his side. Helen was a charming, well-educated, and talented helpmate, who willingly and enthusiastically accepted the challenge of helping Fred accomplish his goals in life. She was part of the team, and, I have been told, a powerful influence.

One of Helen's most important duties as Fred's wife was arranging the social amenities that were required constantly. There was much business entertaining. Dinner parties at the Florence home included two Texas Governors, James W. Allred and William P. Hobby, who also was owner of the *Houston Post*. Mrs. Hobby, who was the top ranking officer in the first U. S. Women's Army Corp and became the first woman cabinet member when named as the first secretary of Health, Education and Welfare, was always a close friend of Helen. In the corporate field, guests included Leonard Wood, Chairman of Sears, and James Cash Penney; and the long list of bankers included James

40

Rockefeller, head of New York's First City National Bank. I have not mentioned any of the distinguished businessmen in the Southwest, but few would be missing from the roster. The Florences' house guests over the years included many well-known and important figures. The Chief Executive of Barclay's Bank in England, Mr. Anthony Tuke, who was subsequently knighted, and Mrs. Tuke spent a weekend at the Florences'. Barclay's is England's largest bank, and at that time perhaps the largest in the world. Fred had met Mr. Tuke and had invited him to visit him and Helen in Dallas. Helen can remember only that this was the year of or a year before the monetary conference held in London. Helen had made careful preparation for the Tukes' visit by buying some new furniture so that they could have separate rooms with bath between. They arrived in the afternoon. Helen had tea ready for her British guests, but as it turned out, they preferred coffee. That evening the Florences gave a dinner party for forty or fifty leaders of the community in the Texas Suite at the Baker Hotel. This was strictly a social evening. A few violinists from the Dallas Symphony Orchestra played at the tables.

The following day lunch was at the Florence home with just Helen, Fred, and the Tukes. After lunch, Mr. Tuke asked Fred if he could get him a small pliers. To Mrs. Tuke's obvious surprise, he asked her for her gold coin bracelet. He snipped off a 1957 commemorative coin which he had received as a gift from Queen Elizabeth herself, and gave it to Helen. Helen was embarrassed and Mrs. Tuke seemed a bit taken aback until Mr. Tuke said that he had received two and would give the other one to his wife when he returned home and could get it out of the vault. Helen put hers on a chain and still wears it very often.

Also a house guest was the great Texas financier Jesse H. Jones. Jones for twelve years was head of the Recon-

41

struction Finance Corporation (R.F.C.) which during the Depression years pumped fifty billion dollars into the nation's tottering economy. After the Texas Centennial Official Opening at which President Franklin Roosevelt was present, Governor and Mrs. Hobby left Dallas' Love Field with Jones in his private plane for Houston. The plane had a minor accident on takeoff. The pilot was injured, but not seriously, and later fully recovered; but all were taken to St. Paul Hospital (the old one on Bryan Street). The Hobby's were satisfied to stay overnight for observation and were released the next morning, but Jones didn't like it. He phoned Fred, telling him to come get him and to take him out to the Florence home. Fred called for him, and Jones selected a pretty nurse to take with him. A police cordon accompanied them to 6525 Turtle Creek and guarded the house all night.

On arrival Jones had no hesitancy in selecting the master suite. He wanted ice cream with raspberries, so when Helen located a cafeteria that had it, a policeman volunteered to pick it up. Helen says the demands for this and that lasted until the nurse came out and said, "Mr. Jones wants a spittoon," whereupon Helen bluntly said, "We have none." Apparently the nurse got the message—this ended the requests.

42

Much of Fred's entertaining was away from Dallas and at conventions. In the thirty-three years of their marriage, Helen made nearly every trip with Fred and always acted as his social secretary and hostess. Fred was ever mindful of the part Helen played in his success. In accepting the Presidency of the American Bankers Association, he said, "She has been a wonderful influence in my life—a wonderful partner. She has subordinated her own life to being helpful to me."

Although Helen may have "subordinated" her life to Fred's, she was certainly not a shrinking violet, useful only for respectability and decoration. The wives of many men of importance bask in their husband's glory, but not so with Helen: she was proud of her man and was a dutiful wife and homemaker, but she was above all an individual. She took time to be president of the Dallas Bankers Wives, President of the Visiting Nurses Association, and during all of World War II was chairman of the Camp and Hospital Committee of the Dallas County Chapter of the American Red Cross.

Helen was very sensitive to her husband's thoughts, sometimes even being clairvoyant. She was always aware of and in sympathy with Fred's thinking, and hence was able to help by making suggestions and by attending to the necessary prerequisites. Not generally known is that Helen participated in the writing of many of Fred's speeches. Having majored in English in college, she was very helpful in putting his thoughts into words. Helen shared Fred's responsibilities and disappointments, as well as his triumphs, and to this day has carried out many of his interests.

After Fred's death Helen took his place on several philanthropic and educational boards, including the Southwestern Legal Foundation and the Board of Governors of Southern Methodist University, which is the executive committee to whom the trustees report. She now serves on the board of the Southwestern Medical Foundation, and for many years was a member of the Mental Health and Mental Retardation board, later serving as its chairman. This institution, operating under the Dallas County Commissioners, had the largest annual social service appropriation from the County. The only social service organization with a larger annual budget is the United Way, which is privately funded. Over the years Helen has

43

increased her activities with the Southwestern Legal Foundation by becoming its Secretary and by serving on its Executive and Administrative committees. There are many more, including her interest in Jarvis Christian College, a black college located in Hawkins, Texas, where she had served as a board member since 1961. Helen is on the Board of the United Cerebral Palsy Research Foundation in New York and is a regular attendant.

Helen's family background and education prepared her perfectly for her role as Fred's wife, enabling her to become the epitome of the "grande dame." Helen was born on October 6, 1905, in Dayton, Ohio, where her father was the Rabbi of the Temple. She came to Dallas with her family in 1920, attended Forest High School in Dallas for two years, and after graduation became an English major at Southern Methodist University. While at S.M.U. she was selected for the "Mortar Board." The ten outstanding Juniors are elected to this society each year. Her graduation in 1927, was really the commencement of her dedicated and continued interest in her Alma Mater.

Helen's father, Dr. David Lefkowitz, was one of Dallas' greatest civic leaders and ranked as a great spiritual leader, not only in Dallas, not only in the Jewish community, but internationally. He was elected President of the Central Conference of American Rabbis, a great honor, and in the late 20's he was offered the pulpit of the largest reform congregation in England, but preferred to remain in Dallas. He was one of the first ministers of any faith to appear regularly each Sunday morning on radio, and later appeared on television. He conducted a short service with a choir and delivered a sermon. His program had a top rating for years, and his audiences of other and varied religious beliefs far outnumbered those of his own faith. He was the first Rabbi to teach Judaism at the Perkins School of Theology at

44

S.M.U. and was awarded an honorary doctorate by the University.

Dr. Lefkowitz was broadminded in all of his activities. He numbered as his close friends the leaders of all the large Dallas congregations and often was a guest speaker at church services. He was faithful to Judaism, but understood and respected other religions. With Dr. W. Angie Smith,* minister of the first Methodist Church, and Monsignor Danglmayr** of the Dallas-Fort Worth Diocese of the Catholic Church, he helped to start a Thanksgiving Day Interdenominational Service. The idea of the inter-denominational service was originated and sponsored by the National Conference of Christians and Jews, of which Hastings Harrison of Dallas was national Vice President and Southwest Regional Director at that time. The first such service was held in 1939 at the Palace Theater and continued there for sixteen years. Dr. George W. Truett, pastor of the First Baptist Church of Dallas, was asked to make the first address. It was the first time in Dallas that Catholics, Protestants, and Jews had joined in one service to thank God for His blessings. This gathering of the three major religions in Dallas each Thanksgiving Day still continues, with the ceremony being held in the recently opened Thanksgiving Square.

Dr. Lefkowitz's activities went far beyond the ministry he was a working participant in virtually every civic and charitable project in Dallas. He served for several years as

45

* W. Angie Smith and his brother, A. Frank Smith, mentioned in Chapter II, both later became Bishops of the Methodist Church. A. Frank Smith was Chairman of the Board of Trustees of S.M.U. for approximately two decades.

** Monsignor Danglmayr also later became Bishop of the Dallas-Fort Worth Diocese.

Chairman of the American Red Cross from Dallas County. He was an active member of the Rotary Club of Dallas, whose tribute to his memory said in part:

> "When death came to Dr. David Lefkowitz on June 5, 1955, it stilled forever the eloquent tongue of one whose voice had become familiar to hundreds of thousands of attentive listeners throughout Texas and the Southwest. But more eloquent than his sermons from pulpit and radio were the many activities and accomplishments of a life dedicated to the betterment of all mankind. Fortunate were they with whom the good Doctor came in personal contact. There was something intimately warming and charming in his nature that caused the very mention of his name to bring a glow to their faces. . . In his passing, the Dallas Rotary Club has suffered an irreparable loss, and Texans have lost one of the most brilliant and one of the most beloved and useful clergymen who ever lived in this state."

Rabbi David Lefkowitz will go down in the history of Dallas as one of its greatest benefactors. His example of "love of man" is reflected in the lives of his daughter, Helen, and her husband, Fred.

46

Sadie Lefkowitz, Helen's mother, was primarily a housewife, and had to care for four children, all of whom went on to college, on the meager salary of a Rabbi. To her great credit, she found time to establish the Sisterhood of Temple Emanu-El and later became national President of all Temple Sisterhoods. She was co-founder of the Visiting Nurses Association in Dallas where she served as President for many years. Helen often refers to her mother in a way that leads me to believe that Mrs. Lefkowitz, in spite of her retiring manner, had a great influence on the success and accomplishments of her children and her illustrious husband. She was an accomplished musician who had taught both voice and piano. She organized the Temple Choir and sang with it. In the seventeen years that Helen and I have enjoyed together, through Helen I have come to know her mother quite well. Her mother was a good cook (we still use her recipes), and she had a keen sense of humor with amusing comments and sage advice. She undoubtedly was a devoted mother and had a modern outlook on the current vagaries of life.

Helen had three brothers, but she was the only girl. Lewis, the oldest, was eighteen months older than Harry, who was eighteen months older than Helen. The youngest brother, David Jr., was six years younger than Helen.

Lewis graduated from high school in Dayton, spent a year at Rice, then transferred to the University of Texas after which he continued at Columbia University Law School in New York until he received his law degree. He returned to Dallas, where, as a member of the Texas Bar, he practiced his profession throughout his life. He married Blanche Mittenthal and they had two children.

Harry finished high school in three years in Dallas and spent only three years at the University of Texas, graduating Phi Beta Kappa. He continued at Johns Hopkins in Baltimore where he received his medical degree, distinguished by being in the top ten in the class. Harry practiced medicine in Cleveland, Ohio until his death. He married Alma Koch and they had two children.

David, like his older brothers, attended Texas University for two years, after which he spent two years at Cincinnati University, concurrently studying for the rabbinate at the Hebrew Union College in Cincinnati. After graduation he became Associate Rabbi in his father's pulpit at

47

Temple Emanu-El in Dallas. I am told that this was the first father-and-son team in the country. Later, David became Senior Rabbi at the reform Temple B'nai Zion in Shreveport, Louisiana, where recently he was honored for thirty years of service. He married Leona Atlas and they have three children. In 1971, he and his wife were the Jewish honorees of the National Conference of Christians and Jews.

Because Helen and Fred both loved children and had not been blessed with their own, they adopted a fine little boy, who was born on July 30, 1931. They named him David (for Helen's father and brother) and Lewis, a middle name, for Helen's oldest brother. David was about three months old when he became a Texan. Two and a half years later, from the same adoption agency in New York, came a charming little girl, born on February 7, 1934, and given the name of Cecile after Fred's mother Celia.

Most of us in our pursuit of a goal must sacrifice something for something else. So it was with Fred who, from early childhood, had the drive that sent him to the top. He adored his family and was always kind, considerate, and generous, but they were secondary to the bank and his civic work. He generously supported those relatives who needed help during their lives, and in his will remembered many, not excluding those in affluence. In talking of Fred, Helen has often referred to his devotion to his mother, whom he either visited or telephoned every day that he was in Dallas, no matter how heavy his business and social commitments. He was tender and demonstrative by nature, and highly emotional and sentimental, often actually shedding tears. Fred gave Helen and the children as much time as his full schedule permitted. The family generally took a short vacation in the spring and the fall when the children were very young, and later when they were at school, would rent

48

a house in California for the summer, during which time Fred would commute to Dallas for short periods. I am inclined to feel that Fred was often torn between his goals and what he would have liked to do with Helen and the children.

David Florence first went to grade school in University Park, and then to the Texas Country Day School that is now St. Mark's School of Texas. He graduated from St. Mark's, which has always enjoyed an enviable reputation for a high standard of education. He spent two years at Westminster College in Fulton, Missouri, and then transferred to and was graduated from Southern Methodist University. He served two years in the Navy, but, since he was stationed in Dallas, it is doubtful that he participated in the sinking of any submarines.

Cecile went through Dallas' exclusive school for girls, Hockaday, and after graduation, spent a year at Mt. Vernon Junior College in Washington, D. C. One of my daughters graduated from another of these so-called *finishing* schools, and I fully believe that they are well named. Cecile, now married to Gene Gall, is a most devoted daughter. Cecile and Gene have two daughters: Denise, now married to Bob Adams, teaches school; and Terry, recently graduated from Texas Tech with a degree in merchandizing, is busy making this her career.

David Florence is now a Director of the Republic of Texas Corporation, a holding company that in addition to owning other banks in full and in part, is the parent company of the Republic National Bank of Dallas. His oldest daughter Kathy attended Oklahoma University and has transferred to Texas. The middle daughter, Shari, attends Jacksonville College in Jacksonville, Florida and the youngest, Helen, is a freshman at Stephens College in Columbia, Missouri. All three girls were graduates of

49

Highland Park High School. David is a capable businessman and is the owner of Normandy Management, Inc., a diversified investment company. He is also co-founder with the late John Edward May and is on the Board of May Petroleum Company. In spite of a very busy schedule of business and social commitments, he finds time to serve actively with numerous charities. David is a most attentive son, and I am proud to have been accepted by him as a new member of the family. With the great admiration I have for his illustrious father, it was a real thrill when David told me one day during a walk together on the beach in Maui that he intended to start calling me Dad.

Between us, Helen and I have ten grandchildren, and when all of our combined family gather for a holiday celebration, there are at least twenty of us. Our family is a great joy to both Helen and me, and we are proud of all of them.

CHAPTER VI
KARL HOBLITZELLE

One man played an important part in Fred's life. This man—Karl Hoblitzelle—was a major influence in everything Fred did. In fact, if we say that Helen, as Fred's wife, stood at his left side, then we could say that Karl Hoblitzelle stood at Fred's right side, and deserves a great deal of credit for his creative ideas and his sound counsel, based on his vast experience as a successful businessman.

Karl Hoblitzelle became a member of the Board of directors of Republic National Bank in December, 1927, and his friendship with Fred grew and deepened throughout the years. Hoblitzelle was not just another stockholder of the Republic Bank, nor was he a figurehead after he became Chairman of the Board in 1945. He knew everything that was happening, and Fred consulted him on most matters of importance. Their relationship was that of two congenial partners with the same goal. Hoblitzelle was an aristocrat and to the manner born, and his chairmanship of the Republic added much prestige to this institution which, with his help, became a model to the banking world. Hoblitzelle had as significant a role in Fred's charitable and civic activities as he did in the success of the bank.

Karl St. John Hoblitzelle was born on October 22, 1879, to Clarence and Ida Hoblitzelle in St. Louis, Missouri. Karl's great-great-grandfather, Adrian Hoblitzelle, was a

Swiss who carried a musket during the American Revolution. His original name was Hableutzel, but in his attempt to Anglicize his name he made an error by changing it to Hoblitzelle, which is German. The descendants of this Revolutionary soldier have been distinctly American in every way. His son, Jacob, married Amy Bell of Maryland, and their son, William T., married Loretta Ogle, daughter of Maryland's Governor Samuel Ogle. Their son, Karl's father, married Ida A. Knapp, daughter of Colonel George Knapp, who founded the St. Louis *Republican*, the first newspaper west of the Alleghenies. Karl's father was Roman Catholic and his mother was Episcopalian, but like Fred, Karl was interested in people of all faiths and particularly those who sought his help. Young Karl was one of ten boys and three girls born to that union. The family's ancestral roots went back to the mountains and the valleys of Switzerland, where the name of Hobleutzel was borne by governors, judges, military leaders, and scholars. In addition to his Swiss heritage, his ethnic background included Austrian and English on the paternal side and English, Irish, and French on the maternal side.

Hoblitzelle's business career began as office boy in the office of Isaac Taylor, who was the director of works during the construction of the Louisiana Purchase Exposition in St. Louis (better known as the St. Louis World's Fair). In 1904, he became secretary to the director, and at the close of the Fair, he was the director in charge of demolition and restoration of the grounds area to its original condition as a part of the campus of St. Louis University.

Despite the fact that young Karl's parents considered the theater "the gateway to hell," his association during this Fair with the show people of the Pike, or the Midway as it is generally called, propelled him into show business. Seeing the great possibilities in the Southwest, he organized a theatrical circuit in that region, the Interstate Amusement Company, which grew to be one of the leading vaudeville circuits in the country. Although the business itself was located in the Southwest, primarily in Texas, he made his headquarters in Chicago and lived there for ten years before moving to Dallas. Hoblitzelle married Esther Thomas, a beautiful actress and singer from Louisville whose stage name was Esther Walker. She became one of Helen's close friends.

Although Karl Hoblitzelle actively guided his Interstate Amusement Company, created in 1933, he will remain in the minds of those who knew him or of him primarily for his vast civic and philanthropic activities. Dallas newspapers described him as "modest and diffident," but he was also forceful and had tremendous vision. His interests were broad, and he was always open-minded. He was never in the foreground, but he was a power behind almost everything that took place in Dallas.

After I married Helen, we spent about ten days of each of our first two summers together visiting him at his glorious home in Cotuit on Cape Cod. I had known him ever so slightly during the twenty years that my company built all of his theaters' signs and marquees. On the Cape, I discovered the gentleness of the man. Although he was eighty-four years old on our first visit, he was keen of mind. While walking with him each morning, I learned of his great vision, which earned him the title "Number One Citizen of Dallas" as the 1939 recipient of the Linz Award as Dallas' outstanding citizen. He told me about the charitable foundation he had funded and even gave me a copy of its financial statement, which at that time showed assets of approximately twelve million dollars. In spite of all the money that he had given the Hoblitzelle Foundation, his personal wealth remained extensive, and I sensed his pleasure in

53

knowing that he could continue to do so much for so many people. By will he left the Hoblitzelle Foundation an additional twenty million dollars. The most recent report for 1977-78 shows this Foundation to have assets in excess of fifty million dollars. During this period they made forty-two grants amounting to $3,402,994.65. The recipients were all qualified as being within their policy of contributing only to educational, scientific, literary, or other charitable purposes. The policy specifically excludes grants for operating funds, debt retirement, research, scholarships, or endowment. An article in the December 1978 issue of *D Magazine* lists 14 Dallas based foundations whose assets exceed $4 million. The Meadows Foundation heads the list with the Hoblitzelle Foundation second.

Of all his charitable activities, perhaps the Southwestern Medical Foundation was nearest to Mr. Hoblitzelle's heart. Also high on the list of his favorites was the Texas Research Foundation at Renner (located just north of Dallas). Renner was unique in its experiments in the whole field of agriculture. The results of their findings, which were made available to those who could benefit, were of incalculable value. At a luncheon of the Knife and Fork Club, Mr. Hoblitzelle addressed the members with a talk entitled "The Law of the Harvest." The following quote well explains his interest in the Renner Foundation:

54

> I believe that nothing is more basic to our welfare as a people than to preserve and restore our land and its natural resources. Our great cities rest upon the broad and fertile prairies. Burn down your cities and leave our farms, and your cities will rise again, but destroy our farms and grass will grow in the streets of every city in the country.

Hoblitzelle gave liberally to this institution and inspired a great interest in it for Fred. This property reverted to the Hoblitzelle Foundation which in turn donated part of it to the University of Texas at Dallas. They have appropriately built the Hoblitzelle Hall, which houses the Southwestern Legal Foundation and also the Andrew R. Cecil Auditorium, on this property. The balance of the property was donated to Texas A & M University, which is using it as a Research and Extension Center.

Karl Hoblitzelle was senstive to any manifestation of beauty. The Hoblitzelle collection of English silver of the Georgian era is one of the world's finest and has been widely exhibited.

In 1946, the story of Karl Hoblitzelle and the development of Interstate Theaters was written by Don Hinga and privately printed in a volume entitled *Forty Years of Community Service*. It is no wonder that after Hoblitzelle's forty years in show business, great leaders like W. P. Hobby and Dan Moody, former Governors of Texas, and the then Governor Coke R. Stevenson, along with the great movie producer Cecil B. de Mille, joined Dr. Umphrey Lee, the President of Southern Methodist University, the great financier Jesse H. Jones, and scores of others in expressing their praise and admiration to be included in this book. Fred Florence wrote the following words:

55

No person has contributed more to the elevation of the theater business to its present standing than Mr. Hoblitzelle. He has steadfastly stood for the finest in ideals and ethical practices throughout the years; but, more important than all of that, he has become and is now recognized as one of the really great citizens of America and is unquestionably the leading philanthropist in the State of Texas. His philanthropy and civil interest extend in practically every direction, and his life's work has been dedicated to the public's interest. As a devoted humanitarian, leader in sound thinking and action, he represents the utmost in the best traditions of American citizenship.

Fred F. Florence
President, Republic National Bank

The author of this book, Don Hinga, makes a very strong point of the moral obstructions that plagued the theater, particularly vaudeville, for many years after the turn of the century. Hinga writes, "A good percentage of the vaudeville acts were being put on in honky-tonk saloons with curtained boxes along the sides and rooms back of the boxes where a man could take a drink and very likely get rolled of his purse if he wasn't careful."

It was Karl Hoblitzelle's ambition to bring respect to an industry which at that time was not even permitted to have performances on Sunday. He demanded decency of his actors and gained the respect of the community. His wanting to do what was right had been instilled in him from childhood and never left him. He was rewarded by financial success, which in turn made it possible for him to live his life dedicated to beauty in all things, to be a patron of all the arts, to have interest in the soil and what it produced; to live his life for all—for the high and the low, black and white, without regard to religion, and for his city, his state, and his nation.

56

Man rises in stature to meet the requirements of his undertakings. So it was with Fred, who possessed all the basic ingredients and had as his helpers his illustrious father-in-law with whom he was very close, his ever-present and devoted wife, and Mr. Hoblitzelle, an outstanding business executive and perhaps one of the great philanthropists of the world. Helen says that in many instances in the building of the bank it was the vision of Mr. Hoblitzelle that Fred carried out. In matters of civic and charitable deci-

sions, there is no question about the vast influence Karl
Hoblitzelle had over Fred.

CHAPTER VII
THE MAN

Since Helen was married to Fred for 33 years, she is an accurate source of information about his personal life—the best, in fact, that any biographer could hope for. What I shall now write is my interpretation of her information, as well as that of others, mixed in with my own evaluation, gleaned from my having known him even longer than she did.

It was easy to tell just from looking at Fred Florence that this man was a perfectionist. Helen describes him as a meticulous dresser; actually, he was almost a dandy, always perfectly groomed, with never a spot. He was fastidious even to the point of a daily visit to the barber shop for a mustache trim and a manicure repair job. His hair never looked either freshly cut or in need of cutting. My barber, who worked in the shop, told me that Fred would take his coat off while on the run, and several times dropped his coat expecting to hand it to the attendant behind him—but who wasn't there. Fred was the only daily customer the barber shop had. On occasion he would take a fresh shirt and suit to his office to change for a late afternoon meeting. So that his clothes would lie flat, he avoided carrying anything in his pockets if possible, and always used a wooden lead pencil.

For years, Fred followed the tradition of wearing the striped trousers and black jacket which were the uniform of the banker's trade. After the wearing of these "morning suits" became passé, he always came to the bank in a dark suit. At work and at home, his clothes continued to be conservative, the colors of his suits mostly blues and greys, and he was probably never seen outdoors without a hat. He always wore white shirts with French cuffs, and Helen tells me that the shirts were sent to Alfred Sulka (the finest haberdasher in New York City, with offices in European and American cities) to be laundered so that there would not be a wrinkle in the heavily starched collars and cuffs.

Fred deliberately cultivated his "banker's image," and I believe he felt most at ease in rather formal clothing because it enhanced this aura of dignity and authority that he wished to project. At any rate, being casual about his dress was apparently a rather difficult indulgence for him, even when the occasion called for it.

Cecile Gall tells me that one of her most vivid memories of her father is of her daughter, Denise, begging her grandfather, just home from work: "Gumbo, take off your coat and tie and play with me." *Gumbo* was the nickname Denise had given him, and the grandchildren still refer to him that way. Cecile says that Denise wanted him to have a romp on the floor with her before dinner. She further says that he did it—reluctantly—and only because he was a real softie where his grandchildren were concerned. He would have preferred to keep his dignity intact and his coat and tie *on*!

Fred was as disciplined about his personal habits as he was about his work. He kept his weight within limits of a few pounds most of the time; he drank socially in moderation and enjoyed it; and I have only been able to uncover one weakness—ice cream! For this he had a craving, and particularly for *coconut* ice cream. When he was in his office, he often sent for a plate of it, and he insisted that the dining room in the bank always have it on hand.

The Man

One somewhat surprising fact about Fred is that he did not drive a car after he married. Helen loved to drive (sometimes tries to drive today while I am at the wheel); so she got Fred out of the habit, and then decided that his mind was probably elsewhere anyway. His driving ended when his marriage began. There seems to have been good reason for Fred to have given up driving. Helen tells me that his older brother Mike had warned her that Fred was a miserable driver. He told her that Fred sometimes would pass a street car on the wrong side. Helen enjoys telling about the time Fred had a brand new Pierce Arrow delivered to him at the bank so that he could drive it home to surprise her. On Field Street (then Orange Street) a half a block after he got behind the wheel, he ran into something and smashed a fender.

Fred could do some things for himself, however, that most successful businessmen cannot: he typed well, and could even take shorthand at a rapid speed, skills he had acquired in business college. He was a good mathematician and could work problems in his head with amazing speed and accuracy.

Fred had no major hobby; in a way, the bank itself was his hobby. Even his reading at home was almost entirely business oriented. He did like to play cards, and especially bridge. I remember very clearly one particular game, many years ago, in which Fred and I happened to be partners. My late wife Horty and I were guests at a dinner at the Dallas Columbian Club, and the hostess had arranged games of gin, canasta, and bridge for our after-dinner amusement. One of these games was especially planned for the few who, our hostess knew, regularly enjoyed playing for high stakes. Fred Florence was one of these. I was scheduled for the small ¼ of a cent game. Just before dinner, however, the man who was to have been the fourth in the BIG game

61

phoned to say that he was stuck in Chicage due to bad flying weather and could not make the party. The hostess asked me if I would fill in for him and play with the "gamblers," since she could easliy find a substitute for my game. She even said that someone would "carry" me (in other words, I would play at ¼ or ½ cent and my partner would assume the difference). I agreed to play but emphatically stated that no one was to bear any of my winnings or losses. Although I had no idea what the stakes were—and was too proud to ask—I didn't see how one bridge game could break me!

We cut for partners, and Fred and I played the first rubber together. We both held enormous hands on the first deal. Our bidding finally ended up at seven hearts (a grand slam), and I was the player. According to our system of bidding, Fred was to have had two aces but only had one; so we lost the hand by one trick. He apologized for his mistake and, with his great and fast mathematical mind, immediately told me that the mistake cost us each $64.00 I then knew the stakes were 5 cents a point. This group did a little extra gambling on the side: for each passed hand 100 points ($5.00) was put in a kitty, and the team who got the first slam, small or grand, took the kitty, often a fairly large sum. I came out lucky that evening—I lost only $15.00.

Fred also enjoyed playing golf. He is often quoted as having said, "Sometimes I play a little golf, but I don't let it get in the way of my banking." From what Helen and his surviving friends tell me, he was what is known in golf as a "duffer," but he loved to play. I think that Helen's scores were too high even to qualify for a handicap; but when they went on vacation, they played together, and both took their clubs to conventions or out-of-town meetings, where generally Fred would play with the men and Helen with the women. According to Fred's Dallas golf cronies, he played

62

every weekend when he could. He knew that he could never make a low score, so was well-satisfied with a few really good shots, a par or two on a round, and thrilled if he made a birdie. One day on the 12th hole at the Lakewood Country Club, Fred got up to his ball on the tee with a 3 iron. Since the hole was only 147 yards long, he was advised by the other players to take a 5 or 6 iron to avoid driving over the green. He kept the original club and, with a mighty swing, hit a shot that headed straight for the little pond that guarded the green. My informants told me that, watching from the tee, no one in the foursome really knew where the ball had gone, and Fred apologized for the poor shot. When they found the ball in the hole, his joy was uncontrollable. Miraculously, the ball had skidded across the water, probably hit a rock, bounded onto the green, and had gone into the hole. Fred never did stop talking about his hole-in-one.

For some years after Fred and Helen were married, they enjoyed horseback riding together, and, for a while, Helen had her own horse. Fred sometimes went fishing and, when he could get away, joined friends for hunting—ducks, quail, wild geese, wild turkeys, and, occasionally, deer. He was reported to be a good shot. Helen tells a story of a close call Fred had involving a hunting trip in 1954. Fred had accepted an invitation to go duck hunting in Louisiana. The morning before the departure by plane, he phoned Helen for advice as to whether or not to go because he had caught a cold. Since sitting in a duck blind is a poor cure for a cold and could turn it into pneumonia, she insisted that he beg off. The hunting party used two planes belonging to the United Gas Company in Shreveport, Louisiana. On the return trip, one of these planes that Fred might have been on, carrying twelve persons, fell into a lake near Shreveport with *no* survivors. This crash was a

63

great personal shock to me because one of my closest friends, Milton Weiss, and his brother, Bernard, were aboard. The Weiss' third brother, Seymour, a very prominet New Orleans citizen, would have been on the plane, but like Fred, did not go because of a cold. Ironically, Tom Braniff, one of the best known men in the aviation industry and founder of Braniff International, was killed in this crash. Darrell Hamric, who was a top officer of Republic and who has helped with this book, was fortunate enough to have been on the second plane.

In the early years of their married life, Helen and Fred spent very few evenings at home alone, although in later years they had more evening leisure. It is easy to understand why their evenings were generally occupied. There was much business entertaining, and the Florences also socialized with two different groups of couples who usually entertained in a similar manner: dinner parties at home or at a club, followed by cards and sometimes dancing, if the party was large. In addition, there was rarely a week in which Helen and Fred did not attend civic or charity banquets, and even when most of the guests were wearing informal attire, the Florences were usually honored by sitting at the head table where formal dress was required.

Both Helen and Fred enjoyed the symphony and the opera and, as both enjoyed the theater, they went to many shows on their numerous visits to New York. On occasion, always with one or more other people, they would go to a night club. In this area Helen has not been very helpful to the biographer, but I surmise that Fred went to be a good sport, danced because it was expected of him, and probably sat hoping that none of his customers would see him. Fred apparently was much more relaxed and less formal whenever he was away from Dallas. For many summers, he and Helen spent a few weeks with the Hoblitzelles on Cape

Cod. Lynn Harris, an associate of Mr. Hoblitzelle, was usually at the home during these visits. While still connected with the Interstate Amusement Company, Lynn became Mr. Hoblitzelle's personal assistant and became a noted authority on fine silver. He is currently the managing director of the Hoblitzelle Foundation. Lynn tells me that when Fred was at the Cape, he was a totally different man, even sporting a pair of colorful Bermuda shorts. In 1958, Helen and Fred took their daughter, Cecile, their son, David, and both their spouses to Europe. They crossed eastbound on the *S. S. United States*, and flew home. During this trip of slightly more than three weeks, they visited Paris, Lucerne, Venice, Rome, Florence, Milan, Berlin, Brussels, and London. Fred was then 67, and this trip was a great joy to him. He got far enough from Dallas to throw off the tension and to play.

Helen talks about parties at home where she was quite the "cut-up," and that there were some parties with discreet friends where even Fred really let his hair down. Although the crowd that the Florences went with were considerably older than my first wife and I, we knew or knew of most of them, and I can safely say that they could not be described as "Mid-Victorian."

One of Fred's qualities that I have admired most was his love of beauty and his excellent taste. From early childhood, I accompanied my parents to fine art galleries and perhaps the finest shops in most of Europe's great cities. I majored in art at college and have considered myself a qualified critic of good or bad taste. When Helen first invited me to her stately home in early August of 1963, I was very much impressed with the paintings and what I was certain had been beautiful furniture before it had begun to show signs of wear. Quite understandably, after Fred's death, Helen lost all interest in entertaining and spent her time in her own quarters on the second floor. During

65

my courtship, we were out a good deal or sat in the upstairs living room when just visiting, so I had not paid much attention to the great number of magnificent possessions of all kinds she and Fred had collected throughout their thirty-three years of marriage.

Merely to keep the record straight, I mention the fact that before Helen and I were married, we agreed to live in her house and to offer both our houses for sale. We had an understanding that if one was sold, we would live in the other until it was sold, and if we could dispose of both, we would rent an apartment or buy another house. I sold my house within a matter of months, so we lived in the Florence home for slightly over two years, after which we moved to our present home. The mansion was sold a few months after we vacated. It was only during the packing and after the move that I discovered and learned of the many artifacts, antiques, and one or more examples of almost everything a collector of art objects seeks. Our present home has built-in cabinets and book case shelves where much is on display, but with our combined accumulations during our first marriages and what we have brought together in the past fifteen years, many things are stored under cabinets and in closets for eventual distribution to our families. These examples of almost every craft or object of natural origin are not just for display, but give us great pleasure. We enjoy looking at them and reminiscing about where or why they were bought. We show them to our visitors, proudly explaining what they are, the name of the artist, the country of origin, or some interesting fact regarding their acquisition.

Often, I asked Helen about their purchases and learned that almost from the first year of their marriage, Fred would meet her on Saturdays at the jewelry counter of Neiman-Marcus or Linz, where they would admire the fine new pieces offered for sale. They would also visit the gift departments of stores at home and on trips. Fred had an innate feeling for the beautiful, and he also worked to increase his knowledge. He spent many hours in museums and viewing private collections so that he could improve his appreciation of art by making comparisons. He came to love fine things, and before making a purchase always gave the matter careful thought. Although able to pay the asking price, he could sense whether bargaining was possible, and was a master at this. He got a great kick out of a good buy, and in 1960 on their trip to the Orient, where bargaining is expected, he had no peer. He also instinctively knew values and that the world was full of exquisite and exotic things, and unless an item completely fulfilled his and Helen's desire at the right price, it was rejected. Helen tells me that Fred went with her when she bought her clothes. I don't; and in the many years of our marriage, I have discovered, with certainty, that equal credit for the good taste in all their purchases should go to Helen.

Fred understood craftmanship, had a sensitive feeling for color complements and an eye for the artistic, as well as a quick repulsion for the mediocre and a shudder for the shoddy, which we all know is in the majority. It was his interest in superiority in all forms of art that led him to seek it and to own it so that he, his family, and his friends could enjoy it.

67

CHAPTER VIII
THE BANKER

"From the day I entered the bank, I never had any thought of anything else except what was related to banking."

—FFF, referring to his beginnings in Rusk

The history of our great industrial giants includes many who, like Fred, came from humble beginnings with no financial help from his family. Perhaps the most difficult obstacle to overcome on the way up is adjusting to a higher scale. However, the transition from a small town bank to a big city bank in no way fazed Fred. Once in an officer's meeting when the bank had reached a billion in deposits, he reminded his staff that there were other figures—like two billion and higher. He believed that even the apex could be exceeded.

The belief that things could always be better—and that it was his personal responsibility to *make* them better—was an important part of Fred's basic philosophy which dominated his thinking and governed his actions. It would be correct to say that Fred was a "conservative optimist." He was realistic—he always had his feet on the ground—but he genuinely believed that things not only could but *would* be better.

Fred never worried about luck or breaks because he knew that with sound business management, the odds were with him. Sound business judgment is generally self-taught by the process of trial and error; with care that the errors are minimal and that each experience becomes beneficial for the next similar situation. Like all human beings, Fred made mistakes. You might think I don't know this by what I have written so far, but he did make them. He used them, however, for what the knowledge gained from them could mean in the future. Many of us tend to look back, an activity which, to my way of thinking, is fruitless, time consuming, and often discouraging. Regrets are regrettable because they only cause unhappiness. Fred wasted no time on regrets, concentrating instead on his goals for the future.

Too many people blame failure on bad luck and credit success to good luck. In practice, luck is by no means the governing force, because in the span of life, we all have our share of good and bad breaks. Success, in a measure, is the ability to avoid or to minimize the bad, and to take full advantage of the good. Fred fully understood the importance of minimizing the bad, as we can tell from an excerpt from his speech before the Illinois Bankers Convention in 1953:

> During boom periods, the seeds are always sown for the difficulties of the succeding eventual downturn, and it is during periods of downward fluctuating activity that credit and financial problems increase and multiply. If we take these problems into consideration in the discharge of our daily work, we will materially lessen their impact when the downturn occurs.

70

It was Fred's solid, fundamental philosophy that allowed Republic to continue on its path of success during times of adversity when many other banks struggled for existence.

We know that Fred had only the most fundamental of formal educations. He did not have the advanced training in economics and specifically in "money and banking" offered by such institutions as the Wharton School at the University of Pennsylvania or The Harvard School of Business. His only formal schooling beyond what he received in the public schools of Rusk, Texas, was a short course at a business college. Considering the limitations of his educational background, I find the soundness of Fred's philosophy, the depth of his technical knowledge of banking, and even his facility with the English language as shown in his speeches, nothing short of amazing.

Let me quote a few of Fred's own remarks which, I believe, best illustrate his banking and business credo:

> The job of banks is to put money to work—to take the money of those who have it and put it into use of those who need it in such a manner that it earns profits for all.
> Banks should meet every sound and legitimate need for credit which they can find. It is not enough in our dynamic society for bankers to wait for business to come walking in; we should go out and find the need where it exists.

And from a speech to the American Bankers Association, May 23, 1955:

> Credit is the banker's stock in trade. The banker is a primary merchandiser of credit. Yet the business of extending credit in one form or another is shared by many others—public and private; corporate and individual; small and large. Bank credit—the life blood of our business—has always held fascination for me, and it has not been a provincial fascination merely cultivated by an atmosphere of growth.

He continued with the following profound advice:

> The mule cannot compete with the tractor; the horse cannot out-run the two ton V-8; and the anvil and forge can-

71

not challenge the mile-long strip-mill. In a world sparked by the drive for better products and better ways of making them, the less efficient, unadaptable units will fall by the wayside.

Fred saw bank credit as a commodity to be marketed, and banking itself as a highly competitive service business in which the bank offering the best service to the customer would come out ahead.

I discussed Fred's banking philosophy with Leland Dupree, who when he retired had been with the bank since 1921. Only one man living at the time of this writing, James Cumby, had served the bank longer. Although Leland began in a humble job, he soon rose to be one of the bank's top executives. He retired as Vice Chairman of the Board of the Republic of Texas Corporation, the bank's holding company. Because of Leland's intimate and accurate knowledge of the development of the Republic Bank, and his close friendship with Fred, I shall quote him often.

Leland told me that Fred repeatedly said, "We never grow; it's our customers that grow and it's our duty to help them grow." Fred believed that the important thing was to serve the customer, whether or not this service was *directly* profitable to the bank. Leland remembered that in the early days, when the Trust Department was small, an officer was talking to Fred about a very small trust that would not (according to this officer) be worth the trouble for the bank to handle. Leland said that Fred chastised this officer severely and told him, "If our cook wanted us to handle her little estate for her, we'll do it no matter how much it costs us."

Leland went on to say the Fred could really "chew someone out" if the occasion warranted it, but that he never held a grudge. After Fred made his point clearly and forcefully, he would usually dismiss the culprit with a pat on the back and a word of encouragement. Leland continued to talk about Fred's fairness with employees. Fred wouldn't listen to complaints from one employee about another behind that person's back. He would call the second person in, and say to the one complaining, "Now what was that you were saying?" So there was no backbiting, no dissension. Leland also said that people *were* fired when there was justification, but he remembered Fred's saying about this, "My heart tells me one thing, my mind tells me another; but I always go by what my mind tells me is best for the bank."

When I asked Leland what he thought was the one thing that made Fred Florence outstanding as a banker, he replied:

> It was not any one thing. It was just that Fred thought that everybody should do business with Republic Bank. And he kept up with everything—he knew *everything* that was going on.

I remember that it was almost as if Fred had E.S.P. because he seemed to know everybody's business. My father, who died in 1937, left two trusts with his New York bank, the Guaranty Trust Company. My brother passed away seven years later and also left a trust to be administered by them. I had moved to Dallas in 1939 and I saw Fred in the bank or at a luncheon from time to time. He rarely failed to tell me how much he would appreciate having me move these trusts to Republic. He knew (how, I don't know) that my mother and I were the trustees, and apparently he genuinely believed that we could move them to Dallas. After obtaining a legal opinion that such a move was impossible, I gave Fred copies of the instruments and the attorney's opinion, not wanting him to think me evasive or uncooperative. I tell this story to illustrate his un-

73

tiring efforts to get new business and his personal knowledge of almost all things that could affect his bank. Fred was an extrovert who enjoyed talking to people, and he was eager to learn from anyone he felt had insights to offer him. According to Helen, he learned much from James and Nat, his chauffeurs. He had an observant eye and a memory for details, but he also had the ability to discard or forget, so as not to clog his brain. It is a rare and precious gift.

Dr. Levi Olan, who is now Rabbi Emeritus of Temple Emanu-el, became the Senior Rabbi on January 1, 1950, when Dr. Lefkowitz, Fred's father-in-law, became Emeritus. Rabbi Olan probably knew Fred as well as anyone besides the family and a few of Fred's closest associates at the bank. Rabbi Olan is a most knowledgeable man, a great teacher, and an excellent judge of people. One day when I was discussing my thoughts about this book with him, he told me that without question Fred had a touch of genius. Now, the word *genius* has always had a peculiar connotation for me: I tend to associate it with a drab, bearded, bespectacled, serious-minded man who knows everything, but whom I wouldn't want to know. We have all heard the saying about there being a fine line between genius and insanity. When I was a boy, I knew a famous surgeon, a man named Louis Berg, who always wore a red necktie. His parents considered him a genius, and therefore in danger of lunacy. They believed the old Jewish superstition that wearing a red necktie would guard against this possibility.

Certainly no one ever characterized Fred as either a Svengali or a lunatic! But the dictionary definition of the word *mastermind* certainly fits: "a person of great intelligence, especially one with the ability to plan or direct a group project." And *genius* may be the correct term for Fred's singular ability to judge people, to hear a story or read a statement and, with speed of lightning, to make an immediate, logical, well-calculated decision. Fred made many loans on the basis of what he thought of the individual, and he made exceedingly few mistakes. He could tell in a moment if a deal was phony or a request was unreasonable, and he wasted no time in turning it down, but usually by telling the applicant that he would think it over and be in touch if interested. He carefully never completely closed any doors because in the future the same person might become a good prospective customer.

Fred instituted a most unorthodox policy on loans. Any loan officer could *approve* a loan within his scope of authority, but under no circumstances could he alone *turn down* a loan of any magnitude. If the loan officer thought an application should be refused, he had to take it all the way to the top. (Sometimes if Fred himself was unavailable, depending upon the circumstances, the decision would be referred to one of the senior executives.) As I have written before, Fred was a superb judge of character, and often, even when a statement was too poor to warrant the loan, he could see possibilities. He often made the loans others considered dubious, and his batting average on collecting the money was unbelievably good. It was almost as if he had a sixth sense that overcame reason, but brought in the results.

Fred was always ready to "work something out" so that he could safely and profitably say "Yes." As an example: If an officer of the bank felt that the ability of the borrower to repay the loan was questionable, he would by policy take the application to Fred before turning it down. Studying the request, Fred might see the possibility of making the loan a desirable one by restructuring the deal. The borrower might have set his sights and ambitions beyond realism, so that a smaller loan would be acceptable to the

75

bank and adequate to satisfy the need. Or an improvement in the collateral, a change in the corporate structure, the use of a business insurance plan, or some other sound idea could accomplish the purpose of making the loan safe. Fred was a past master of such techniques, which served the customer and made money for the bank.

There was, of course, the other side of the coin where the loan officer was fully justified in his opinion that a loan should not be made. In these cases, Fred had a most gracious way of saying "No." Although disappointed, an applicant always knew that he had his inning in court, had seen the boss, and in most cases, that the bank was right. He left with regrets, but not with malice.

Fred wanted broad holdings of the bank's stock, and he made a great effort to have his stockholders attend annual meetings. He insisted on dividends being paid monthly instead of quarterly, so that his stockholders would have a continuing reminder of their interest in the success of the bank. Fred thought it was extremely important for the stockholders to take a personal interest in the bank. Fred checked all transfers of the bank's stock, and, whenever a new stockholder of consequence appeared on the list, Fred usually phoned to welcome him. Fred always did his homework before talking to anyone, either in his office or over the telephone; so before making such a call, he would review for his own information the stockholder's activity with the bank. This personal touch was the best possible public relations. Often when I buy stock in a company, I get a letter from the chief executive officer or the president welcoming me as a stockholder, usually enclosing a brochure of the company's most recent statement. I know that the letter is just a form, but it neverthelesss is impressive. Fred's personal phone call was even more effective.

76

Besides keeping up with new stockholders, Fred knew daily how each department of the bank stood. He was informed about deposits, withdrawals, and loans, and reviewed the daily list of new accounts. If he spotted one that appeared to represent a potentially large customer (or if he had been alerted to that fact), he would place a welcoming call. Who wouldn't be flattered to have a prominent banker call and specifically offer his services? Everyone likes recognition, and everyone likes to know that his business is appreciated. Often that one phone call increased the new bank account, resulted in a good loan, and possibly created a good long-time customer.

Fred also did this in reverse. If a large depositor, all of a sudden, let his account get very low, or he closed it, Fred let no time go by before he had the man or woman on the phone. Generally there was a logical reason for the customer's action, such as a mistake or a misunderstanding because of lack of communication. We must remember that until we depended upon computers and before hiring practices were regulated, people rightfully felt that a bank should not (or hardly ever) make an error. The phone call had two important purposes. First, it gave Fred information from an outside source about a possible deficiency of the bank or of an employee, requiring further investigation. If the complaint was justified, corrective action could be taken. Second, ruffled feathers could often be smoothed, and an account saved. If the reason was valid but the condition subsequently changed, another phone call might bring the customer back into the fold. In 1932, when I was still living in New York, Republic refused to renew one of our company's notes. I was very impetuous at thirty-one years old, so I sold some gilt-edge bonds at a 10 percent loss (mighty little during the depression), mailed the bank a cashier's check from the Guaranty Trust Company of New

77

York, paid off the loan, and closed our Republic bank account. No sooner had the check arrived than Fred had me on long distance. He scolded me for not having called him personally, and said that he was returning the check, and, of course, would renew the loan. I shall never know whether the cashier's check was what improved my credit or whether the turndown was someone else's doing. In the many years that followed, I never asked.

I wish to comment on two particular rules Fred followed which today seem to be observed by relatively few people. Perhaps it was these unshakable principles that I admired most in Fred, because the absence of them has always irked me most. During my many years in business, my evaluation of an employee often was determined by his promptness and his dependability. Maybe our lives would be more pleasant if there were no timepieces, so that we would eat when we are hungry, sleep when sleepy, and do what we say we will do only at our own convenience or when the spirit moves us. Well, unfortunately, the hourglass and the sundial upset the apple cart. We work, sleep, play, and eat by the clock; we anticipate prompt answers to our mail, look for an "as soon as possible" reply to a phone call, and expect to have debts paid to us when due. Many never care much about these annoying necessities for a successful life, but the man I knew for 37 years was impeccably prompt and almost never forgot to do anything that he had promised. If he was late, it was not intentional and always genuinely unavoidable; and if he forgot any obligation, it was a rare happenstance.

Fred got up each morning at 7:00 A.M. and arrived at his office quite promptly at 8:00 A.M. Helen tells me that he had unlimited vitality, and his friends and associates still wonder how one man got so much done, so well. Fred was involved in so many civic and charitable activities that it is hard to understand how he ran a great business and still had time for all his other assignments. It is a mystery to me how he managed to know so much about every detail in the bank and also keep abreast of what was going on in the other organizations and institutions in which he was interested. In addition to his formal commitments, Fred was constantly being sought out for advice on all kinds of matters, and he not only made himself available for such inquiries, but if he agreed to help, he could be counted upon to give sound advice, usually with little delay.

I think that Fred's organized way of doing things— plus, of course, his extraordinary personal energy—helps to explain how he kept up with all his responsibilities. So many people procrastinate in doing everything that their minds become cluttered and eventually, nothing is done. Fred made quick decisions, shirked nothing that he had undertaken, and kept an orderly mind. He wasted no words, and he always asked direct, intelligent questions. Helen says that Fred always came home with stacks of reports. My guess is that he had devised a method of scanning these reports to spot items of interest almost automatically, the way a typewriter stops at a margin control. Fred did everything fast: even walking with him on the street, with his speedy gait, was proof of how this 6-foot man, who stood as straight as an arrow, could set a pace hard to follow.

79

Fred surrounded himself with capable assistants in whom he had great confidence, and he allocated many matters to them for research and recommendations. They would give Fred the facts and their opinions, and Fred would make the final decisions—sometimes in accordance with their advice, sometimes not. Although Fred was gracious and mild-mannered and always listened to his associates, the final decision was his and he made it. Since ultimate responsibility for the bank rested with him, he always did what in his opinion was right. One of my informants described him as being autocratic. I dislike the word "autocrat" and like to think of the boss as a "benevolent dictator." Often using one's authority is unpleasant, but in good management it is vital.

Darrell Hamric, a longtime employee of Republic in the Oil Division, told me a story that illustrates an almost uncanny ability which Fred possessed that undoubtedly provided much-needed short cuts in his busy days. Hamric said he had been asked to prepare a report on a particular company in regard to a loan request. When he finished compiling the lengthy report, he took it in a folder to Fred's desk. Without even opening the folder, Fred began asking questions. Hamric said, "Fred's questions took up where my report left off. It was as though he had already read every word of what I had written."

Fred also had two capable secretaries who helped in many ways, saving him time by doing work which they could do on their own, and by reminding him of things that needed to be done that might have slipped his mind. Dewey Dean, who is now Senior Vice President of Republic Bank, began his career as Fred's secretary (male secretaries were more common in those days than they are now). Dewey told me that Fred dictated as fast as he walked and that there was no way he could possibly keep up with him, although his shorthand was rapid. The way he managed was to understand the gist of what Fred wanted to say, write down whatever key words he could, and then reconstruct the whole thing from memory. Fred's secretaries had to be rather special people!

Although I was by no means a steady visitor to Fred's office, I learned a trick from him that I copied in my own office. Fred never told me his strategy of ending an interview, but being observant and having had it pulled on me, I figured it out. So often, when a man or woman finally gets to see an important person, the visitor likes to sit and pass the time of day even after business is concluded. Fred had no time for small talk or trivialities, and there was always someone waiting in his reception room or a meeting to be attended. His two efficient secretaries made quite accurate estimates of the length of time to allot each appointment, and were able to set the calendar to give each visitor sufficient time and to give the boss a little time for dictation, phone calls, consulting with his associates, or reviewing reports. When a visitor's business was concluded, Fred would rise from his chair and offer his hand, whereupon most people would find their way to the door. Most times, Fred would walk with the visitor to the door, a gesture that showed warmth and good manners. If his next visitor was already on his feet, Fred was at the door to greet him with a welcoming handshake. Often, if the departing friend or customer was important to the bank, or if Fred wished to show special interest or appreciation, he would walk all the way to the elevators.

People dislike being kept waiting; when Fred would step to his door and see a good friend or a good customer, he would greet him with the assurance that his wait would not be long. Such cordiality made those waiting feel that everything was being done to speed things up, but, most important of all, the incoming visitor knew that time was of the essence and therefore would get down to business and be as brief as posssible.

Fred had a special method of discontinuing nonproductive interviews. If after a few minutes, it was obvious that the meeting would be of no value to either party, Fred would press a button that was fastened under his desk and out of sight. A buzzer on his secretary's desk was a signal to which she was accustomed. She politely came to Fred's

81

desk to tell him that he had a long distance call from some far-away city. Fred took time enough to tell the visitor that he would think the matter over or send him to someone else, or sometimes, suggest that he come back at another time.

Conversely, some wondered how they could always get Fred on the phone even though they knew how busy he always was. His one secretary generally answered the phone while the other took care of typing and other office matters. The private secretary (if I may make a distinction) pretty well knew the names of all the directors, large stockholders, and substantial customers. She had some way of alerting Fred that this call was important if he was already talking to someone else. Fred would tell the person to whom he was talking on the phone that he had long distance on another line and would call back; or, if someone was at his desk, he could apologize for the interruption and take the call. If the call was confidential, he could excuse himself and take the call on another telephone. Even though Fred had this method of giving priority to calls from important people, he was not at all hard to reach by not-so-important people. I am told that he returned all calls promptly (with, of course, some discretion on the part of his secretary to screen out cranks and people she knew positively would merely be wasting Fred's time).

Fred's real finesse was with the good customer who, seeing no one in the waiting room and having plenty of time of his own, decides to add a little social visit. If, when Fred arose from his chair, his visitor had taken root, Fred would suggest that he would like to show his guest a Steuben vase which he had recently acquired, or a silver bowl that the bank employees had given him for some occasion. Not surprisingly, the object was always on a table near the door or in the waiting room—and the battle was won.

82

The Banker

It all worked wonders, and, even today, people tell me that Fred Florence got more done in one day than any ten men normally do. I am sure others do the same as Fred, and if we could ask him, he probably would say that he learned it from so-and-so. With it all, no one ever felt rushed; and the empty desk top, the fresh flowers in a vase, the comfortable and elegant decor of the office, and Fred's warm, gracious manner made all feel important and, at least during their visit, that they and their business had Fred's undivided attention.

Researching material for this story has brought many pleasant surprises. It has made it possible for me to meet many interesting and charming new people and to visit again with old friends, some of whom I had not seen in many moons. Some have told me about their experiences with Fred that merely confirmed what I already knew about his character and his ability as a banker. In all cases I could feel their pride in having known him. Much of what they told me was repetitious, but I permitted myself to be reassured of my own evaluation, and ever so often someone would describe Fred in a way that tickled me.

J. Neil Mancill had been head of the National Accounts Department of the Republic Bank for many years. One day at lunch Charles Pistor, now Chairman of the Board of Republic, suggested that I ask him to tell me the story about the Franklin Life Insurance Company of Springfield, Illinois. I had not seen Neil in many years, so I was especially pleased when he came to my office looking and acting like a 60-year old, but in fact 82. We had a nice reunion. The Franklin Life story is just like hundreds of others except that in the late forties, this million dollar loan to Charles Becker in San Antonio was an unusually big one. Fred handled it himself. Becker used the money to buy the life insurance company, paid off promptly as planned, maintained a substantial minimum balance—and the Republic had a good long-time customer. Neil Mancill said that Charlie Becker never forgot what Fred had done for him. My spry, jovial visitor left with this comment:

> I don't think there was a greater banker in the United States anywhere than Fred Florence. I think he was tops. His men were loyal to him one hundred percent, and they'd do anything in the world for Fred Florence. He was right with them—he wasn't pushing them, he was pulling them!

The following story is a perfect example of Fred in action. It was told to me by Jake Mossiker, a personal friend. In the early 1920s, Jake and another young man, Arthur Voekel, joined the firm of Paul's Shoes, ladies' retail shoe stores. The company got its name from the founder, Paul Baerwald, who was married to Jake's oldest sister. As the years went by, the operation became a big success, with a number of new stores added; and Jake and Arthur each acquired an interest in the company.

In or about 1944, Paul Baerwald decided to join the Consolidated Dry Goods Company of St. Louis and move his home to that city. At the same time (and I do not know exactly for what reason), he determined to acquire the stock that Jake and Arthur held in Paul's Shoes, and had made them an offer. Although the terms of the sale apparently had been pretty well agreed upon, Jake insisted that the three parties meet with Fred Florence in his office at the bank, to discuss the details of the deal and to make the closing. Jake was a close friend and great admirer of Fred, and he wanted his assurance that the transaction was handled properly.

To the surprise of both Jake and Arthur, Fred immediately made the suggestion that perhaps, instead of

Baerwald buying their shares, he might prefer to sell his interest in the company to them, at the same price per share. Paul said he would be willing to sell out (as Fred somehow must have known), but that Jake and Arthur didn't have the money. "They do now," Fred replied, "I'm going to lend it to them."

Fred knew that both men were of the highest integrity, were hard workers, and good businessmen. He further knew that if Paul bought, the bank would probably not do as well with absentee ownership; and by lending the purchase money to the Dallas men, he would get a good, profitable loan, keep a good customer, and hold a Dallas-based firm. It worked out just that way. Paul sold; and the firm, under the new owners, grew substantially until they sold the business in 1959 to the International Shoe Company.

Several stories illustrating Fred's ability as a banker came to me from a slightly mysterious source, but I have decided to include them anyway. In the files of the bank's Public Relations Department I found five typewritten pages about Fred, with the following message typed in the top margin on the first page:

> John—here is a series of thoughts expressed in the rough rather than in story form, both for the conserving of time (no pun) and for the fact that I know I'm not as familiar with Time style as you are . . . Bob G.

85

The page bears the date "4-17-46." Apparently this material was notes for a proposed *Time* magazine article about Fred, but a thorough search in the library revealed no such story ever published. I have not been able to learn the identity of either "John" or "Bob G.," although I have asked Leland Dupree and others who were with the bank in the forties.

The part of these notes that I want to quote here begins with a story about Fred and R. J. (Mike) Morfa, who was then President of the Missouri, Kansas and Texas Railroad, known as the Katy:

> Behind scenes in Katy deal: Morfa expressed consideration of need for refinancing while casually visiting in Florence's office. Quick as the proverbial rabbit, FFF told him that he (Florence) believed that Texas banks could and would do it—and at a saving for the Katy. In a matter of a couple hours (telephone connections were slow in some cases) he had commitments for over $8,000,000, well over the $4,750,000 needed by the railroad—all on FFF's personal say-so to bankers.

To understand the full significance of such a deal, we must remember that up to this time, over thirty years ago, most of the really big deals in Texas had been made with the big money banks in New York and Chicago. Fred set out to change this situation, as illustrated further by the next two stories from Bob G.'s notes:

> On Washington's birthday (this year) Eugene B. Smith, head of Eugene B. Smith & Co. came in, said, 'Fred, the government is going to put some Commodity Credit Corp. cotton - 320,000 bales of it - on the market in New Orleans Feb. 28. We'd like to try to buy a little of it.'
>
> Florence: 'Well, Gene, how much do you want?'
>
> Smith: 'Don't know yet, Fred - we'd like to bid on whatever looks good to us.'
>
> Florence: 'OK, Gene, give 'em a check for it, and we'll clear it.'
>
> That check, for commitments of cotton deliveries for the next six months to domestic mills in this country, was for $8,500,000. Florence called a few correspondent banks, gave them a 'piece' of the loan, took up to the legal limit for Republic (national banks by law may lend only 10% of their capital and surplus - Republic's capital and surplus is $20,000,000).

The Banker

A few days later Rogers Lacy, slight, round Santa-Claus-looking Texas oilman walked in, said, 'Fred, you know I owe you and some of your folks (banks who correspond with Republic and participate in loans with it) $6,000,000 -well, Fred, I need another $10,000,000.' 'What are you planning, Rogers?' FFF wanted to know. 'Well, I want to build a couple new refineries, one at Big Sandy, Texas, and one at Rogerslacy (just been named) Mississippi, where I am helping develop some new properties. And then, too, I want to do a little further development at my gas fields in Panola and Harrison counties (also in Texas), the East Texas oil field, in Louisiana and Mississippi.' He laid blueprints on Florence's desk of the above and of holdings in the Hawkins and Quitman fields - well known oil properties in Texas. Florence's petroleum engineers and geologists were called in (he has three full-time specialists of this type). 'Okay, Mr. Florence,' they said, and the deal was consummated.

The mysterious Bob G. continues with the following evaluation:

It isn't happen-chance or irresponsible banking, it is the exemplification of a perfectly coordinated banking machine, with broad experience and judgment based on years of experience in their fields by Mr. FFF and his staff. In cotton, oil, commercial fields - it makes little difference, the bank is capable of handling any type of application and fast. Bank losses on loans are infinitesimal.

87

When I began interviewing old friends of Fred's, Helen insisted that I go to El Paso to talk to Mr. Sam D. Young, Sr., the Chairman of the Board of the El Paso National Bank. Mr. Young in his early years had been a bank examiner in East Texas, and later it was he who presented the Guaranty Bank and Trust Company (Republic's original name) its first charter. I had become acquainted with Mr. Young after

Helen and I married, and on several occasions Helen and I visited with him and his family in La Jolla, California, and in El Paso. I agreed that he might have some interesting stories to tell about his early association with Fred.

I left Dallas on an early morning American Airlines flight to El Paso, and Sam was at the airport to meet me. I returned home at about 4:00 p.m. and found Helen anxiously waiting for my report. She asked, "How was it and what did you learn?" I told her how Sam had picked me up in his brand new beautiful car. His bank had recently completed a handsome new building of which he was justly proud. After the V.I.P. tour we sat in his spacious, tastefully decorated office and spoke until lunch. At noon we had a sumptuous meal; and after visiting with Sam, Jr., President of the bank and our son David's very close friend, I was returned to the airport.

After listening to all of this in somewhat greater detail, Helen said, "That's great, but what did you learn?" I told her that I had learned a great deal about Sam, which I enjoyed because he is a delightful person; but I had learned nothing about what I was really seeking, which was information about Fred's early banking career when he and Sam had been closely associated.

However, during my visit with Sam he did tell me this interesting story about a big deal in Mexico in which he and Fred were both involved:

> The story of the purchase of the Mexican telephone system by Mexican nationals, joined by a few select American friends, really began in the early '20s. Eloy S. Vallina at that time was a clerk employed by the El Paso branch of the Federal Reserve Bank. I was a young bank examiner assigned to the El Paso district. Our friendship grew closer as the days came and went, and in its midst many air castles were built, only to be punctured totally or to emerge

partially successful. After many years, Vallina had organized a successful and prosperous banking institution in Chihuahua, Mexico. He proposed to further his ambition to arrive at the level of a great industrialist and banker by attempting to purchase for himself and a group of followers the telephone system in Mexico, which was in a state of deterioration and decay. The former owners were the International Telephone and Telegraph Company and L. M. Ericsson Telephone Company of Sweden. Vallina spent much time and effort in preparing figures of every description, including pro forma statements of assets and liabilities, operating statements, etc.

Vallina's plan, as Sam Young described it to me, was for him and a Mexican syndicate to join with a few American friends in attempting to purchase the telephone facilities from the present owners in order to get the control back into the hands of Mexican nationals. Vallina realized that a plan to take over this huge enterprise from two substantial companies was not an easy task. As Sam further told me,

The proposal, while firmly based, was somewhat like treading on thin ice. However, with the passing of time, the intricate pieces seemed to fall in place. When Mr. Vallina seriously proposed the plan to me, it was firmly entrenched in financial circles along the border and with some of the larger city bankers, and Vallina suggested that I set out to explore the possibility of arranging credit on satisfactory terms for the purchase. My attention automatically went first to my close and devoted friend, Fred Florence, President of the Republic National Bank, with whom I had enjoyed intimate ties over a period of years since the two of us were young men together in the Dallas Circles back in the early twenties. Fred Florence, after scanning the matter, briefly concluded in his inimitable way that the idea was sound, and, tasting the meat in the coconut, pronounced it of good flavor, add-

89

ing that the proposition was meritorious for further exploration and development. This was all the incentive Eloy Vallina needed to pursue it vigorously and then, joined by his comrade in other ventures, Don Carlos Trouyet, he began apportioning the proposed stock acquisition among his associates. Simultaneously, I began supplying Mr. Florence more and more information in support of the legitimacy of the proposed deal. Things were dragging along over the slow and tedious route of negotiations between Stockholm, New York, and Mexico City.

In 1954, Sam and Betty Young, and Helen and Fred, went on separate European tours. Sam had been advised that the telephone deal was fast coming to a head; and although Sam was in Strassburg, Austria, he found Fred in Lucerne, Switzerland, and they had a telephone discussion. It was agreed that when Fred returned, he would carefully analyze the proposition to determine the feasibility and justification for this huge loan of $25,000,000.

On Fred's return, he was presented with the proposed deal. He turned the investigation over to Mr. Oran Kite, who had been with the bank for many years and in whom he had great confidence. To make an intelligent decision, careful analysis was necessary. Oran tells me that Fred presented him with the figures early one morning with instructions to have the analysis back on his desk by 3:00 p.m. To complicate matters, everything was in Spanish and all the figures were in pesos. This meant that Oran required the services of an interpreter, and he needed to convert the pesos to dollars.

The task completed, the parties involved met in Dallas, where many problems needed to be solved. When everybody connected with the deal was satisfied, the loan was made, the takeover was concluded, and the project was a success.

This deal was most unique in American banking because it involved lending money for the purchase of stock and therefore was not a self-liquidating loan. Furthermore, lending a large sum for a Mexican project was frowned upon by the New York banks.

Sam Young summed up this very interesting deal with the following few remarks:

> This is another confirmation of the great insight, the clarity, and the alacrity of Fred's thinking power, and his tremendous capacity in deciding what was and what was not a wise business deal, acceptable for bank financing. Needless to say, the deal was successfully concluded, and its operations over the years proved out almost to the penny the projections and estimates of Eloy Vallina.

Not only did the bank get a good loan, but their wholly-owned subsidiary, the Howard Corporation (whose story follows) became owners of 113,824 shares of Telefonos de Mexico, S.A. In 1979 it paid a semi-annual dividend of 401,730 pesos, which at an exchange rate of 22.75 pesos to the dollar is $35,317 a year. The cost to the Howard Corporation was $1.545 a share. It sold on the Mexican Bourse on September 26, 1979, for $2.66. This asset of the Howard Corporation was transferred to the Republic of Texas Corporation, which in turn owns the Republic National Bank.

91

Until I began writing this biography, all that I knew about the Howard Corporation was that it belonged to the Republic National Bank and paid huge dividends into their coffers every year. In researching for this story, I have become convinced that the formation of the Howard Corporation was the most important management decision that Fred made throughout his many years as a banker.

The history of the Howard Corporation involved some complicated consolidations, name changes, and trusteeships. To be sure that my facts are correct, I quote from *A Special Report to Shareholders of Republic National Bank of Dallas on The Howard Corporation et al*, dated December 1, 1964:

Origin and History of the Corporations
Republic National Company

On June 6, 1928, Republic National Bank and Trust Company was organized as a consolidation of two existing banks: Republic Trust and Savings Bank, a state-chartered institution, and The Republic National Bank of Dallas. Prior to the consolidation, the state bank owned all the shares of another corporation, Republic Mortgage Company, which had been organized under charter issued by the State of Texas in 1924. By a charter amendment on June 13, 1928, the name of Republic Mortgage Company was changed to Republic National Company. The name of Republic National Bank and Trust Company was changed in 1937 to the current one: Republic National Bank of Dallas.

Under its charter, Republic National Company was authorized, among other things, to accumulate and loan money; to hold, sell and deal in stocks, bonds and securities; to subscribe for, purchase, invest and otherwise deal in stocks, bonds, debentures and other securities; and to borrow money and to issue debentures for carrying out its purposes. The stock of the Republic Mortgage Company (Republic National Company) was an asset which was not eligible to be held by a national bank. Thus, as part of the consolidation with The Republic National Bank of Dallas, it was agreed that the stock in the Mortgage Company would be set aside in a separate trust for the benefit of the stockholders of the consolidated bank.

The decision of the management and the shareholders not to dispose of the assets ineligible for retention by a national bank, but to preserve them for the benefit of the

92

Bank's shareholders, demonstrated foresight and confidence in the development of the Southwest.

Over the years the trustees have been succeeded by new trustees, each of whom also has been an executive officer of the Bank. W. O. Connor, as one of the original trustees, has been succeeded in the following order by Leslie Waggener, Oscar Bruce, and James W. Aston, who is currently also serving as President and Chief Executive Officer of the Bank. Wirt Davis, as another of the original trustees, has been succeeded by Karl Hoblitzelle, now Chairman of the Board of the Bank, while the third original trustee, Fred F. Florence, has been succeeded by Leland S. Dupree, presently Vice-Chairman of the Board of the Bank.

The Howard Corporation

On June 24, 1946, the Howard Corporation was organized. The Republic National Company transferred its petroleum properties to this new corporation in exchange for all of its authorized capital stock. The Howard Corporation derived its name from Howard County, Texas, where some of the properties were located.

The stock of The Howard Corporation was held by Republic National Company until 1955, when in order to simplify the capital structure, such stock was transferred to a new and separate trust under a trust agreement substantially identical with the trust under which Republic National Company had operated since 1928, and with the same trustees. 93

Since its organization in 1946, the investments of The Howard Corporation have consisted largely of oil and gas interests, diversified as to area, with principal holdings in Texas, Illinois, Utah, Wyoming, Louisiana, Oklahoma, New Mexico, and California. The Howard Corporation also has held from time to time investments in real estate and corporate stocks.

The oil and gas interests consist largely of mineral rights owned or acquired through fee title to lands, and leases and other properties acquired and developed in collaboration with, and operated by, a number of oil companies.

This report was the first detailed public accounting of Howard's operations. According to an article by Richard Curry in the December 4, 1964 issue of the *Dallas Times Herald*,

> Stockholders of Republic National Bank got an early Christmas present Friday when they learned that the long-secret Howard Corporation holds assets worth in the tens of millions of dollars.
>
> James W. Aston, one of the three trustees of the Howard Corporation, et al., which is a group of corporations whose shares are held in trust for the ratable benefit of Republic Bank shareholders, told reporters in a late Thursday press conference that this trust relationship is unique in commercial banking in the United States.
>
> To get an idea of the success of this trust relationship and its value to Republic National Bank stockholders, the report shows that Howard Corporation, et al, has made payments to the bank totaling $20,120,000 on an initial investment of $100,000 in 1928 and a subsequent investment of $500,000 in 1949.

By using these funds and others to increase its capital accounts, Republic National Bank has become one of the nation's top 20 banks in terms of capitalization.

Wallace D. Montgomery, a former executive of the Howard Corporation, told me one of this company's "success stories." The Calcasieu National Bank in New Orleans had gotten into trouble, and a Mr. W. E. Walker was able to acquire their assets by being the highest bidder at the sale. Republic National Bank loaned Mr. Walker the money, and Howard received a half interest in what was known as

Walker Louisiana Properties, a company that owned thousands of acres of land in Louisiana, some of it in oil production and some in rice production. When the Howard Corporation was sold in 1976, Mr. Montgomery said, these Walker properties were worth approximately ten million dollars.

It was in connection with the formation of Republic Bank's holding company, Republic of Texas Corporation, that the Howard Corporation was sold. Texas is one of only 11 states that do not permit branch banking. To get around this restriction legally, the large Texas banks began forming holding companies to buy smaller banks. On October 23, 1973, the Federal Reserve Bank granted Republic permission to form the Republic of Texas Corporation. However, one of the requirements was that they divest themselves of the non-banking assets of the Howard Corporation. This was not easy to do without a sacrifice, in spite of the Howard's great assets and large income. James W. Aston, who became President of Republic in 1957 when Fred assumed the position of Chairman of the Executive Committee and Chief Executive Officer, was on the board of directors of American Airlines. He was able to work out a deal for a subsidiary of American to acquire all of Howard's assets except stock in other Texas banks. It was a splendid deal for both parties. Republic got 60 million dollars before taxes for their $600,000 investment.

The subsidiary of American Airlines was the AA Development Corporation. Under the terms of the original agreement dated February 1, 1977, Republic of Texas Corporation was to purchase an option to acquire preferred stock of the AA Development Corporation at the closing of the deal. The option price was to be determined at the time when American has recovered its investment in the Howard Corporation assets with interest. In July, 1977, R.

95

L. Caldwell, president of the AA Development Corporation, stated that major emphasis was being placed on increasing the value of their assets which consisted of substantial oil and gas reserves, a half interest in the fee ownership of more than 34,000 acres of land in southern Louisiana from which it derives oil and gas, farming, and timber sales. It also owns the capital stock of Round Rock Lime Company, one of the oldest and largest in the Southwest.

For many years the mysterious Howard Corporation created large cash profits for Republic, and from a reliable source I am told that the option may someday become an asset as great as it was at the time of the sale to AA Development Corporation.

Earlier in this chapter I said that Fred did sometimes make mistakes. The road to success is full of obstacles, and no one's judgment or actions are perfect or beyond reproach. Certainly Fred approved some loans that ended up with a loss. Undoubtedly he employed some people who later were a disappointment. His decisions and policies were not *always* right. A successful person is one whose track record is better than average and, in business, superior to his competitors.

The July 8, 1937 issue of *Newsweek* contained a scathing article entitled "A Banker's Troubles" with the caption "Fred (Fromowitz) Florence" under an extremely unflattering picture which accentuates his nose, shows heavy five o'clock shadow, and has him apparently wringing his hands. The first paragraph refers to him as Fred Fromowitz, although this was 27 years after he legally anglicized his name. The article emphasizes that he was the son of Russian immigrants, mentioning it not once but twice, and says that he changed his name when he "saw himself rising." The tone is derogatory throughout, and the story probably infuriated Fred more than any previous happening in his life. Helen says that he was really upset.

The article tells of "the biggest setback of his career" resulting from a banking transaction in 1933. He and the bank were sued by a Chicagoan who claimed that he had been damaged by Fred's action in connection with a bond deal. The text of the article speaks for itself, so I quote:

In that year Republic paid a Chicagoan named R. E. Crummer $416,101 for bonds with a face value of $824,453. Three years later Crummer sued the bank and its president for damages. He had let the bonds go at a cut rate, he alleged, only because Florence had told him that was an RFC loan requirement. Charging 'false' representations, Crummer accused Republic of paying other banks and insurance companies full face value for similar bonds.

Dallas knew little or nothing of this because Florence called on the editors of the four daily newspapers, who agreed to print nothing. They even kept mum when the Federal District Court tried the case last year and awarded Crummer $160,933 damages.

But the city seethed with rumor, and curious citizens bought out the newsstand supply of out-of-town papers. The case became the most talked about and least printed in Texas legal history, and Florence finally realized that gossip was more damaging than open publicity. So he passed the word—and the newspapers reported his unsuccessful plea to the Fifth Circuit Court of Appeals.

Last week the newspapers printed brief press dispatches from Washington; the Supreme Court of the United States had turned down Florence's last appeal.

Since the court awarded the plaintiff sizeable damages, we must conclude that the bank had done something wrong. It was a civil action—no criminal charge was involved. At the time the *Newsweek* story appeared, rumor had it that Fred's arch rival, Nathan Adams, head of the First National Bank, was behind it, but we all know that rumors can be vicious. There is no evidence that there was any truth to this rumor. However, the rumor itself is evidence of the intensity of the competition between the two banks.

When I looked for this article at the Dallas Public Library, I had no difficulty finding the correct issue of the magazine, but I was quite surprised to find the page with the article missing. Perhaps a good friend decided it was not constructive reading or that this would please Fred. Maybe Fred himself decided that this page would better serve him if it were in his trash basket! I finally found a complete copy in the McDermott Library at the University of Texas—Dallas.

In researching the fifty years of Fred's career for this biography, I was amazed that I found no other stories of this nature. As track records go, Fred's was really quite amazing. In my evaluation, Fred's remarkable success can be attributed to a dozen factors:

* He had a most methodical mind and was almost a mechanical calculator in the mathematical field.

* His judgment of people was almost uncanny.

* From early childhood he was straightforward and people believed him, believed in him, and had his confidence.

* He never lost his dignity and very rarely his composure.

* He bore no prejudices, and harbored no grudges.

* He exercised discrimination, in that he wanted only the best, whether in the ability of his employees, the quality of a gem or a work of art that he acquired, and including the careful planning of a dinner party or the selection of a gift for an occasion.

* He could say "no" as well as "yes" and when he did he meant what he said.

* His commands were gentle but firm, and he rarely—if ever—vacillated, although he was willing to change his mind.

* He was generous, almost to a fault, always genial and friendly, and he could, when the occasion demanded, turn on the ultimate in charm. Consideration for others was all important.

* He was untiring and almost always moved in a trot. This was a characteristic that has never been forgotten by those who knew him and exemplifies his spirit and his attitudes.

* He always looked ahead, never backward, and planned for the future with the courage to act on his own judgment and convictions.

* His basic philosophy of life, business, and charity and his devotion to his family were sound and unswerving.

In short, Fred Florence possessed a fortuitous combination of intelligence, personality, character, and a philosophy that made it virtually impossible for him *not* to succeed.

CHAPTER IX
THE THIRTIES AND FORTIES

We have learned a great deal about Fred, his background, his family, many of his habits, and his amazing energy and vitality. Now we must return to the year when he became President of the bank and examine how he used his special talents.

No one can attribute all of the phenomenal success of the bank to his guidance, but certainly he did shape its growth to a greater extent than any other one person. We know that he had many capable and dedicated men and women who made important contributions. We also know that most profitable enterprises can impute their success to management. Maybe it is one man, maybe a team, but the key is strong leadership. Management achieves results by setting the example, by demonstrating their willingness to work, by using good and well thought-out judgment, and by being open-minded toward innovations whether from within or from without. I emphasize, luck plays no part over the long run. There is ample of both bad and good. The trick is to minimize the bad and maximize the good.

Fred Florence's banking career spanned some very dramatic times: years that saw boom, panic, war, and a rapidly changing world. The complete story of his career and the growth of Republic Bank from the time he became President in 1929 until his death in 1960 would have to cover much the same facts as a comprehensive economic history of Dallas and the entire Southwest. Such a complete history is beyond the scope of this book. Therefore, in this chapter, instead of even attempting a chronological history of the bank, I will highlight what seem to me to be the most significant happenings of the 1930's and 1940's in terms of the growth of the bank: first, weathering the depression, and second, the development of the various departments that made Republic Bank truly a "full service bank."

WEATHERING THE DEPRESSION

Fred was named President of Republic Bank on January 8, 1929. In retrospect, this was hardly an auspicious time for him to have taken the reins. On October 28 and 29, 1929, the country plunged into the worst financial panic in its history. Overnight, wealthy people lost everything. Brokerage houses and banks struggled to stay solvent. Many could not survive, and men and women jumped out of the windows of their Wall Street offices, took their own lives in various other ways, or lost their minds. Following the crash, business throughout the country suffered; banks and commercial enterprises folded. Bread lines, the forerunner of welfare, could be found in all cities and towns.

Half a century later, the memory of this disaster may have dimmed even for those who lived through it. As with any other happening, there are many explanations as to its cause. Every day we read in the newspaper why the stock market rose or fell the day before. The answers were clearer in 1929 than they are today. My own theory is that it was avarice, coupled with over-optimism.

On the Saturday before the crash, my late wife and I, with Lester Moss, a very successful stock broker, and his wife, Edna, were riding on a special all-pullman train from New York to Philadelphia to attend the Penn-Princeton football game to be played in Franklin Field. I can

102

remember our conversation as if it were yesterday; in the light of subsequent events, this was one that could not be forgotten. Lester begged me to let him have $50,000 on Monday morning for the purpose of buying stocks for me on margin. He promised that within a year I would have made a million. However, I personally did not have the money, and furthermore, I was scared to ask my father for it. He was a bond man, very conservative, and I was afraid that he would give me hell.

Usual margin requirements were only ten percent, so with fifty thousand cash you could own a half a million dollars market value of common stock. Here is how it worked. Assuming your stocks averaged $25 a share, you would own 20,000 shares. If the average market price of the stock you bought increased only $5.00 a share, you would have made a $100,000 paper profit. Had you sold, you would have made this tidy sum in cash.

In business, greed plays an important role and over the years has been a prime factor in causing failures. The speculators, goaded on by the brokers, could see only higher prices and greater profits, so the paper profits were used to buy more stock on margin, and the pyramid kept building. Safety and income were not even considered. With a $100,000 leverage you could buy another million dollars in stock. (Capital gains taxes had not yet been dreamt up.)

103

The market had been rising for months because the whole concept looked like the best "get rich quick" scheme yet discovered. As people saw others get richer, more and more bought at the higher prices to get in, so stocks kept going higher. Paper profits snowballed. Some brokers, eager for commissions and with no regulations, required *no* margin from trusted friends.

Early in October, 1929, stocks began to fall, but optimism still prevailed. Today an occasional bad day or two are normal, and nothing much would happen even if this continued for a week or more; but things were different then. When some of the big traders decided to take profits, prices began to plummet and buying dried up. Few wanted to buy in a falling market, and it takes a buyer for every seller. Brokers became nervous and asked for more margin. If the customer did not have the cash, the broker put his stock up for sale, causing the Exchange to be flooded with sell orders. Monday the 28th was a record bad day, and on Tuesday the 29th (Black Tuesday) stocks took a nose dive. Brokers and traders panicked. They would take whatever price they could get. The paper profits disappeared, and the result was the worst crash in Wall Street history. The tragedy was that many who had only gambled with a small part of their fortune could not believe that the drop would continue, so they took money from their savings, quickly mortgaged their homes, and sold their wives' jewelry at a sacrifice to protect their paper profits. The market kept on sliding downward. I was not entirely lucky. That Friday I buried my good friend Lester Moss. He had joined the many who had jumped out of their office windows.

In 1929 Texas was much further from Wall Street than it is today because of differences in transportation and communication. Only a relatively small number of Texans in 1929 ever thought about, or had even heard of, the New York Stock Exchange; so the impact of the crash was not felt immediately.

Fifty years later the Dallas *Times Herald* on Sunday, October 7, 1979, featured a number of articles recalling these events. Under the heading, "Crash of '29 Pulled Reluctant Dallas into Depression," Stephen Good wrote:

Fifty years ago, the great stock market crash shook Dallas like an earthquake tremor from the East Coast—causing nothing more than a low rumble. Local business leaders downplayed the crash. But its aftershock pulled Dallas into the Great Depression, stifling economic growth and throwing thousands out of work. Although Dallas suffered less than other parts of the country, its recovery took most of a decade.

Helen remembers that Fred was extremely upset by the market crash. Publicly, however, he was optimistic, as were most business leaders and public figures at the time. And, for a while, everything was indeed "business as usual." Republic Bank went right ahead with plans for a new building and for the consolidation with North Texas National Bank. I was interested to find that the minutes of the bank's directors meeting on November 12, 1929, which was just about two weeks after the crash, mentioned absolutely nothing about this financial catastrophe; they voted on the consolidation of the North Texas National Bank with Republic, and they approved action "to consider, promote, and complete plans for the erection of a building adjoining the present bank building on the West for the purpose of providing more adequate banking quarters."

105

In the period immediately following the Wall Street crash, the Dallas newspapers (which I examined on microfilm in the public library) showed relatively little concern. On Sunday, November 3, 1929, just a few days after the crash, the main headline on the front page of the Dallas *Morning News* was not about the stock market at all, but read: "Million-Dollar Annex Announced for Republic Bank and Trust Co.," with a large drawing of the proposed building. On Monday, November 4, 1929, the following article by Stuart McGregor appeared on the financial page, headlined "Business Confidence in Texas Unshaken; Best Indices Point to Good Condition This Winter":

> A search through the pages of thirty-odd large and small daily newspapers covering all parts of Texas reveals hardly a single note of pessimism in the interviews of business men respecting the stock market crash. The prevailing opinion seems to be that Texas, not being directly in the path of the tornado that hit the exchanges, will suffer little direct bad effect and the indirect effect will be negligible. Throughout the Nation there is a prevailing opinion that the stock market damaged nothing much but itself when it fell through, and if this is true, of course the business conditions of Texas will not be adversely affected. But even if there is general depression in the North and East as a result of the market upset, it will not be felt greatly in Texas according to business men.

And, for a time, all *was* well. At a meeting of the bank's directors held January 14, 1930, a few months after acquisition of the North Texas National Bank had been approved (and a few months after the stock market crash), Fred proudly announced:

> We are now not only the 2nd largest bank in the 11th Federal Reserve District in invested capital, but also in deposits. Ours was one of the few large banks to show sizable gain in deposits over last year, taking into consideration combined deposits of merged banks.

This was to be the last gain in deposits that the bank would show for several years.For of course,depression *did* come, and Texas and the Southwest, even Dallas, *were* affected, though probably less than other parts of the country. The effects of the Great Depression were worldwide, and no one was exempt from its wrath. Business generally was bad, causing many bankruptcies, serious unemployment, and an ever present atmosphere of gloom. This continued for several years. Building and Loan societies, financial institutions, and many banks closed their doors leaving many who were not even involved in the stock market in desperate straits with life savings and needed operating funds wiped out. There is no need for me to try to describe just how bad things were: those of my readers who do not remember the Great Depression have undoubtedly read about it or heard about it from those who did live through it.

President Herbert Hoover attempted to stem the downward tide, but his efforts were mostly feeble and unsuccessful. However, it was Hoover who signed the legislation creating the Reconstruction Finance Corporation in January, 1932, although this agency is generally associated in people's minds with Roosevelt's "New Deal." During the dark days of the Great Depression, the R.F.C. loaned and invested billions of dollars to rescue banks, railroads, and all types of businesses from ruin. Jesse Jones was with the R.F.C. for thirteen years and headed it for twelve, and wrote a book entitled *Fifty Billion Dollars: My Thirteen Years with the RFC (1932-1945)*. I am very proud of the copy which he personally autographed for me. Jones should know better than anyone what transpired in American banking during the depression; so I shall quote several passages from this book. According to Jones, problems in the banking system were clearly evident before the depression began, but rapidly became worse with the nation's economic decline. Jones explains:

> The breakdown of the American banking system, which came to a complete ten-day stop in the nation-wide moratorium of March, 1933, was not a sudden catastrophe. Ugly signs and warnings of the disintegration had continual-

107

ly cropped out in one spot after another on the nation's map long before the depression crept across the country in the wake of the stock-market break of October, 1929. A chance-taking, expanding, and optimistic people, we Americans had always had more than our share of bank failures, in good times as in bad. From 1904 through 1920 some 1,170 banks failed. Between 1921 and the end of 1929 there were 5,642 suspensions.

The general depression accelerated both the pace—3,635 failures in 1930-1931—and the size of the average loss to depositors, creditors, and stockholders. Deposits affected by the failures in those two years totaled $2,624,000,000, or about $900,000,000 more than all the deposits in all the banks that failed in the entire decade of the 1920's.

Nearly all the banks that went broke during the ten boom years of the twenties were small. Only 12 per cent had a capitalization above $100,000, and 40 per cent were village establishments started with less than $25,000. Most of these should never have been opened, for the capital investments were too small. With the shrinkage of all values—real estate, commodities, and everything else—which followed the stock-market break of 1929, middle-sized banks began to show up alarmingly in the ever lengthening roll of business failures. Before the snowball stopped rolling downhill in 1933, it had taken with it to destruction some banks capitalized in the millions.

108

Jones describes the events that led to the nation-wide bank closing in greater detail than we need to go into here. The following excerpts are enough to give us an idea of how, in state after state, the banking structure collapsed almost like falling dominoes:

As Christmas approached (1932), sporadic runs troubled country banks in various parts of the Midwest and in

Pennsylvania. In January this epidemic spread to some of the larger cities—Memphis, Little Rock, Mobile, Chattanooga, Cleveland, St. Louis. By early February the fever had appeared in Baltimore, Nashville, San Francisco, New Orleans, and Kansas City. On February 9 we (R.F.C.) were informed that the banking situation in Detroit, which we previously had aided with loans, was critical. Dried out of liquid assets, the larger Detroit banks were tinder for a conflagration that soon got beyond control. . .

The debacle in Michigan soon affected the entire country. In one state after another the lights of finance flickered and faded so that it became necessary to declare a nationwide bank holiday until government help could be arranged. . . All the banks in Michigan had been closed by Governor William A. Comstock on February 14. On the 24th Governor Albert C. Ritchie proclaimed a three-day holiday in Maryland: withdrawals from banks and trust companies in Baltimore had drained some large institutions to the danger point.

Before the following dawn the legislatures in Ohio, Pennsylvania, and Delaware amended their banking laws to empower the state banking authorities to control withdrawals by depositors . . .

On March 1 bank holidays were declared in Alabama, Louisiana, and Oklahoma. The next day all banks were ordered shut in seven other states—Texas, Oregon, Arizona, Idaho, Nevada, Washington, and Utah. Visitors arriving in Washington for the inauguration of President Roosevelt found notices in their hotel rooms that no checks on out-of-town banks would be honored. On March 3 the Ford interests abandoned their plans to start two new banks in prostrate Detroit. Four more states—Missouri, Wisconsin, Georgia, and New Mexico—declared holidays. After midnight, a few hours before the sunrise of Inauguration Day, state moratoriums were declared in New York and Illinois. That was the knockout blow. By breakfast time every state that still had any banks in operation ordered them closed.

109

On that unforgettable Saturday morning, as Herbert Hoover and Franklin D. Roosevelt rode together to the Capitol for the great moment of a presidential succession, the economic sun was in total eclipse over all the United States. The time had now come to build a new foundation for the financial structure and to make permanent improvements.

Fred Florence was president of the Dallas Clearing House Association during the nation-wide banking moratorium. Leland Dupree recalled that during this time,

> Fred was going night and day! But he was optimistic—*optimistic!* I remember one time he made a talk to us, while the banks were closed, and he said, "We're on the bottom, we've got only one way to go and that's up!" He was optimistic, all the way through.

James Aston, who succeeded Fred as president of the bank, recalled:

> I was at the City Hall at the time and therefore not privy to all the goings-on in the banking community; but I'm told that Fred Florence was really the leader in the period of crisis, when Roosevelt declared the bank holiday in 1933. We had some banks in trouble, a bank that went broke; and they met every morning (the Clearing House Association) and Fred was the spokesman—he was the quarterback.

Aston told me that Fred and Republic made every possible effort to help other banks because, in his words, "It was considered a black mark against the banking community in the city for a bank to go under." Using the

Republic Mortgage Company* as a vehicle, Republic made investments in other banks. "That's how we bought the Oak Cliff Bank and still own 30% of it," Aston said.** He continued:

> This is an important part of Fred's career—his leadership and contribution to banking. And it was an unselfish thing. He looked at it more as a civic responsibility than as a profitable enterprise. Fortunately, some of these things turned out to be profitable.

I have also been told that during the depths of the depression, Fred visited a great many of the small banks throughout Texas, generally at their request, to help them with advice and often with the money they needed. By doing this he made many friends—and new customers for Republic's Correspondent Banks Department.

Several days after the beginning of the moratorium, Roosevelt announced that only sound banks would be permitted to reopen. According to Jones' book about the R.F.C., the decisions as to which banks were sound were made by the Comptroller's office, the Treasury, the banking departments of the individual states, and the R.F.C. As President of the Dallas Clearing House, one of Fred's chief concerns must have been to see that everything possible was done to assure the prompt reopening of all Dallas banks. Apparently there was only one casualty. I found the following interesting commentary in *Dallas Guide and History, American Guide Series, Writer's Program* (a

---

* A subsidiary that had been formed for the purpose of owning assets that could not legally be owned by the bank.

** In late 1980 Republic of Texas Corporation owned it 100%.

W.P.A. project), in the Texas Collection in the public library:

> The solvency of Dallas Banks has on the whole been exceptional, as was demonstrated again in the severe and prolonged crisis which followed the Wall Street crash in 1929. Eleven bank failures were recorded by the Dallas Federal Reserve Bank in the early 1930's. Of these only one was in the City of Dallas, however. This was the State Trust and Savings Bank, which was liquidated in 1933.

On March 9, 1933, a special session of Congress passed a bill authorizing the R.F.C. to invest in the preferred stock of commercial banks and trust companies. The purpose of this was to permit banks to improve their capital structure. It gave them much needed cash at a reasonable rate of interest. Jesse Jones wrote about this bill, in the book previously quoted:

> In one stroke Congress had turned the tide toward recovery. But it took many months of hard work and much persuasion for us to convince the banking fraternity that this was so.

Jones wrote further that getting the banks to participate in the preferred stock program was surprisingly difficult, and that the program moved at a very slow pace. He finally asked the American Bankers Association for permission to speak before their convention in Chicago in September, 1933. About this speech, Jones wrote:

> My speech to the convention—in which I advised the bankers to "be smart, for once," and without stint to go partners with the government—was not well received. I was followed on the program by Eugene R. Black, Sr., who had

but recently resigned his membership of the Federal Reserve Bank in Atlanta. A good part of his time was devoted to apologizing for my speech.

After a dinner that evening, Jones was unexpectedly called upon to speak again. About this, he wrote:

> ...I was called upon, but declined. The crowd insisted, and I finally arose. As best I can recall, I said "off the record" that I had addressed them once that day, and that they had not liked my speech. I added that all I had to say on this second appearance was that more than half the banks represented at the gathering in front of me were insolvent, and no one knew it as well as the men in our banqueting room. I then sat down.
> That blast started the rush into the preferred stock program. From then on until the end of the year we often processed and authorized purchase of capital in as many as one hundred banks in a day.

The R.F.C. encouraged banks that did not really need the money to issue preferred stock also, and promoted participation in this program as the "patriotic" thing to do. Republic's Statement of Condition for December 20, 1933, shows, for the first time, "Capital—Preferred" in the amount of $2,000,000; and a check of the minutes revealed 113 that this was authorized at the December 16 meeting of the board. The minutes show only the action taken, and contain nothing about the discussion preceding it. We can only speculate about whether Fred's friendship with Jesse Jones had anything to do with this decision, or whether they wanted to improve Republic's capital position in order to be able to help out other banks. There is no question of Republic's own solvency—they certainly did not *need* the money. But the fact is that they did issue $2,000,000 in preferred stock; and, for whatever it is worth, I was able to find out that the First National did not do this.

A speech Fred made in 1931 gives us some idea of the principles he and Mr. Connor followed to make Republic strong and enable it to come through these hard times in stable condition. This speech, entitled "Present Day Banking," was given at a meeting of District No. 1 of the Texas Bankers Association in Galveston on February 17, 1931, and printed in the March 1931 issue of the *Texas Bankers Record*, the association's official publication. This speech reveals Fred's own view of the banking situation at that time, and his ideas about sound banking practices. I would like to quote several passages from this speech, from which I learned a good deal about banking and about Fred's philosophy:

> Bankers in any community, large or small, occupy positions of unusual public trust. Deposits represent coined and crystallized fruits of years of labor on the part of depositors. Savings cannot be measured merely in terms of dollars—but also in terms of toil. It is the first responsibility of bankers to return depositors' money when the depositors want it.
>
> The causes of bank failures are numerous and it is easy to place undue emphasis on any one of them. In the small bank which fails, some of the situations commonly noted are these: faulty management by men with limited training; scant attention paid by directors to the bank's affairs; local prejudices and favoritisms; excessive personnel and overhead expenses, not justified by small resources. Yet, bad management alone does not account for all bank failures. Officers of suspended country banks have usually been honest and conscientious. In most instances they were capable—but not capable enough to keep their institutions healthy in the face of economic changes which came over

114

the whole community. Good roads, for example, have taken to larger centers both the farmer's trade and the farmer's deposits.

The other part of the banker's problem—to find profitable occupation for the community's funds—has also presented difficulties...The present day banker should appropriate the suggestion and advice all of us have so freely given to the farmer—diversify. All of our loans should not be local, but a part of the portfolio should be represented by loans and securities not affected by purely local conditions.

Those bankers who have created a diversified portfolio are comfortable and sanguine, while those who have invested their bills receivable in purely local securities are, more than likely, feeling themselves quite frozen and gloomy. Present day banking requires the investment of funds in liquid securities and bonds and other forms of indebtedness of unquestioned safety. Many bankers in Texas, under the old style of operation, wanted their note case to depend entirely upon the growing cotton crop—and with the the entire capital stock, surplus, undivided profits and even furniture and fixtures. Too, there was usually considerable borrowing of money in addition to all of the bank's own funds. Then, if the price of cotton or the yield was poor, the bank's assets were completely frozen and therein rests the inception of many of the difficulties which we have encountered in recent years.

The large number of bank failures throughout the 115 country during the past year is a blight upon the financial and business life of this country...The opportunity for correcting this situation rests largely with us, just as the responsibility for it falls upon us. Certainly we have learned that there are too many banks and too many people engaged in the banking business. Fewer banks and better banks would have a stabilizing effect upon the situation . . . *There should never be a satisfactory reason for the loss of a penny of a depositor's money.*

The banker who has not learned many lessons during the period of the business depression is certainly without imagination or intelligence. It is quite evident that the artificial prosperity created by the booming stock market had an untold number of avenues through which the banking and business interests of this country were made to suffer. However, we have learned that "when you get something for nothing—you, in fact, get nothing for something." Present day banking should not depart from the lesson that the business cycle follows—expanding credit and contracting credit. Expanding credit supposedly creates good times and contracting credit creates depressions. There is no necessity for a contraction of credit, except in cases where it has been extended too freely. Yet, it seems that no legislation or act of the Government or any of its agencies, have been able to meet the situation of establishing and guiding the credit structure on an even keel. Therefore the cycles in business, the eras of prosperity and depression, come and go as the aspiration and energy of mankind cause men to seek too far—to dare too much—and to produce too abundantly. When that happens, and we realize that credit has expanded too far and the process of contraction sets in, production practically halts and there is created the national bread line, which is a disgrace to the intelligence of American industry. However, we must have faith in our automatic salvation, for, as production ceases, consumption begins to forge ahead of the available supply created by production. We are then consuming more than we are producing, which condition carries us back to normalcy.

116

Whatever reservations Fred may privately have had about the government's efforts to hasten this return to normalcy, publicly he took a position that was totally optimistic and supportive. On April 24, 1933, he gave an address before the East Texas Chamber of Commerce, entitled "A New Deal in American Banking," in which he said:

Great history is in the making, and our people look with confidence to our President to safely, though gradually, guide us out of the woes and hardships of the depression, without leading us into another disaster. Such courageous leadership is now necessary, and only with safe steering will our security be restored and endure.

A New Deal in American Banking should, and I am confident will, provide safe-guards against the costly and dangerous experience of the past. At this time there are under consideration certain fundamental and drastic changes in the present banking system. In the future, banking in the United States will be on a vastly different basis. Great reform will come from within. Regardless of what sort of legislation is passed, the experiences of the last few years will have the evolutionary effect of working out reforms which can be depended upon to make banking safer and better. There has been a complete rebirth of that healthy suspicion and cautiousness which must always characterize sound banking. This evolution is a positive thing, and the law of the survival of the fittest may be expected to be constantly at work to generally improve the entire banking structure.

In this speech, Fred went on to discuss the various measures that were under consideration at that time, including the highly controversial topic of insurance or guarantee of bank deposits. The editorial position of the *Texas Bankers Record* on this subject had been one of unequivocal opposition—the following had appeared in the January, 1933 issue:

117

We of Texas know what a nightmare and mockery and basically unsound thing this guaranteeing of deposits is. We have had about 18 years experience* and the good and sol-

* Texas had tried deposit insurance on a State level.

vent banks in our state were taxed $25,000,000 to pay for the mistakes and mismanagement and crookedness of people who should never have attempted banking. All Texas bankers have long since agreed that such a scheme will not work—that it encourages more and poorer banks and more and poorer bank managers.

In contrast, Fred's speech—while he did not come right out and say "I'm for it"—presented both sides of the argument, and stressed the importance of protecting the depositor. I quote:

> The opponents of any such plan point primarily to the responsibility of the Federal Government in its operation, and to the fact that those well conducted banking institutions, composing a large majority of the banks of this country, are put on a level with those operated by the less judicious and less competent bankers. They feel, therefore, that the Government should not condone this system, as they regard it as being contrary to the spirit of Americanism.
>
> On the other hand, those in favor of such a measure definitely cling to the belief that it is of paramount importance that consideration be given to the depositing public, a large number of which are not thoroughly conversant with banking to the extent that they should be held accountable for the mistake of depositing their money in banking institutions operating under unsafe policies. It is viewed, therefore, as a piece of legislation not for the banks but rather for the millions of depositors. It is necessary that our banking system provide absolute safety for depositors, and unless supervision can immediately and unquestionably guarantee the safety of the banks of this country, it will fall to the responsibility of our Government to design a form of insurance or other guarantee to afford full protection to depositors and to create absolute confidence in all banks licensed to transact business. There is no single factor which

will stimulate sound business as much as the full and complete confidence of the public in the banks operating throughout this country.

The *Texas Bankers Record* in its May 1933 issue reported on Fred's speech as follows:

> Mr. Florence's speech received wide acclaim as a constructive address. His listeners were impressed with the sincerity of his attitude. The American people are aroused over the banking situation, he says. He believes Congress will work out a new system of banking that will be advantageous to all concerned. His reaction to all proposed reforms is one of optimism.

Fred's ability to provide positive, constructive leadership even in the most troubled times did not go unrecognized among Texas bankers, who elected him President of the Texas Bankers Association in 1935.

The one word that seems to characterize Fred best during this period is "optimistic." But as I have said before, his optimism was realistic—he never played ostrich. Yet no matter how bad things seemed, he always looked on the bright side. Jesse James, the recently deceased veteran Treasurer of the State of Texas, told me an amusing story about Fred's optimism. One time during the depression, Fred was talking to Mr. James, who was telling Fred that he thought the country was headed for its worst year in history. Fred just smiled and said, "This is going to be a great year." Shortly thereafter, Mr. James was in New York talking to David Rockefeller, head of the great Chase National Bank. When Mr. Rockefeller began to sing the blues, Mr. James repeated Fred's statement.

"Who told you that?" asked Mr. Rockefeller.

"Fred Florence in Dallas," was the reply.

119

"Would you believe him instead of me?" Mr. Rockefeller asked.

Mr. James said he *did*, whereupon Mr. Rockefeller said, "Well, maybe you are right."

If Fred was talking about 1933, he *was* right, at least for Republic Bank, because by the end of that year things had begun to turn around. Total deposits, which had declined by almost 25% between December 1929 and December 1932, were back up almost to the 1929 level by December of 1933, showing an increase of over 11 million dollars for the year. From then on, there was a steady increase each year. Republic had weathered the storm. The dramatic growth that characterized the bank during the 20's, interrupted briefly but not halted by the depression of the 30's, would be even more spectacular in the years to come.

DEVELOPING A FULL SERVICE BANK

Never at any time in his career did Fred want to let one single piece of desirable business go to a competitor. He wanted Republic to be able to handle all the needs of its customers and to be able to solicit new business by offering every type of service. From conversations I had with Fred, I knew that his ambition and goal was to have a bank in Dallas that could compete with the giants in New York, Chicago, and Los Angeles—the "money banks," as they are called. These banks were enjoying some of the business of the Southwest because of their facilities to serve special needs, not available locally. Fred knew that if banking facilities in Dallas could meet all needs, it would encourage industry to leave the North and East and settle where good labor was more easily available and where living conditions were more relaxed.

Fred's desire to compete with the larger banks reminds me of a story I heard when I was in the advertising business. Many years ago a small advertising agency was competing with one of the giants, Batten, Barton, Durstine and Osborne, for a large account. The small agency's principal argument was that being small they could render personal attention to this account, as it would be their largest and would command preferential treatment. The advertising manager asked B,B,D & O if they had an answer to offset this. The reply was simple: "Is anyone small through choice?"

Fred probably never heard this story, but he knew the enormous value of being large, particularly in a fast growing area. He knew that to compete and to make money for his stockholders, his bank would have to be able to furnish a customer everything to satisfy his needs. Of recent years banks in this category are called "Full Service Banks."

In my studies about Fred, I interviewed many who knew him well. All were willing to discuss their experiences with him and to attempt, at least, to pinpoint the underlying reasons for the bank's great progress. Putting all their comments together, I think the secret of the bank's success boils down to one basic belief: if someone else can do it, we can do it, and maybe better. No one told me that Fred ever said this, but I believe that the story of the development of the bank's major departments clearly indicates that this was the way Fred felt. All of Fred's personal characteristics which I have previously described were important; but this belief that "we can do it" was crucial. For Fred, it was never enough for the bank merely to maintain existing levels of service. He was always reaching out to provide more different kinds of services for more people. The result was growth, at a truly extraordinary rate. 121

Needless to say, the bank had Loan and Savings Departments from the very beginning, and a Correspondent Banks Department very early. To meet all the needs of their customers, Fred began developing various other departments. I will trace the origin and importance of several of these, specifically the Trust, the Agricultural or Commodities, the Petroleum, and the International Departments, telling a little about each, because Fred's life and the development of Republic cannot be divorced. Those who manned these departments and their staffs deserve much of the credit for the prominence that each gained; but everyone, and there were many, told me that Fred's interest in them and what they were doing, and his daily contact with them, helped them immeasurably.

The Trust Department had its origins in the Republic Trust and Savings Bank, the state bank that was formed in the early 20's because of the limited trust powers and real estate loan powers the national banks were permitted at that time. As I have previously written, the state bank was absorbed into the national bank in 1928 when the restrictions on national banks were eased. A trust department was an important service to the bank's customers. Additionally, this department could keep whole families as customers even after they became heirs of a rich relative. Trust funds were often large and a good source of profitable revenue.

122

C. B. Peterson, Jr., who was Executive Vice President and Chairman of the Trust Committee when he retired December 1, 1978, told me that Robert G. Storey was the first Trust Officer of the bank. Storey served as head of the Trust Department for only a short time, succeeded by R. L. McBane, and later by T. J. (Tom) Moroney. Peterson became head of the department in 1960. Pete, as his friends and associates call him, made a most interesting observation about the Trust Department:

I think one of the most significant points that might be made is that, generally speaking, across the country, when trust departments became the recipients of properties—real estate, oil, objects of art—they usually liquidated them and put the money into stocks and bonds—something they could handle, and that was marketable. But this Trust Department—and there were others who did it, too—held on to these assets—oil, real estate—because they knew that they could enhance as much or more than stocks and bonds. And that is why these trust departments in Dallas, and particularly Republic, were so big in real estate management and oil management. They recognized that these assets would enhance.

For sound and intelligent management of this type of holdings, it was necessary to have men who understood them. Therefore, the Trust Department developed its own real estate and oil divisions. The Trust Department also needed its own investment analysts and economists, and the facilities to sell their customers all types of non-equity investments such a commercial paper, certificates of deposit, government bonds, treasury bills, tax exempt bonds, etc. Today there are so many different types of investments that even the sophisticated investor is constantly learning of something new. Even Fred, if he were alive today, would have much to learn about bankers acceptances, Euro-dollars, money market certificates, etc. Today we are in a brand new ball game from what it was during Fred's regime, so it is incumbent upon management to stay constantly abreast of the times.

When Fred came to the Republic Bank in 1920, cotton was king. As David Nevin wrote in his book, *The Texans:*

123

The first of the really big action was in cotton. There is an old saying that Texas began on hide and horns—the produce of the range country—but it didn't. It began on cotton. Long before the Civil War, East Texas was plantation country, the great cotton tracts inching westward until they reached the blacklands south of Dallas. As the terrain expanded, Texas cotton production went up until by itself it formed an important part of the world market.

The successful cotton men owned plantations, gins, and compressors, or traded in cotton seed, cotton seed oil, or cotton futures. They owned many of the great mansions in Dallas, some of which are still being occupied by wealthy families or have now been designated as "historic landmarks."

Dallas, the largest city adjacent to the cotton belt, which was concentrated in East Texas, naturally became the banking hub for the cotton traders. When Republic Bank first began, it was not in a position to take large loans, being limited by its capital. As it grew in assets and deposits, cotton gave them a great opportunity for lending money. By 1947, cotton loans had become such big business that the bank employed Albert L. Long to head the Commodities Department. Long, now retired, was kind enough to come to my office where I could record much of what I write here. Before he came to Republic in 1947, he had been with the National Bank of Commerce, then the largest bank in Memphis, Tennessee. He stayed with Republic until he retired. During our lengthy interview he told me many interesting things about a business of which I had little knowledge.

Apparently lending money on cotton was huge business and very desirable because the risk was low.

Money was loaned on a crop that was ready for market. The cotton man borrowed 80% or 85% of the sale value. The cotton was the collateral, and to prevent the fluctuation in the market from affecting payment of the loan, it was hedged in the futures market. According to Long, the bank's only risk was trusting the man to whom they made the loan. He needed to have the ability to know the grade and staple of the cotton, and to be a good salesman, a good businessman, and above all a man of integrity.

Long told me that when Republic Bank began to get into cotton loans, one of the older banks already had most of the cotton business. In order to compete, Republic concentrated on service. Long explained:

> Republic got the new business, and a lot of the business from the other banks, by giving them service. And by service I mean—a cotton man who has a chance to sell a thousand bales of cotton worth a hundred thousand dollars has got to know in ten or fifteen minutes whether he can borrow the money or not. And he could call up Republic and get an answer *right now*—he still can.

Long further told me that it was to Republic's advantage that there were no cotton men on their board. "Each one of the cotton men doesn't want the other one to know what he's doing," Albert said. However, the cotton man did want a banker who understood the cotton business and wouldn't make a decision that would hurt him, and a banker that he could sit down and talk to. With his East Texas background, Fred was better qualified than most of his competitors; and though Albert modestly denied that he was the best man available for the job when Fred brought him to Dallas, his own words indicate to me that he was:

125

I wouldn't say I was the best man available. I'd say there were five men that could have done the job; but you've got to consider, I was from the South, the cotton belt. The others were from New York and Chicago. You realize, thirty years ago, you didn't bring a man in from New York to be a big shot! We brought one or two in and it didn't work out. they just didn't fit in the commodity business.

The Commodities Department was not exempt from Fred's rule that a single officer could not turn down a loan without taking it higher. When we discussed this, Albert told a little story. He said he wanted to turn down a $5,000 loan, and then Fred approved it. Fred told him that he knew the man's daddy and added, "He'll pay it," and sure enough he did. "Looking at that thing on paper," Albert said, "it wasn't worth the paper it was written on; but Fred knew his daddy!" Albert was the first person to tell me that if Fred knew someone, and knew that suing him for a small loan would put him in dire straits, he would write it off.

Although I knew that Fred stayed close to all of the bank's operations, before this interview I had not thought about the need to watch the loan position from the standpoint of where the money went: that is, by departments as well as individuals. Fred insisted on an intelligent balance of oil, cotton, and industrial loans, and loans to corporations and individuals. He himself kept track of everything to be sure that this desired balance was maintained. Albert told me:

126

Fred was a one-man bank. As far as the percentage of oil loans, and everything else that was made—he knew! He'd come down some day and he'd want to know my estimate for how much cotton loans would be. For the winter months, this was some time in August every year. And I'd have to sit down and try to figure it out. You can't guess it exactly, but you can estimate it. If it's a small crop, you're not going to need as much money. If it's a large crop, you're going to need more money.

I never did leave myself in a position to be told that I had over-extended the bank in any way, because that was part of my job, to see that the bank didn't get too much in one thing, too much in another.

Albert told me that Republic could have handled more cotton than they did, but to get the money to do so, they would have had to take something away from loans to oil or industry. The careful balance of loans in various areas, which Fred worked so closely with his department heads to achieve, undoubtedly was very important to the overall success of the bank.

Oil was first discovered in Texas near Beaumont in 1901 when "Spindletop," as the well was named, brought this great industry to Texas and the Southwest. This well was a giant, but even more important, especially to Dallas, was the discovery of oil in East Texas in 1930, when on October 3, an old wildcatter named "Dad" Joiner brought in a well known as the Daisy Bradford#3. This was the beginning of the largest oil field in the United States. Until this time, there were no restrictions on the amount of oil that could be pumped from a well. Naturally, many prospectors, anxious to get their wealth in hand, depleted the supply quickly. From a banking standpoint, this meant that the only loans that could safely be made to oilmen were short-term loans (thirty days, or at the very most, ninety) based on the amount of oil to be produced in that time, or small loans against equipment. The absence of regulations created absolute chaos in the East Texas Field, where conditions became so bad that something had to be done. David Nevin describes the situation so well in his book, *The Texans*, that I would like to quote him rather extensively:

127

By July of 1931 there were 1,300 wells in production and they were pouring out an incredible 1.4 million barrels of oil a day. (There were 3,612 producing wells by the end of 1931 and the figures went to 25,976 by 1939.)

The result was chaos. The nation was in depression and already there were the beginnings of a glut. With the new oil supply, prices collapsed. There came the day when oil sold for a dime a barrel (a barrel holds forty-two gallons; there were instances of penny barrels) and for many there simply were no buyers. But there were no regulations then. If you didn't take your share, your neighbor pumped your share out from under your land. If he pumped, you did; if anyone did, everyone did. Storage space was exhausted and people dug big tanks with earthen walls to hold the oil. They put earthen dams in canyons and stored the oil behind them. Sometimes the dams or the tanks would break and send a cascade of crude oil bubbling down the river killing fish and birds and ruining for decades large sections of that lovely piney woods country . . .

The East Texas Field was running wide open when, on August 17, 1931, the Texas National Guard was called out to shut it down. It had been wild. Production had hit 1.4 million barrels a day and was still climbing, though the market had broken and some oilmen could find no buyer at any price. When oil was stored in earthen tanks its most valuable parts tended to evaporate and dirt and debris contaminated what was left. People watched offset wells running continuously despite the glut and draining oil from beneath their land. Tempers rose, fights broke out and there was a dangerous air over the big field.

Armed cavalrymen went on patrol in the deep pine forests. Troops in trucks wound along the red dirt roads up to the hidden wellsites. It was hot and steamy and the soldiers sweated and cursed as they moved across the field and well by well pinched off the endless flow of oil. As a restless, uneasy quiet hung over the field, the state established and prepared to enforce a system of proration.

The "market demand act," passed by the Texas legislature in the next year, 1932, gave the Railroad Commission the power to regulate oil production so that it would not exceed anticipated demand. This proration had two main advantages: it stabilized prices, and it conserved the oil supply (if oil was pumped too fast, a well could stop producing with most of the oil trapped in the ground, never to be recovered). But proration changed the situation dramatically in another way. Now that the rate of production was regulated, the oil reserves still in the ground became a bankable commodity. It was possible to make excellent estimates as to how much oil could be expected, and banks could know with fair accuracy how a loan could be amortized. Firms like DeGolyer and McNaughton, geologist and engineers, became of great value to the industry as appraisers for bank loans.

The increased "bankability" brought about by proration was a good thing for the oilmen, because financing was becoming increasingly important as finding oil became more difficult and more expensive. To quote Nevin's *The Texans* again,

> This was the situation when the Dallas banks stepped into oil, a move that in terms of the meaning of oil to Texas probably was second in significance only to the actual finding of the oil. The leader of that move was a slender, gentle man named Fred F. Florence, who may have been a financial genius.

Nevin also gives credit to Nathan Adams at First National and R.L. Thornton at Mercantile, as well as Florence, and concludes:

> So these were the men with the financial foresight, the resources, and, most of all, the downright courage to take the next step in oil: they began lending against the reserves.

129

I was very fortunate to find many men who had been in Republic's Petroleum Department, in executive capacities, who gave me generously of their time discussing the bank's role in oil. Darrell Hamric, Rushton Ardrey, and John R. Scott were particularly helpful. Jake Hamon, one of the country's most successful independent oil men, and J.W. Rutland, an eminent petroleum attorney, both good friends of mine, gave me enough information to write a separate book on this subject alone. I often became so fascinated with a phase of the bank's activity that I needed to remind myself that this is the story of Fred Florence, a legendary banker.

All of my sources seemed in agreement on the point that, while Republic may not have made the very *first* oil production loan (apparently Nathan Adams and the First National can claim this distinction), Fred and Republic Bank still played a pioneering role in oil financing. Republic and the First National were developing oil departments at about the same time. According to John R. Scott, Republic made its first oil production loan to the East Texas Refining Company in 1932. This loan, the forerunner of the founding of Republic's Petroleum Department, was handled by Fred and Doug Forbes, a senior vice president of the bank who later headed the department. As time went on, Fred saw to it that they had the best staffed oil department that could be found. It was an innovation for a bank to employ geologists and engineers, but Fred knew the importance of technical advisors. By the late 1940's the bank had made several hundred million dollars of oil and gas loans, and the department had four vice presidents assigned to it, as well as three or four geololgists on staff. Each of my informants told me that Fred not only knew exactly what the department was doing, but was in on the big deals.

130

Apparently Fred quickly became well known in the oil industry because when he was elected President of the Texas Bankers Association in 1935, *East Texas Oil* magazine used his picture on the cover of their August issue, with the caption "In Good Hands" under the picture. The accompanying article was entitled, "East Texas Furnishes Bankers Another President Who Understands Oil Industry." In July, 1950, Fred's picture appeared on the cover of the *Texas Oil Journal*, along with an article about plans for Republic's new building. The Editorial page of this issue refers to Fred as a "giant of finance." It is indicative of Fred's importance as an "oil banker" that this journal of the oil industry considered Republic's new home a newsworthy item.

J.W. Rutland and others told me that Fred's most significant contribution in the area of oil financing related to something that came to be called the "ABC" transaction. Republic Bank pioneered this type of financing, using a most ingenious method that was worked out by J.W. Bullion, an attorney, and Algur H. Meadows, a founder and then Chairman of the General American Oil Company. Al Meadows, who was killed in an automobile accident in 1978, lived directly across the street from the Florences, and all were good friends. The "ABC" method was a plan for financing proven reserves by lending money on "interest bearing oil payments." The deals that Republic made with Meadows and his affiliated companies were enormous, bringing in large profits on almost 100% safe loans. Al's company prospered to where it is today classified as a major oil company.

131

The clearest explanation I could find of the "ABC" method was given by W.L. Perryman, Jr., in an address he delivered to a meeting of the Newcomen Society in New

York City in 1961.* Mr. Perryman explained the "ABC" transaction as follows:

> In a typical "ABC" transaction, property owner *A* sells to *B*, the purchaser. *B* pays a part of the agreed value in cash, usually from 10 to 25 percent. *A* conveys the property to *B* but reserves a production payment in a face amount equal to the remaining value plus interest on unliquidated balances. A percentage of production, usually 80 to 90 percent, is dedicated to the production payment and the balance goes to the buyer to cover operating expenses. *A* then sells his reserved interest to *C*, a third party, for cash equal to its face value. *A* has now received the full value of his property and realized capital gain on the two sales.
>
> *C* either uses its own funds or borrows to buy the production payment. It takes cost depletion equal to the face amount of the payment and reports the interest factor as income.
>
> The benefits of these transactions are manifold. For income tax purposes the buyer reports only the free income, which is offset by the cost of operations. There is little tax paid on income until the production payment has been liquidated. Thus, payout is shortened considerably. There are no fixed payments or maturities, and since production payments are similar to nonpersonal liability notes, *B*'s liability is limited to his cash investment and the obligation to develop and operate the property.

132

---

* Mr. Perryman's address to members of the Newcomen Society in North America on March 16, 1961, marked the 25th Anniversary of the General American Oil Company of Texas. Mr. Perryman became president of this company in 1960. The Newcomen Society is named for Thomas Newcomen (1663-1729), a British inventor who earned lasting fame in the field of the Mechanical Arts.

Since many people felt that this was a "tax caper," Mr. Perryman continued:

> To a casual observer this may appear to be an avoidance of taxes. This is not so. It is merely a postponement insofar as the purchaser is concerned. Because of a shorter payout, the buyer can pay a higher price. This results in greater profit to the seller and encourages more sales. He pays a capital gains tax at the time of sale, but loses the depletion allowance which he would have taken on the income if he had retained the property. After the production payment has been extinguished the buyer reports and pays tax on the income. We believe that the government receives more tax revenues because of these transactions. Their validity has been recognized by the Internal Revenue Service and upheld by the courts for many years.

The tax laws were subsequently changed, so the "ABC" method is no longer used. However, it was extremely profitable for both the oil company and the bank.

In the same speech quoted above, Perryman gave credit to Republic Bank for contributing to the success of General American Oil Company:

> I cannot fail to emphasize the part which our friends in the financial world have played. Without them much of our success would have been impossible. Many are here tonight, and to them we say "Thank you for your confidence and support." We do business with many financial institutions and we are grateful to all of them. I would like to pay particular tribute to the Republic National Bank of Dallas. This is fitting in connection with General American, since they have been our bankers since 1938. They have pioneered the way for other bankers in many areas of oil financing. Rushton Ardrey, now the head of Republic's Oil Department, and then a very young man, loaned the money for the purchase of the first interest bearing oil payment.

133

When I decided to title this biography "The Texas Banker," I did so because I knew that the Florence name would live on for generations in the history of Dallas and the Southwest. The role Fred played in the development of the oil industry is an important part of the legend, as shown by the following quotation from an article in *Town and Country* magazine, September 1979—nearly 20 years after Fred's death:

> Dallas has been Texas'—indeed, the Southwest's—financial center since early in the oil boom when Fred Florence built Republic Bank into the State's biggest by bankrolling wildcatters. Florence used the then innovative technique of taking oil in the ground as loan collateral. Today Republic is twentieth among the nation's 300 largest banks.

I learned about the bank's International Department from Nicholas F. Roberts, Executive Vice President and now head of the very important Funds Management Division of the Trust Department. Nick, whom I have known for many years, came with Republic in 1943. He was not only the first employee of the International Department but, at that time, its only employee.

Before I go into what Nick told me about the International Department, I would like to quote verbatim what he said about his early relationship with Fred:

> I don't know of anyone outside of my own family that I thought more of than Fred Florence, and I was personally considerably concerned when he died—much more so than you would imagine. I guess the reason is that when I came into the bank, I hadn't graduated from college, and I wanted to go back to school at night. J.M. Hadra was the head of the Cotton Department at that time—he was about 63 or 64

years old then—and I was talking to him one day, and told him what I'd like to do, to go back to S.M.U. at night school. He said, "Well why don't you go up and talk to Mr. Florence? He occasionally will give some scholarships to S.M.U." And I said, "Well, he doesn't even know that I work here." He said, "Well, I'll call him and tell him," which he did. I went up to see Mr. Florence, and told him what I'd like to do, and he said "That's fine." He said, "You go out there and register and tell them to send me the bill." I did, and I took several courses.

Every semester, when it came time to re-register, I'd show him my report card, so to speak, what courses I'd taken and what my grades were, and he'd say, "That's fine, go ahead and just tell them to send me the bill." And he paid my tuition. Of course, I never knew whether he paid it personally—I kind of think he did, but nevertheless, it was taken care of and this enabled me to go back to school and study law. I told him I'd like to study law, but I did not intend to be an attorney, that I wanted to know what would be helpful to me here in the bank. So I went on through S.M.U., and then about 1949 he transferred me into the investment side of the bank.

Nick told me that the International Department, which was first known as the Foreign Department, was an outgrowth of the Commodities Department. Although Nick was raised in Dallas, he worked for a time in New York City, where he handled commodity loans for the Chemical Bank. When he returned to Dallas, he was employed by Republic to work in their Commodities Department. In New York, Nick had also acquired some know-how in foreign matters because at the Chemical commodities were a part of their Foreign Department. Hence in 1944, when Republic needed someone to handle their cotton business with Mexico, he was selected, and as he modestly put it:

135

When we began to get some inquiries about Mexican business and letters of credit and some inquiries from the Mexican banks about an account back and forth with each other, it was turned over to me to handle simply because I'd had some previous experience. The thing began to grow then, and we began to get several Mexican bank accounts and more and more interest in confirming their letters of credit to shippers in this state who were shipping goods to Mexico or who were importing merchandise from Mexico, either way; so as a result the department grew of itself, mainly from customer demand.

Whenever Fred saw a need that the bank could fill, he always moved quickly to do so. It seemed natural that Republic be the first bank in Dallas to handle the needs of domestic customers doing business beyond our borders, as well as supplying a convenience for foreigners and the needs of their business. It is possible, since Houston is a port, that the banks there preceded Republic in this market, but it appears that Republic was the first to offer this service on a broad scale in the Southwest.

Nowadays hiring minorities is commonplace and by law a requirement. It was not so when Nick needed someone who could speak Spanish to help him. He hired a Mexican girl, the first Mexican on the payroll. Some of the other girls in the bank said, "I am not going to work with a Mexican, I'll quit first." Nick says he simply asked, "When are you leaving?"

The record shows that in only five years the Nick Roberts-one girl department had grown to 10 or 11 employees and business had more than doubled each year, this in spite of its beginnings partly having been during World War II and the early postwar years. Ten years after Fred died Republic led all Southwestern banks by establishing a full-fledged branch in London and now has several banks and offices throughout the world, all under the direction of the International Department.

Barry Mason, now head of this department, advises me that he employs 125 persons in the U.S. and 60 abroad. One can easily see how this department can be of enormous service to its correspondent banks and, today, to the banks owned by Republic of Texas Corporation and to their customers. I have personally found it to be a great convenience in buying foreign currency when going abroad and in cashing what I have brought back into dollars. I have even used their services to buy or sell American Deposit Receipts or stock in foreign companies.

To describe all of the services available at Republic would end up by being a treatise on banking. However, there are two services that are especially interesting to me because Republic pioneered both of these in the Southwest. They are the Traveler's Checks and the Lockbox.

On August 16, 1938, the Republic became the fourth American company to issue traveler's checks, the other three being American Express, the First National City of New York, and the Continental National Bank of Chicago. Later, the Mellon National Bank of Pittsburgh and Bank of America of San Francisco established a similar service. Today, both the Mellon and Continental banks have discontinued the service, again leaving, to my knowledge, only four in this business. There are other institutions outside of the U.S. such as Barclays Bank of London whose checks are accepted worldwide. As of this writing, Master Charge is considering entering the field.

137

It is interesting to note that it was Republic's vast interest in oil loans, and oil investments in their Trust Department, that gave Fred the idea of using this device to help the men in the field and to supply safe money to the bank's many oil company customers who had their personnel located in the far reaches of the world. After the end of World War II, tourism, stifled for many years, again came into its own, and the Republic had worldwide recognition and many agents selling their checks.

The bank also sold money orders and, in order to market them throughout the United States without being in violation of unit banking laws, the bank formed Republic Money Orders, Inc., on March 13, 1959. Effective January 1, 1971, this company acquired RNB Traveler's Checks, which then became known as Republic Money Order, Inc., Traveler's Checks, payable through Republic National Bank. On November 30, 1977, Republic Money Orders, Inc., became a wholly owned subsidiary of Republic of Texas Corporation.

In 1969, Helen Poe and Mary Broad collaborated to author a book, *Never Take Nyet for an Answer*, in which they wrote about landing at Nakhodka, a very important naval base, 30 miles east of Vladivostok in Siberia. They wrote:

> Although the entire trip is paid for you, never travel without currency of the land. Like travel in any other country in the world, you need money for entertainment, tickets, taxis, and gifts.

138

Describing the Money Exchange as a barn-like building, they continued:

> We presented a traveler's check from our local bank. The Intourist cashier was hesitant and apologetic because it was not the well-known American Express. We were about to bring out our dollars when the young assistant, who had been thumbing through a stack of papers, came up triumphantly with a large white sheet of paper. In the center was

glued the identifying check of the Republic National Bank of Dallas, Texas. It was like a telephone call from home. Halfway around the world in the most remote corner of Siberia was the familiar traveler's check from our hometown. the Intourist girl was more relieved than we were and quickly handed us the rubles.

Each year, the Republic renews its arrangement with the "Bank of Foreign Trade and Commerce," which is the official bank for the U.S.S.R. Republic also holds a contract with the U.S. Army and Air Force.

The traveler's check has many advantages for the bank, the principal one being the large float of free money. Checks are paid for in advance and many people keep unused checks after a trip, or at all times, for an emergency or a quick unplanned trip. It is true that some of the money to pay for the checks comes from accounts in banks in the Republic of Texas Corporation family; but most depositors attempt to keep their usual balances, and many buy with cash given to them as gifts or with checks on other banks.

By far its most important function is to advertise the Republic's name throughout the world. Many firms in Europe, both wholesale and retail, carry bank accounts in the United States, and their knowing of and handling Republic's checks familiarizes them with the bank. Many of the thousands of banks at home and abroad display the little plastic facsimile of the Republic check or have one under the glass top of the counter.

139

A "Lockbox" account can make a good deal of money for a corporate depositor, especially when interest rates are high. The concept dates back to 1947. Radio Corporation of American (R.C.A.) in cooperation with the First National Bank of Chicago and Bankers Trust of New York were the first to use it. In 1954 Republic became the first bank in Texas to make this service available. Here is how it works.

The bank acting as the corporate agent of the corporation has a box at the Post Office. Customers' remittances are mailed to this box. The bank picks these up every hour during business days and every two hours on weekends. The money is credited to the corporation's account immediately. The bank clears the checks and routes the paid invoices to the corporation. The corporation has the use of their money two or more days earlier than they would if they had the money owed them sent to their own office. The bank charges a fee for this service, but the Cash Management Division at Republic estimates that their largest customer using this device saves close to a million dollars a year.

Republic is not unique in being a "full service bank" except that it really is what the description says, while many claim this distinction if they can only take care of the normal requirements of a large segment of the people.

CHAPTER X
THE FIFTIES

THE AMERICAN BANKERS ASSOCIATION

Fred's active affiliation with the American Bankers Association began in 1934, when he was appointed to the Committee on Banking Studies. He remained on this committee for three years, after which he served for four years as a member of the Committee on Federal Legislation and the Subcommittee on Taxation. From 1941 to 1944, he served on the National Defense and War Loans Committee, followed by the Chairmanship of the Postwar Small Business Credit Commission. In the year 1947, he was elected to a three-year term on the Executive Council, Administrative Committee, and Small Business Credit Commission. During the 1950-1951 year, he became Chairman of the Credit Policy Commission, considered by him to be the most important committee of the Association. This group was composed of the top ranking bankers in the country. He then served as Executive Council Chairman of the Credit Policy Commission. In addition to his offices in the A.B.A., he had been President of the Dallas Clearing House Association and the Texas Bankers Association, and since he had met nearly every banker of any importance in the country, he needed no introduction at an American Bankers Association convention.

One of the best known men in the financial world was W.A. Philpott, Jr. of Dallas. He had been secretary of the Texas Bankers Association for thirty-seven years, and was the editor of its official publication, *The Texas Bankers Record*. He had also been a regular attendant at A.B.A. meetings. He was likable, lively, and extremely capable and a close friend and golfing partner of Fred. It was he who thought that Fred would make the A.B.A. a good president.

F. Raymond Peterson was the President of the Patterson (New Jersey) National Bank and a most influential man in Eastern banking circles. He knew Fred well and was one of his ardent admirers. In the fall of 1953, prior to the A.B.A. convention in Washington, Philpott approached Peterson to solicit his help in getting Fred nominated for Vice President at the next year's meeting, the election to which would be tantamount to his being made President the following year. Philpott told me, during an interview, that he knew Peterson would be of immeasurable help. They agreed to work together, but their first move was to get Fred's approval. In view of the fact that Republic was building a new home (described later in this chapter), there could have been some doubt about his wanting to take on any additional work at that time. However, it is unlikely that anyone would pass up the chance to be the President of one of the oldest (1875) and one of the most powerful associations in the country. I am certain there was no real doubt in the minds of the sponsors as to Fred's answer, but they needed his acquiescence.

During the convention in Washington, Philpott arrived at the Florences' suite, where Fred and Helen were taking a rest before dinner. Fred greeted him at the door and invited him in. Philpott jokingly told me that Helen wasn't in on the deal—she slept through it. What Philpott failed to tell me during our interview, Helen, my biographical adviser, now tells me, is that he and Peterson had visited her previously (knowing that Fred was in a meeting) to enlist her cooperation. Fred's answer, as expected, was an

142

enthusiastic "yes," and the wheels were in motion. Helen has often told me that she can never remember Fred as ever being tired and that he always had time for everything pertaining to the bank.

While much work was required, the first step was to get him nominated. It was necessary for the Texas Bankers Association to endorse him, and a unanimous vote was almost a requirement. We all know that jealousies exist and that others must have had candidates, but Fred had thoroughly ingratiated himself with all the Texas bankers, and all knew that he above all Texans had the best chance for election. Thereupon, the Association's secretary was empowered to send a letter to the secretaries of Bankers Associations in every state, and to Hawaii and Alaska, containing the following endorsement:

As fellow bankers, business associates, and personal friends of Mr. Florence, members of the Texas Bankers Association, assembled in 70th Annual Convention in San Antonio, May 18, 1954, proudly present his name to the bankers of the United States for the office of vice-president of the American Bankers Association.

We recognize Mr. Florence's capabilities as a banker, we value him highly as a leader in the business life of Texas and the nation, we respect and esteem him as a man. Fred Florence has the qualifications and the competency necessary to occupy the high official posts of the A.B.A. and to direct its policies and work. He served with distinction as president of the Texas Bankers Association in 1935-36.

Therefore, we heartily recommend Mr. Florence to the bankers of this nation as a man worthy of their approval, confidence, and regard. And we hope in October, 1954 when his name is offered for vice-presidency of the A.B.A. that he will be chosen by unanimous acclaim.

143

Philpott was not only known throughout the banking fraternity, but, of more importance, he was very popular. He and Peterson worked hard, so when the 80th convention was held in Atlantic City, Fred's election to the Vice Presidency was a foregone conclusion. Helen tells me that Fred had told his sponsors that he would not permit his name to be put in nomination unless he was assured that his election would be unopposed. Fred's feelings of gratitude were so perfectly expressed in his letter to his friend Phil that it is worth repeating. Fred was always a skilled letter writer, and this letter shows the warmth that was characteristic of all his correspondence:

October 29, 1954

Dear Phil:

Have been thinking I would see you, but you were away—and now since your return, I wanted to drop you this note to express again my very, very deep appreciation to you for all of the things you have done for me throughout the long years—but particularly in relation to my election to the vice presidency of the American Bankers Association. You have always been my stalwart friend—advocate—and generalissimo—and I will have to say that certainly in this instance you accomplished the desired objective without even a casualty. I really do appreciate it, Phil, very, very much. Am sure you know I do, and while among close friends, we can normally take things for granted—I did want to drop this note to you to thank you again and again.

Helen joins in sending our dearest love,
Affectionately,
Fred

144

Philpott's reply is equally worth including because it so clearly shows his pleasure at the victory:

November 1, 1954

Dear Fred:

The finishing words have just been written to a story the November Record will carry, reporting how the bankers of the nation honored you on October 20th. The writing of this gave me personal pleasure and satisfaction.

Now comes your cordial (from the Latin, *cordis*, heart) and affectionate note, dated October 29, and my inner glow is intensified. Your appraisal of my work with the "campaign" is greatly inflated, I fear. But your declaration of friendship, appreciation, and good will toward me, personally, is taken at *face value*—because your capacity for gratitude, for loyalty to those you esteem, for steadfastness in friendships, has long been recognized by your intimate associates—among whom I humbly list myself.

Concerning recent happenings, culminating in your election as A.B.A. Vice President, there is one moral to be pointed: get behind a "winner" and you can't fail! Truly, this was the status of those of us behind you: we pick a *winner*!

You and Helen please do remember that you have a friend and admirer in me who is ready to go to any extremity (short of murder or mayhem) in furthering your case and cause.

I am deeply flattered that in these busy days for you, you should brush aside manifold and pressing matters in order to address me such a warming note of affection. I shall treasure it always.

To you and Helen,

Ever thine,
Phil

The following statement praising Fred appeared in the *Dallas Times Herald*, November 30, 1954, shortly after he became the Vice President of the A.B.A.:

145

The brilliant, aggressive Texas banker was attracting National attention and offers—some for sky-high salaries in the East—but his devotion still was to the Southwest. He brought Wall Street to the area, in effect, by becoming its most important and astute financier.

During Fred's year as Vice President, preceding his automatic election to be A.B.A.'s first, and up to this writing, the only President from Dallas, he served on a large number of banking and credit commissions and was a director of many great business institutions. All firms, particularly banks, seek directors with two basic qualifications: (1) their occupying a position by virtue of which the company would benefit from a sales standpoint, and (2) their capacity for sage and experienced advice. The ideal director is one who adds the ability of leadership, the interest in securing new business, and the advantage of being widely known and respected. Fred had all these qualifications and was untiring and conscientious in furthering the success of the institution. He always reached for new goals. Therefore, it is no wonder that he was invited to join more boards of business, charitable, and educational institutions than he cared to join. Fred instinctively knew which organizations in each of these categories were well managed and could be expected to succeed or progress. Hence, he was never associated with any organization that failed or that in any way embarrassed him. He helped many over some rough spots, and the time and wisdom that he gave returned a great reward to him personally and, to a great measure, to the success of the Republic National Bank. (At this time, Republic National Bank had $24 million in capital, $26 million in surplus, with $508,077,834.48 in total deposits.)

During his Vice Presidency of A.B.A., Fred was on the board of some great companies: Austin Bridge Co., Cosmopolitan Hotel Corporation, Baker Hotel (one of

Dallas' finest), Dallas Power and Light Company, Dallas Railway and Terminal Company, Missouri-Kansas-Texas Railroad Company (known as the Katy), and Wyatt Metal and Boiler Works. He was also Chairman of the Board of the Lone Star Steel Company.

The President of the A.B.A. during Fred's apprenticeship to the top job was Homer J. Livingston, then President of the First National Bank of Chicago. He had been a close friend and an ardent admirer of Fred and lent a very helpful guiding hand in preparing Fred for the procedures and details of his job. When Mr. Livingston passed away in Chicago in 1970, Helen flew to Chicago for his funeral and visited for a while with his widow.

In November, 1954, the *Texas Oil Journal* said of Fred, "Leading bankers of the nation have just conferred a high honor upon one of the most powerful and influential friends the Petroleum Industry has ever had in banking circles of Texas and the Southwest." They further described him as "a creative banker who came out of the piney-woods to show Texans how to finance their own fantastic dreams of empire—and to put that empire together in terms of industrial growth that has lifted a whole sectional economy by its bootstraps to the No. 1 wealth-producing area of the nation." They editorialized with the climax: "The Florence philosophy has tended to step up the whole tempo of American banking. Over 20 years ago, R.N.B. was already offering fifty different services to their customers, and was actively merchandising them."

Frank X. Tolbert wrote the following in the Dallas Morning News about the meeting in Chicago in 1955 where Fred became the President:

147

The place smelled like money. Maybe this was because there were 6,000 bankers milling around, talking about interest and other interesting things. Many of the bankers were also talking about Fred Farrel Florence, who, in his twenty-seventh year as President of Dallas' Republic National Bank, has been given banking's highest honor.

One banker said, "Mr. Florence is tops in the broad field of finance. He knows how to get the most out of money when it is plentiful. He knows how to find money when it hides—he knows money. Bankers, good bankers, know their rafts are not going to sink, but most of them don't know where their rafts are going. I think Mr. Florence knows where the rafts are going."

Most of the 6,000 bankers in Chicago are men of a stately, measured gait. In contrast, Fred Florence moves along at a bouncing, running walk. He has been moving on the double ever since he was a school boy in Rusk, Texas. He then had the nickname of "Teddie"* and he went through the public schools in Rusk in a sprinting fashion. He started at the age of 7, was double promoted three times,** and took his high school diploma at 15.

Being praised at home is even more gratifying than being a hero abroad. The *Texas Bankers Record*, October, 1955 issue, commented on Fred's becoming the first Dallas banker ever to head the American Bankers Association:

Let it be remembered he has had a hand in every forward, worthwhile movement for the betterment of Dallas every year since—well, since he first came to Dallas in 1920.

Electing a Vice President to serve for one year and then automatically become President the following year is a widely used policy with trade associations. The two years

*I have been unable to authenticate this.
**Maybe.

of executive status with the big ones like the American Bar Association, the American Medical Association, or the Bankers, represents a great honor, of course; but even more so, it imposes a tremendous responsibility and means a great deal of hard work for the one elected. Those who earn the honor are generally chosen because their history has been that of an energetic leader.

During the two years that Fred served, he attended nearly every State Bankers Association convention, and Helen almost always went with him. Helen says that Fred was in great demand as a speaker; so, being conscientious (and, I suspect, also anxious to keep the name Republic in the minds of the banking fraternity), he tried to accept every invitation. I asked Helen if Fred used the same speech at successive meetings. She said that each speech was slightly different, usually covering the same subjects but somewhat rearranged, with a few timely new comments. She told me Fred had someone who helped him a bit with material for his speeches and that she was his sounding board and helped him with things like grammar and sentence construction. Essentially, though, the speeches were his own.

A few of the annual meetings took in two or more states at one time, but the various conventions were definitely not scheduled for a convenient circuit tour. As a result, Fred and Helen spent a lot of time during those two years almost literally bouncing from one side of the country to the other. Furthermore, the meetings were not always held in the state's principal city or one where air travel was readily available. For example, West Virginia might select the beautiful Greenbriar Hotel in White Sulphur Springs, an ideal location in many ways but very difficult to reach in those days by either train or plane.

Helen recalls a particularly hectic trip that included meetings in Sun Valley, Idaho, Sheridan, Wyoming, and St.

149

Louis, Missouri. The selection of Sun Valley for the Idaho meeting could not be questioned from any standpoint—except access!—and most of the Idaho bankers could simply drive their cars. Fred and Helen, coming from Dallas, had to fly to Salt Lake City, where they rented a car and drove the rest of the way. They had expected to drive back to Salt Lake City and fly into Sheridan, Wyoming, where Fred's next talk was scheduled; but there was no service available whatsoever. Sun Valley did have a landing strip for small planes, so Fred phoned his good friend, Toddie Lee Wynne, who sent his private plane to their rescue. Even so, Helen remembers that the trip to Sheridan was rather uncomfortable—the pilot had used up all the oxygen on the plane en route to Idaho and had not been able to refill his tank (or didn't have time, or forgot!). They made it to Sheridan, however, and the plane waited for them and then flew them on to St. Louis, where another speech was closely scheduled. On arrival at their hotel in St. Louis on June 5, 1955, Helen received the sad news that her father had died. Dr. Lefkowitz had suffered a stroke more than a year before, and had been hospitalized for a very long time at Baylor Hospital.* For months he had been unable to talk or, possibly, even to know what was happening around him.

Fred wanted to return home with Helen, but she talked him into staying because he was scheduled, immediately following his talk to the bankers the next day, to award diplomas to the graduates at Westminster College in Fulton, Missouri and at the same ceremony to receive an honorary doctorate. Helen tried to get a commercial flight to Dallas, but none was available for a long time. She phoned to find out whether the Wynne plane was still at the airport, and

150

*In happier days, Dr. Lefkowitz had participated with Dr. George W. Truitt in Baylor Hospital's dedication.

was told that it had been on its way for about 30 minutes. Purely by chance, Helen had memorized the plane's identification numbers—she said she guessed she had just sat and looked at them for so long during the flight—so the dispatcher was able to make contact with the plane. It returned to St. Louis, and in short order Helen was on her way home. Son David went to Fulton to see his father receive the doctorate (David had attended Westminster College). They returned together in time for the funeral.

Most of their trips were easier than that one. Wherever they went, their hosts did everything they could to make them comfortable and happy. The ladies almost always had a luncheon for Helen, which she usually enjoyed, although she remembers that it was not always easy to be charming to so many women she had never met. Accommodations were not always truly deluxe, but they generally received the best available. In one of the smaller cities, Helen said, they were given a room with three king-size beds for the two of them! Helen told me about one trip when she was happily anticipating the suite they had been told they would have, because she was very tired and wanted to go immediately to bed even while Fred was still visiting with the bankers in the living room. When they arrived at the hotel, the "suite" turned out to be what is called a "semi-suite," with the living room and bedroom combined; so there was no privacy for Helen to hop right into bed. Also, their hosts had thoughtfully provided a fully stocked bar and decided to stay and help them use it! The party went on for several hours while poor Helen struggled to stay awake.

At the end of Fred's year as President of the A.B.A., he was presented with an illuminated manuscript, hand-lettered in black, red, and gold, and beautifully bound in a brown leather book inscribed in gold, as an expression of thanks from those he had served with untiring energy and

151

without pay. It was signed by Erle Cocke, the new President of the A.B.A. and Vice Chairman of the Board and Chairman of the Executive committee of the Fulton National Bank of Atlanta, Georgia; by J.C. Wellman, new Vice President of A.B.A. and President of the Bank of Kennett, Kennett, Missouri; and by George R. Bayles, Treasurer of A.B.A. and Chairman of the Board and President of the Merchants National Bank of Chicago, Illinois. The inscription read:

> In recognition of his leadership as President of the American Bankers Association during the year 1955-56, after many years of helpful service to the Association, this testimonial of appreciation and affection is presented to
> FRED F. FLORENCE
> for his dynamic energy, for his eloquence as a spokesman for American Banking, and for his warm, friendly personality which he has shared so generously with his legion of friends throughout the country.

It had been a tiring two years for Fred and Helen. Often they would only be home long enough for Fred to visit the bank and for them to re-pack and start out again. But the experience was exciting, the honor was rewarding, and from Fred's viewpoint it was worth any effort. It was good for Republic.

152

THE NEW BUILDING

> I understand there's a new bank being opened here, I believe it's called the Republic. Well, I knew the Republicans would start opening banks around the country pretty soon!
> —Bob Hope on his arrival in Dallas for the opening of the new Republic National Bank Building.

On Sunday morning, April 17, 1949, the Dallas newspapers published a story about the new Republic Bank building, predicting that its completion would make Dallas' skyline the highest in the South. A $2 million property transaction made way for the largest bank and office building in the Southwest. The ground space covered about 45,000 square feet, or slightly more than an acre. At that time, Fred was greatly criticized for this choice of location because it was outside of the concentrated business district. People were particularly shocked because they believed in Fred's judgment, and this seemed foolhardy.

In the very first announcement, Fred said that the new building would have garage facilities within the main structure, designed along the lines of the most successful parking facilities in the country. This was another first for Dallas and is indicative of Fred's farsightedness thirty years ago.

It took five years of careful planning and daily supervision to fulfill the dream of the stockholders and directors of the bank. The architectural firm of Harrison and Abromovitz was employed to design the structure. This firm was selected because of its outstanding work, which included the United Nations Building in midtown Manhattan; Rockefeller Center; the Trylon and Perisphere, central symbol of the New York World's Fair; the 40-story United

153

States Steel Corporation Building, and the Aluminum Company of America Building, both in Pittsburgh. In cooperation was the firm of Gill and Harrell. Grayson Gill had been a leading architect in Dallas and is now retired, but his son is continuing and enjoying the same splendid reputation. Harrell, who joined Gill in 1950, had come from New York, having won first and second prizes in the Libby-Owens-Ford "Modernize Main Street" competition at the New York World's Fair. His firm is currently one of the most prestigious in the nation. The J.W. Bateson Company, based in Dallas but active in building nationwide, was the general contractor.

This building was needed to house this fast expanding bank and to help fill the need for first class downtown office space for the city's growing economy. The building was to be unconventional in many respects, but also very functional. Once the building got underway, the eyes of the construction fraternity watched eagerly for the finished product. As many as 750 men worked on the site, while plants throughout the world worked to produce materials, decorations, and equipment. Marble was brought from France, Italy, and Spain to complement the beautiful Calacata statuary marble from our own State of Georgia.

Its 598-foot height, including the neon tower, made it the tallest building in forty-five of the nation's then forty-eight states, and only three cities—New York, Chicago, and Cleveland—could boast of taller ones. It is interesting to reflect that in 1931, when Republic added an addition to its banking headquarters on Main Street, that building then became the largest in Texas in square footage. The new building became the world's tallest building faced in aluminum and glass, with its forty stories and a 150-foot ornamental tower on top of which is a beacon light which rotates twelve times every minute and has a strength of five million candlepower. At that time this beacon was surpassed only by a lighthouse on the Florida coast with 5,500,000 candlepower. The purpose of the beacon, which engineers estimated was visible for 120 miles, was threefold: to protect aircraft from hitting the building and to help guide them to Dallas, as well as to be a powerful advertisement for the bank. More than two miles of neon tubing, powered by 1,516 transformers connected with seventeen miles of wire, changed the Dallas skyline. Of the beacon, one bank official commented, "It would be visible farther but we're limited by the curvature of the earth," and was rather put out to think that the curvature of the earth would go around limiting things like that in Dallas!

Perhaps the smokeless smokestack would have created more comment today, with our pollution-conscious public, than it did twenty-five years ago. This flue starts fifty feet below ground and emits boiler gasses for 500 feet. The screen-covered stack carries the smokeless fumes from the natural gas powered equipment over the Dallas skyline without smoke or smell.

Having been brought up in the advertising business (I resent its being called "game"), I was intrigued with "SPEMBSE," which stands for "Society for the Promotion and Encouragement of More and Better Sidewalk Engineers." The bank built headquarters for the society—a bleacher unit, high above street level, from which visitors watched the excavation in comfort. An awning shielded them from the sun as they occupied seats covered with red plush cushions. Cold drink machines and telephone booths added to the convenience of the visitors. The stand was opened in April, 1951, and closed on June 26, 1952. Visitors signed a guest book, and during these approximately fourteen months, the gallery was visited by 112,000 people from every state in the union and from more than twenty foreign countries.

155

This epitome of showmanship gave the public a feeling that here was a bank with something besides stone walls and "fashion plate" officers with ice water in their veins. SPEMBSE became a conversation piece, and kept the interest in the progress of the building alive. It was a great piece of publicity which, for little cost, made the public aware that the bank was interested in them—not just their money.

At the time, a humorous story did the rounds. It was reported that a SPEMBSE visiting lady from out of state saw where a barrel of oil had been overturned in the pit, by accident. She informed her children that there was the start of another Texas oil well. "See, they've struck oil on the way down," she said, "but they'll go ahead with the building. I'm sure they'd rather have a nice new building than just another oil well."

For as long as I can remember, Dallas had—and still has—a "Bonehead" Club—serious business men who gather each Friday for lunch with the only purpose "fun." Each meeting mourns or celebrates something that has to do with Dallas, a prominent citizen, or an event. They have an annual Christmas party in July with an upside-down tree. The Boneheads celebrate another yearly event at their Friday luncheon before the opening of the great Texas State Fair during the second weekend in October. At this time the members, aboard Dallas fire engines, go to the fair ground to *close* the Fair. Another popular stunt is to invite a luncheon guest to the podium to make a few remarks. As soon as he begins to talk, everyone gets up and leaves.

The Boneheads may have been ahead of their times. Fifty years ago they could not have foreseen the growth of downtown Dallas, yet they planned to build a 21-story building and to start the 21st floor first and build down toward the first floor, hoping by the time they got the building completed to be able to find a lot to set the building on. For one of their meetings during SPEMBSE, the Boneheads assembled on the bleachers to help the excavators. They announced as the purpose of the meeting: ''To get the Republic Bank out of the hole!''

The building is sheathed in anodized aluminum panels, each with the design of a four-pointed star. This grey building was a symbol of strength, and the star later (after Fred's death) became the bank's widely known trademark. All members of the bank's 2,400 or more staff wear a pin portraying the star, and much of its advertising includes this insignia. Today, the bank's emphasis is on rendering ''Silver Star'' service.

In line with Fred's insistence that ''only the best, newest, and most modern'' would be good enough, the new building surpassed in many ways all others then in existence by using some completely original ideas and many unique innovations then unknown to the Southwest. Installed were 23 ''autotronic'' operatorless elevators. Those to the upper floors travel at more than 1,000 feet per minute, the highest speed that had ever been achieved for automatic elevators at that time. On the second floor was the palatial banking room with a ceiling twenty-three feet high constructed of acoustical material with recessed fluorescent lighting. The area designed to house the tellers, loan officers, and customer's service, is 287 feet long and is reached by fast-moving escalators, stairs, and elevators. Above this huge banking floor is a 333-foot balcony emblazoned with 3,300 square feet of 24 karat gold leaf. which cost $30,000. 157

To illustrate how no details were overlooked, newspaper notices before the opening called attention to the three specially made, 15 × 25-foot flags, each containing forty yards of material, to fly from the flagpoles over the main entrance. The flags are those of the United States,

Texas, and the house flag of Republic Bank. The latter is gold colored and bears the bank's seal. When the James Templeton Company delivered the order for 5,000 yards of chenille carpet for the floors, it was the second-largest order in their 149 year history. The larger order had been from the Aga Khan for 6,000 yards. Buyers for this Scottish firm visited wool markets throughout the world gathering materials, and it took the full output of their plant to produce the bank's requirements in time for the opening. One carpet measured 85 × 32 feet—one of the largest in the world, requiring ten men and a block and tackle to install this 3,000 pound floor covering.

In the banking quarters on Main Street, Republic had been the pioneer in Dallas in furnishing time and weather 24 hours a day to those wishing to dial one of the special numbers. Today, this kind of service is common, but then it was another "first" for Republic and unique in Dallas. The popularity of this service supplied by Audichron was so great that it was continued and expanded in the new building, and today utilizes an entire telephone exchange. In response to dialing 844 plus any four numbers, a pleasant voice delivers a short message about the bank, or a special greeting or charitable appeal, and then gives the correct time and the current outside temperature.

158   No important project is ever accomplished without problems and headaches. During the course of construction, there were four separate fires, the last one of which, at first, seemed so serious that Fred donned a hard hat and, with the representatives of the various organizations involved, personally inspected the building, as there was a grave question as to whether the steel structure had been impaired to an extent requiring the building to be dismantled and rebuilt. Fortunately, all was well.

The gold leaf rail on the third floor, which provides a horseshoe-shaped opening to view the banking floor, also created quite a problem. Once the architects elected to have the frieze gold leafed, they discovered that there was not that much gold leaf readily available, and to get it applied on schedule, it would be necessary to employ the labor of most of the gold beaters in the United States. This was done, and the 24 karat gold leaf was applied. At the time the gold leaf was applied, the cost was $30,000. Today, with gold selling near $500 per ounce, that same gold leaf would cost over $460,000.

During the opening of the bank, many thousands of people visited this balcony and many commented that it looked like real gold leaf! Like people testing wet paint, they would run their fingernails across it, which, of course, tore the gold leaf and damaged it. Even before the opening festivities were over, the contractor put up a sign, "PLEASE DO NOT TOUCH THE GOLD LEAF." Unfortunately, many had already torn pieces off, and a number of places had to be repaired.

Fred knew that this magnificent building would be a great stimulus to the growth and importance of Dallas. He was fully aware of the national publicity that would accrue for the benefit of the bank. He was assured that this handsome structure would stand as a symbol of strength, would 159 instill confidence, and would prove to everyone that Republic was progressive and that they were large enough to handle any and all kinds of business.

Earlier I wrote that the site selected was considered a poor one. Fred miraculously visualized this location being the hub of the city. How could he have known, in 1954, that in twenty-six years the site that was thought to be on the fringe of the city would be the very center of the seventh largest metroplex in the country?

A year or so after Fred's death, the Board of Directors authorized a further expansion because they needed more banking facilities, and, because office space was in demand, a new 50-story office building adjacent to the original building and called The Tower was opened in 1964. It is similar in construction to the original building and is covered with identical aluminum panels of the same design. The bank had also acquired the Medical Arts Building that occupied the southeast corner of the property where both the "Building" and the "Tower" are located. A few years ago this building was razed and a new eight story building matching the other two has been opened to house the bank's expanding needs.

The growth of Dallas both downtown and in the suburbs has been exciting and almost unbelievable. Fred's "end-of-the-town" location is now the hub. Surrounding the Republic complex we find the Sheraton and Plaza of the Americas hotels and many multi-story office buildings, many not yet complete. The new buildings when completed will almost completely block the view from the upper stories of Republic. Most of these buildings are or will be connected by underground passageways with shops or by bridges over the streets. This area is dotted with small parks and far exceeds Fred's wildest dream.

160   The entire project of planning, constructing, and opening the new building in 1954 was the crowning achievement of Fred's banking career, and he wanted it perfect in every respect. All successful business men are salesmen. Fred was by no means the exception. He knew what he had, what it could do, and he set forth to merchandise it by having the most elaborate and exciting opening that had ever been staged in Dallas.

THE OPENING PARTY

> In conclusion, I want to pay tribute to two of my closest personal friends, Karl Hoblitzelle, Chairman of the Board of the Republic, and Fred Florence, its President. They have been my friends for many years, in good times and in bad. They are two of the finest citizens I have ever known, progressive, far-sighted, always dependable and always in the front ranks in meeting the needs of our community.
>
> —Honorable Robert L. Thornton, Mayor of Dallas at the Dedication Ceremony, December 1, 1954

The formal opening ceremony was staged on the corner of Ervay Street and Pacific Avenue, where the main entrance to the bank is located. Crowds jammed these streets in all four directions, all vehicular traffic having been rerouted. The weather was threatening and it looked like rain, but as some wag pointed out, *it didn't dare!* The Master of Ceremonies on that memorable morning was Robert G. Storey, Dean of the Southern Methodist University Law School and founder of the Southwestern Legal Foundation. The invocation was given by Bishop Thomas K. Gorman, Bishop of the Dallas-Fort Worth Roman Catholic Diocese, and the benediction by Rabbi Levi A. Olan of Temple Emanu-el. The Honorable Allan Shivers, Governor of Texas, was the principal speaker. The dedication of the building was made by Bishop A. Frank Smith, Fred's longtime friend, who was then chairman of the Board of Trustees of Southern Methodist University. A bit of ad-lib humor by the inimitable Bob Hope, and two of the world's greatest singing voices, Miss Mimi Benzell and Mr. Gordon MacRae, accompanied by Ted Weems and his orchestra, added to this important occasion.

Mr. Robert L. Thornton, Mayor of Dallas and also Chief Executive Officer of the Mercantile National Bank, which until the new building was completed had been the tallest bank building in Texas, made the following welcoming remarks:

> While this building is somewhat taller than I would have wished for, I will have to admit that it does boldly penetrate our beautiful skyline and is a wonderful asset to this great Southwestern city.
>
> As mayor, I welcome this vast assemblage here this morning—a big audience—which I understand exceeds any opening of any other bank that has ever taken place in our country. To our visitors from out of the city I would like to say this: If any of you by accident or otherwise find yourself in our county jail and I can't get you out, then I will get in with you, because I am in dead earnest about wanting you to have a good time while you are in our city.

Both Mr. Hoblitzelle and Mr. Florence made acceptance speeches on behalf of the bank. Mr. Storey introduced Hoblitzelle as follows:

> Now, I present one of our greatest citizens and public benefactors—a businessman, financier and philanthropist, Mr. Karl Hoblitzelle, Chairman of the Board of the Republic Bank.

162

Mr. Hoblitzelle:

> It is not my intention to dwell on the material aspects of this great institution, but to call to your attention the more important forces that have made this great accomplishment possible; the vital and human elements that have welded this institution into an organization that has consistently cast its bread upon the waters and had it returned many-fold.
>
> Therefore, I think you will agree that the inscription on the plaque on the Ervay Street entrance of this structure is

symbolic of the Republic Bank Family. I quote the inscription: "This building is dedicated to the principle that no institution can long endure that fails to faithfully and unselfishly serve its Country, its State and its own Community."

Mr. Storey, in introducing Florence, said:

The magnificent edifice which brings us together this day is the result of the hopes, dreams, aspirations and energies of one of the great leaders of the Southwest, the President of the Republic National Bank of Dallas, Mr. Fred F. Florence.

Mr. Florence:

This building symbolizes the great growing Southwest, and the eternal spirit of America. It is the product of a great force of loyal men and women, who through the years—by devotion and hard work—in a community of wonderful people—have created an institution as nearly human as possible—which will live on with genuine consideration for the well-being of our citizenship, our institutions, the area we serve, and the nation.

A great bank must be delicately attuned and responsive to the pulse of the people, in leadership and service, if it is to project the spirit, vitality, and strength of America.

The responsibility of banks—and we say of this bank in particular because we feel it so sincerely—is to serve their people soundly, constructively and courageously. This we will do with all of our vigor and strength.

In Texas and the Southwest, we have the greatest wealth-producing area in the country. This tremendous production of wealth from the natural resources with which we are blessed, carries with it great responsibilities of conservation, utilization, and clear judgment.

163

This Bank, along with other important banks and financial institutions of our country, will supply the credit to meet the sound and worthy requirements of this area, and of America's expanding economy. These combined resources are a bulwark of strength to America's business, and to the defense and security of our nation.

Here at the Republic Bank, we are dedicated to the policy of keeping the stream of financing open so that worthwhile and useful things of life will flow in greater abundance to all people; and so that our economic advancement will speed onward with a mighty rush to uplift us as individuals, strengthen us as a Nation—to the glorious end that as a free people we will measure up to the responsibilities of our rich heritage of American citizenship.

The crowd on the street at the dedication was estimated at 15,000, and in addition, countless thousands watched it live on T.V. The Apache Belles from Tyler Junior College, who have appeared nationwide and have often been featured in the great Macy Christmas parade in New York on Thanksgiving Day, performed their intricate dance routines for the admiring and appreciative audience. The dedication was concluded when Miss Benzell sang the "Star Spangled Banner;" and MacRae sang "Bless This House." Together, they led the crowd in singing "The Eyes of Texas."

164

The opening festivities lasted for two weeks. There were so many thousands of congratulatory flowers that the handling of these created a problem. The bank called the executives of the Dallas Allied Florists Association into consultation, and they in turn contacted their members, arranging for deliveries to be spread out during the ceremonial days to make certain that flowers would be fresh at all times. In view of the fact that flowers were ordered in cities nationwide and locally, it was a real challenge and quite an accomplishment for the local

Rusk Bank. The man on the far left is unidentified but the others are Mr. Fromowitz, E. J. Bateman, John Whiteman, Marvin Simmons, Fred and E.C. Gregg (President).

The Fromowitz home in Rusk. It was here that Fred grew up.

Fred in his World War I uniform.

*The Fromowitz
store in Rusk.*

*Dr. David Lefkowitz.
Helen's father.*

The Boger Building. This was torn down in the early years to build the annex.

Republic Bank's first home on Main Street.

The family leaving for a European trip in 1958. Top left to right. David, Gene Gall, Susan Florence. Bottom left to right. Fred, Helen, Cecile Gall.

Spembse . . . grandstand "getting Republic out of the hole".

◄——*The Bonehead's in the grandstand.*

Ground breaking ceremony for Texas Centennial Exposition on Friday, February 28, 1936.

The Florences with Jesse and Mrs. Jones at a football game.

The Honorable Sam Rayburn and other dignitaries in the Piney Woods of East Texas. They were assembled here for the ceremony at the coke ovens. 1. Mr. Gus F. Taylor, President, Citizens National Bank, Tyler, Texas; 2. Mr. W. W. Lynch, Vice President, Lone Star Steel Company; 3. Mr. W. A. Thomas, Collector of Internal Revenue, Dallas, Texas; 4. Mr. Fred F. Florence, President, Republic National Bank of Dallas; 5. Mr. J. W. Carpenter, President, Lone Star Steel Company; 6. Hon. Wright Patman, Congressman of the First District of Texas; 7. Mr. John D. McCall, Attorney for Lone Star Steel Company, Dallas, Texas; 8. Hon. Sam Rayburn of Texas, Speaker of the House of Representatives.

Fred and Karl Hoblitzelle, chairman of the board, before opening of the new building.

The building completed. Note its isolation away from the central business district.

Fred in front of Florence Hall at Southern Methodist University.

Fred with George Dealy, founder of the Dallas News.

Mayor Bob Thornton and Fred on the occasion of Thornton's 80th birthday.

Conrad Hilton with Fred and Governor Hobby when Dallas' first new large hotel was planned.

Medallion of Queen Elizabeth given to Helen by Anthony Tuke.

Halliburton Day in Duncan, Oklahoma. Fred sought the big ones.

Private audience given to Florence Family in 1958 with Pope Pius XII.

Benemerenti Gold Medal.

Cruet. Gift to Helen From Teddy Kolleck.

The Thompsons' and Florences'. First stop, Hawaii on their around the world trip.

florists. Not only were the florists involved, but the growers as well. The florists had arranged with the growers in California and Hawaii to have the flowers sent by air and when they arrived, they were stored in the automobile parking basement, then not in use. The flowers were then displayed on many tables, and with expert crews under the supervision of a firm in Houston, were counted and rearranged so that they might be put in vases and placed in locations in the bank most suitable for their display. Flowers arrived throughout the fourteen days. Even as late as five days before the festivities were over, orchids and other flowers were coming by plane from Hawaii to be put on exhibit the following morning. Replaced flowers, still perfectly fresh, were sent daily to hospitals throughout Dallas. This was not only thoughtful and appreciated, but good PR.

Banking operations began in Republic's new home on Monday morning, December 6, 1954, but the festivities began on Sunday, November 21, with an open house for the Bank Family (attendance estimated at 3,000). For a whole week, officers of the bank conducted tours and gave press conferences. On Monday evening, November 29, a special cocktail and buffet party entertained approximately 1,000 out-of-town guests. Throughout the entire week of open houses and receptions at the new building, the officers and their wives were an active reception and tour committee. This committee included Helen, who has told me that punch and cookies were always being served in the vault. The cookies were especially baked somewhere in New Jersey and were so delicious that the thousands on hand were quickly consumed and a new batch had to be flown to Dallas. Although the bank footed the bills (estimated to be $325,000), it was also a party for Dallas and will live within and beyond the memory of all who attended. The city was justifiably proud of having this great bank

165

with its forty-story tower of gleaming aluminum reaching high into the skies. It stimulated and excited civic pride beyond imagination.

Mr. Hoblitzelle, the Chairman of the Board, was a showman. The *Post Dispatch* in St. Louis, where he began his career, published a report on December 4, 1954, which characterizes him so well that I shall quote the words of the author, John Keasler:

> "Intelligent showmanship is the great asset in banking," Karl Hoblitzelle had told us the previous day. The courtly 75-year old chairman of the board of Republic National knows about showmanship. Hoblitzelle, a native St. Louisian, is a financier, agriculturist and philanthropist and, for a long time now, a theater man. He said, "You want to present your story to the public in the most interesting way—to capture the imagination."
>
> He leaned back in his chair in the bank lobby and said, "I've gotten a great kick out of this."
>
> Karl Hoblitzelle's first St. Louis job, after raising vegetables and chickens, was a $5-per-week office-boy position at the World's Fair. Three years later, at only 23, he was the man in charge of operations in taking down the huge exposition. He had saved $2,500, formed the Interstate Amusement Co., with his brother, George, and in 1905, opened theaters in Dallas, Fort Worth, Waco, and San Antonio.
>
> In 1929, he sold his theaters to RKO Studios and "retired." But soon he was back again as owner of Interstate. So, as a combination banker and theatrical man, he eyes with admitted delight the atmosphere of warmth and hospitality in the new bank building. He doesn't think banks should be stuffy, anyhow.
>
> "That was for the Victorian Age," he said.

There were 150,000 invitations for the opening sent out from Dallas to people across the nation. This list was the remainder out of the original list of half a million. Great care needed to be taken to eliminate duplication. Engravers in Dallas said that this was the biggest such order ever done by them. Reservations for 4,000 out-of-town dignitaries were made, grabbing up every hotel and motel room in and around the city. These "special guests" were carefully chosen because not only were they entertained when they got to Dallas, but a great many received their transportation with the compliments of the bank and, to their surprise, when checking out of their hotel, were told that the bank had paid the bill. A half-million copies of a special rotogravure section were distributed by Dallas' newspapers, and a copy was given to each visitor at the various open houses at the bank building.

If anyone suspects that this opening was even slightly haphazard, I suggest he read the 50-page (legal size) instructions headed "General Plans and Detailed Committee Functions for the Formal Opening," which is in the bank's archives and which, prior to the opening, was distributed to the hundreds of employees who were to participate. Like a well-trained army, each one knew his job and was proud to serve.

Prominent Texans invited to the opening included Jesse James, State Treasurer of Texas; J.M. Falkner, Banking Commissioner of Texas; and Olin Culbertson, Railroad Commissioner of Texas. Out-of-state notables, to mention only a very few, included Stewart Baker, President, Bank of Manhattan; Clark Beise, President of the Bank of America; Ray M. Gidney, Comptroller of the Currency; H. Earl Cook, Chairman of the Federal Desposit Insurance Corporation; Erle Cocke, President of the Fulton National Bank, Atlanta, and Fred's successor as President of the A.B.A.; Howard

167

Sheperd, Chairman, National City Bank, New York; Charles E. Baldwin, Jr., Treasurer, New York Life Insurance Company; L.E. Briggs, Treasurer, Ford Motor Company; Donald V. Fraser, President, M-K-T Railroad; L.F. McCollum, President, Continental Oil Company; H.J. McKenzie, President, St. Louis Southwestern Railroad Company (Cotton Belt); and C.R. Smith, President of American Airlines. Among the many others of equal importance was Fred's close friend, Homer Livingston, President of the First National Bank in Chicago, whom he followed as A.B.A. President

After the first open house, there were conducted tours each afternoon for special groups such as architects, contractors, and suppliers, for the press, and for the more than 6,000 stockholders. There were luncheons and cocktail parties, but the climax was the dazzling, indescribable party on Tuesday evening, November 30. Unfortunately, my wife Horty was ill and could not attend, but I went with friends and so can attempt to describe a party that is outstanding in the annals of the bank and of Dallas and shall live in my memory forever.

At 6:00 p.m. the guests began to arrive at the tremendous Automobile Building in Dallas' Fair Park. To have selected a group to stand in the receiving line from the many who were the bank's officers, directors, or important friends would have been impossible without creating some hard feelings. It was decided that to eliminate any possibility of noses being out of joint, only the President and his wife would be the official greeters. Helen and Fred shook everybody's hand as they entered the building. At that time Helen had been a banker's wife for more than twenty-six years and had trained her memory to remember names and faces. She knew a vast majority of the guests, and she and Fred rarely had to signal for assistance when they saw someone in the long line who was unfamiliar. Officers of the bank from different departments knew virtually all the guests. Although the line moved rapidly and many decided to by-pass it and greet the Florences later, the officers, when necessary, were able to convey the names to Helen and Fred so that each person was pleased by being recognized. The attendance was limited to 4,300 because of the capacity of the adjoining Music Hall where the party was later entertained. Few of those invited were missing; so what was probably one of the largest private parties ever given in our country, and certainly the largest ever hosted in Dallas, was underway on a festive though rainy evening.

Outside of the automobile building stood six cowboys and cowgirls at attention, holding the six flags under which Texas has lived. The show inside outdid P.T. Barnum: he only had three rings, Republic had dozens. First, imagine a cocktail party for more than 4,000 people, all eager to celebrate and to toast the bank's further success. If ever the expression "Texas Style" was appropriately used, it was on that November night in 1954. The two main cocktail bars were each 350 feet long, and manned by eighty bartenders. A cowboy band playing typical Texas music stood at the entrance to the canopy which led into the huge building that had been transformed into an old-time saloon. A bar on each side of the room stretched its full length. The walls were decorated with cattle brands. On unique stages hanging out from the walls over the bars, continuous entertainment included magicians, cancan girls, jugglers, acrobats, cyclists, and almost everything imaginable. In the center of the building were the fronts of buildings of a frontier Texas town which were removed promptly at 7:30 to permit the guests, with drinks in hand, to enter a virtual fairyland simulating an outdoor garden, with an eight-foot hedge of magnolia leaves hanging from white fluted columns that were topped by huge bowls of white chrysanthemums. On

169

entering the 50,000 square foot dining area, one approached a large golden cowboy holding a replica of the new building.

Tables were set to allow all the guests to enjoy their feast in comfort. The many buffet tables were covered with silver cloth and offered a most delectable meal. For a moment, imagine the scene: forty-three hundred people, almost all in formal dress, the ladies with their finest gowns and extravagantly bejeweled. At the far end of the room was the full Dallas Symphony Orchestra, conducted by the well-known maestro, Walter Hendl, playing selections from Lizst, Tchaikovsky, and others. The great Chilean pianist, Claudio Arrau, served as soloist.

Two tons of prime roast beef, one and a quarter tons of the white meat of turkey, a half-ton of ham and two hundred pounds of assorted cheese, fifty crates of lettuce, tomatoes, and celery, plus great quantities of lamb, shrimp, and lobster were on the menu. For dessert, there was ice cream molded in the form of enlarged $20 gold pieces and cookies baked in the shape of the new building. Three hundred gallons of coffee and the best cigars made a fitting end to this superb buffet. A happy group was then ready to walk under the canopy that stretched a good city block from the Automobile Building to the Music Hall, then known as Fair Park Auditorium. Even during the walk under the canopy, entertainment was provided by the Tyler Junior College Band, and while the guests were finding their seats, Dallas' own popular private party band led by the baton of Hyman Charninsky played in the orchestra pit.

Guests had been issued reserved seats to enjoy a beautiful show that started at 9:00 p.m. Ted Weems with his band on stage introduced the Messrs. Hoblitzelle, Florence, Livingston, the Honorable Mayor of Dallas, R.L. Thornton, and the Governor of Texas, the Honorable Allan

Shivers. When the overflowing crowd, with several hundred extra chairs, settled down, the show began. Miss Benzell, the Metropolitan Opera Star, sang "Siempre Libre" from "La Traviata," and the popular songs "Over the Rainbow" and "Kiss Me Again." Gordon MacRae, then one of America's most popular singers, sang "Luck Be a Lady," "Old Man River," and "I Believe." The stars were supported by the variety acts of the Barrancas, Latin dancers; the Honey Brothers, comic acrobats; and Eddie Gerson, ventriloquist. The entire show was delightfully entertaining, but the high point of the evening was the appearance of the incomparable Bob Hope.

Bob Hope was a particularly good choice for a predominantly Dallas audience because it was in Dallas' Majestic Theater that he made his debut into big time vaudeville. Bob O'Donnell, the General Manager for Mr. Hoblitzelle's Interstate Theaters (owners of the Majestic) had brought Hope to Dallas. It is said that Hope has never forgotten his beginning, and has recently shown his appreciation by giving a grant which built the "Bob Hope Theater" in the Southern Methodist University Arts Complex.

From the time Hope reached Dallas' Love Field until his plane departed, he spread joy and laughter with his unsurpassed humor. Everything he said was funny. But, that has been true for years, so I shall repeat only a few of his witicisms. At the dedication he said, "In Texas, they don't open banks with ribbon cutting, but they stretch a snake across the door and the President bites it in two," and quipped that Governor Shivers claimed his golf was good enough to qualify him as a presidential possibility (this was during the Eisenhower administration). As an autograph seeker rushed at him with paper and pencil, Hope took it and turned it over in his hands. "I always look at these to make sure they're not checks, " he said. With a big smile he spoke sagely about his host: "I like banks. I always say it's

171

nice to put your money in the bank. You can't take it with you, but it sure is nice to see where it's going." Of the party, he said it was "Quo Vadis with Tums."

The show lasted until midnight, when the men in their tuxedos and the women with their mink stoles, gowned in brocade and taffeta, with their formal length gloves and somewhat withered orchids, went home from a party never to be forgotten. Sitting before the television cameras waiting for his flight to be called, Hope's parting remark was, "Man, I don't pose this long for Paramount!"

At noon on the Wednesday after the party, the great crowd that jammed the streets for the formal dedication proudly went back to work, remembering the sincere words of the bank's chairman: "This vital force did not come into being by accident, but is the result of the unselfish leadership and inspiration of one man—a man not only of vision and judgment, but of outstanding citizenship."

The bank physically moved from Main Street to its gleaming new quarters between 1:00 p.m. closing time Saturday, December 4, and its reopening at 9:00 a.m. on Monday, December 6. During that weekend, approximately seventy-five mammoth vans loaded and unloaded everything from a 1,500 pound proof machine to a one-ounce box of paper clips. The first day in the new building was "business as usual" with one important difference. At the head of each escalator and stairs stood one or more top officers of the bank, greeting and welcoming all customers and visitors. This continued at least throughout the first week, and I have been reliably told that one man was nearly always in sight—Fred Farrel Florence.

THE PINNACLE OF SUCCESS

Fred would never have agreed that a "pinnacle" was ever reached. Whenever Fred achieved any goal that he had set for himself, or for the bank, he immediately began looking toward even greater horizons. As I have said before when discussing his banking philosophy, he believed that even the apex can be exceeded.

The fact remains that everyone enjoys the fruits of hard labor. No one is above the joy of knowing that the job has been well done. Success in anything does not go unnoticed, and the saying that "nothing succeeds like success" is and will continue to be true. No one is too blasé to want recognition, if earned, or to enjoy a little flattery, if sincere. It must have given Fred great satisfaction when the November 10, 1958 issue of *Time* magazine included an article about him and Republic Bank, entitled "Winner & Champion," from which I quote:

> Taller than egos, Stetsons or oil rigs, the tallest things in Texas are banks. Busting out all over in an unparalleled boom, their huge buildings dominate the skyline in Dallas, Houston, San Antonio, and Fort Worth. Texas has more banks than any other state: 968 with total deposits of $10.4 billion, combined resources of $11.6 billion. Texas bankers succeed by fighting for business like warring supermarket operators on a Saturday afternoon—while also wearing Homburg hats and speaking in muted tones. The man who best combines such Texas talents is taut, wiry, fiercely competitive Fred F.Florence, 67, head of Dallas' Republic National Bank, who for years has been locked in an epic duel with Dallas' First National Bank. The prize: the title of No. 1 bank in Texas.
>
> Last week Banker Florence, who clinched the title this year, moved Republic out of the Texas League into national banking. First National (total deposits $728.4 million) made

the first move, upped its capital and surplus from $51.1 million to $60 million, allowing it to lend $6,000,000 at a crack. But then Florence's Republic (total deposits: $798.4 million) for the ninth time in nine years, boosted its own capital and surplus from $87 million to $100 million, jumping its single loan authority to $10 million. Republic's new total resources: $948 million, v. First National's $817 million.

Texan Florence can now compete for loans far from home, perhaps even in New York, where, he concedes, he was born.

Fred Florence aims to make Republic far more than a bustling regional institution. Hanging in his sumptuous third floor office is a painting of cowboys rounding up wild horses, entitled *Bringing Them In*. "When it comes to business," says he, "that's my motto."

Fred's picture accompanied the article, with the caption: "Dallas' Florence—From the Texas league to the majors." By the end of 1958, Republic had passed the $1 billion mark.

Often men reach the peak of their career and then fade into oblivion or feel that, their mission in life accomplished, they can rest on their laurels. But not Fred Florence. I can only surmise what happening in Fred's business life was of the greatest importance to him. Often bringing a small undertaking to a successful conclusion can be more gratifying, because at the outset it may have seemed impossible, than an accomplishment of greater magnitude that may have seemed a foregone conclusion. I can only guess what might have been to him his crowning glory. Being President of the American Bankers Association certainly was an ultimate accomplishment; but the four years between Fred's retirement as head of A.B.A. and his untimely death were his most fruitful and rewarding years. The banking world never forgot him: he was as great an influence out of office as during his stewardship. Fred Florence was always counted where the "power group" assembled. In 1959 Fred was a delegate to the Monetary Conference of the American Bankers Association held in London. One of the fringe benefits Fred and Helen enjoyed was an elaborate banquet given by the Committee of London Clearing Bankers in Grocers Hall, one of the many great Guild Halls in London. Helen still has the attractively bound Menu and Program from this banquet, which contains a list of the guests and a seating chart. To name the dignitaries at this great banquet would be like reciting the "blue book" of world banking. At the great head table were seated thirty-eight of the honored guests, including many ladies. The men were not seated next to their wives. There were eight tables perpendicular to the head table, each with approximately twenty-three people. At the ends of these tables were seated the General Managers of all of England's great banks. Fred sat next to the head table in front of the Honorable Per Jacobsson, Managing Director and Chairman of the Executive Board, International Monetary Fund. On his right sat M. Fernand Collin, Chairman, Kredietbank, Brussels; and across the table, H.E. Prot. Constantino Brescani-Turroni, Chairman, Banco di Roma, Milan. I searched the chart of table assignments to find Helen. To my surprise, she was seated at the head table, between Mr. A.W. Tuke, Chairman, Barclays Bank, and Mr. E.K. Stewart-Smith, M.D.E., Master of the Grocers' Company, who autographed the program that Helen has. The honored guest was H.R.H. Prince Bernhard, Prince of the Netherlands.

Music during the banquet was provided by the Orchestra of the Grenadier Guards. There were ceremonial toasts and responses and, after the elaborate dinner, the ritual of the Loving Cup which was described as follows in the program:

The Loving Cup is a delightful feature of the Hall-feasts of the City. The Cup is filled with spiced wine, immemorially termed "Sack."

Immediately after dinner and grace the Chairman rises to drink the assembled company a "hearty welcome." The guests on his right and left also rise. The Chairman takes the cup, turns to the guest on his right and bows. The guest removes the lid; the Chairman drinks to him and then applies the napkin to the mouth of the cup; the guest replaces the lid, takes the cup and turns to the person on his right and repeats the ceremony. The Chairman then takes the second cup and drinks similarly to the guest on his left. At the same time the persons with cups at the end of the sprigs rise (the guests on their right and left also rising) and each turns to the guest on his left and drinks to him. The same procedure is then followed with the guest taking the cup and turning to the person on his left and so on.

There are always three people standing, one in the middle drinking, and the other two on either side pledging his safety—a reminder of ancient days when the act of drinking was sometimes made the occasion for assassination.

In 1970, Helen and I attended the opening of Republic's branch at One Moorgate in London, directly across the street from the Bank of England. We were invited to a banquet at Livery Guild Hall, where we participated in this traditional ceremony.

176

Fred had relinquished the Presidency of Republic Bank to James W. Aston in 1957, in order to assure a smooth continuation of executive leadership. But as the *Time* magazine article quoted above indicates, Fred was still the "head" of the bank, and he remained so until the day he died. As Chief Executive Officer and Chairman of the Executive committee, he was still right on top of everything that went on at Republic.

CHAPTER XI
CITIZEN FLORENCE

I would not like for a moment to live with the thought that I have been taking more away from the world than I have been giving to it.

This remark of Fred's, which has been quoted over and over in articles written about him, aptly expressed the attitude he held toward mankind from his youth until the day he died. I like to think that the person who cannot even remember the many things he has done to make life happier for someone else is the true philanthropist. If he remembers he hasn't done enough. Even with Fred's excellent memory, certainly he could not have recalled even a fraction of what he did. Furthermore, there is no doubt in my mind that he met his own standard of giving more than he took away, not just by donating his money, but more importantly, by his deeds.

A large volume would not hold the full story of what Fred did for the city of Dallas, the state of Texas, the nation, and people throughout the world. His personal interest, as well as his money, touched all who were within the wide scope of his public and private philanthropy. And the scope was wide, indeed, as illustrated by the following list of Fred's affiliations in various fields (which, long as it is, is not guaranteed to be complete):

Civic and Business-related Organizations:

American Bankers Association, President, 1955-56

American Road Builders Association, President
of Banking and Finance Division, 1957
Dallas Chamber of Commerce, Director
Dallas Citizens Council, Director
Dallas Clearing House, President six times—
1933, 1934, 1940, 1945, 1951, and 1957
International Chamber of Commerce, Board of
Trustees, United States Council
Texas Bankers Association, President, 1935
Texas Centennial Exposition, President, 1936
Texas Law Enforcement Foundation, Director
Texas Mid-Continent Oil and Gas Association,
Director

Charitable and Social Service:

Dallas Community Chest, Director and member
of Executive Committee
Danciger Foundation, Chairman (founded by
Dan Danciger of Fort Worth)
Salvation Army, Dallas Board, member of
Advisory Board

Education:

178

Academy of Political Science, City of New York,
Life Member
National Merit Scholarship Corporation
St. Marks School of Texas, Trustee
Southern Methodist University, member of
Executive Committee
Southwestern Legal Foundation (Fred was one of
the founders of this organization, whose
stated purpose is to conduct programs in the
field of continuing education for the benefit

of the legal profession, the business world, the public, and the government.)
Westminster College, Fulton, Missouri, member of Board of Directors

Medicine and Health:

National Foundation for Infantile Paralysis, Lifetime Chairman, Dallas County Chapter
Pilot Institute for the Deaf, Director
St. Paul Hospital, Lay Advisory Board, Chairman
Scott and White Hospital, Temple, Texas, Director
Southwestern Medical Foundation, Treasurer and Trustee
United Cerebral Palsy Association of Dallas County, Director

Youth Organizations:

Boy Scouts of America, Circle Ten (North Texas), Council Director
Camp Fire Girls, Director
Junior Achievement

Fraternal Organizations:

179

Dallas Scottish Rite Body—awarded the KCCH Investiture in 1958.

Cultural (The Arts):

American Heritage Foundation, Trustee
Dallas Grand Opera Association, Director
Dallas Symphony Orchestra, Director

Agricultural Research:

Texas Research Foundation, Trustee, Treasurer,
member of Executive Committee, and
member of Endowment Committee

Fred's philanthropies extend beyond his lifetime. On December 24, 1956, he and Helen created the Florence Foundation. It began with $5,000 cash, to which he continually added during his lifetime. He started the Foundation in order to have a vehicle for continuing to support his favorite projects after his death (which to him at that time must have seemed very far off). During the four years between the establishing of the Foundation and his death, he added bank stocks and mineral interests that he and Helen owned. At Fred's death the Foundation had already become quite formidable. Until a change in the tax laws, private foundations were an excellent vehicle for people to contribute appreciated assets without having to pay a capital gains tax. They could deduct the full market value of the gift from their income rendition.

By will and a trust, Fred made provision, out of his portion of the community estate, towards the maintenance of members of his family who were not affluent. He also carved out of the income a portion for a trust set up for his five grandchildren. The Foundation also receives a slice of the income until Helen's death, when all the corpus of the trust will go to the Foundation. Fred had made generous provision for his two children, David and Cecile, during his lifetime.

The Florence Foundation is carefully administered by its trustees and the Republic Bank. Helen is chairman and they meet twice a year. The purpose of the trust is to effectively assist and promote the welfare of humanity and, particularly, the residents of Texas.

The by-laws of the Foundation determine the guidelines for the eligibility of organizations who may be

180

the recipients of grants. Briefly, its income is earmarked to be used for "promoting and aiding scientific research for the advancement of human knowledge, for increasing the productivity of the soil and animal life, for elimination of disease and alleviation of human suffering, for the care of the sick, the aged, the needy and helpless." It specifially restricts "carrying on propaganda or otherwise attempting to influence legislation." The Board of Governors have determined not to make contributions for endowed scholarships or for the operating funds of charities.

During the eighteen years since Fred's death, the Foundation has made contributions of over $560,000. The largest single gift was for $100,000 for the Southwestern Medical Foundation for the Florence Bioinformation Center.

From the time he was treasurer of the Rusk City Band while he was still in high school, Fred enjoyed being a part of everything. Some of the earliest newspaper clippings in the Florence family archives show that Fred was chairman of the Dallas Community Chest fund raising campaign as early as 1926. Another clipping from April 8, 1927, shows that Fred first became a Director of the Dallas Chamber of Commerce when Louis Lipsitz, a noted Dallas business man and philanthropist, died suddenly, and Fred filled the unexpired term. Other clippings from this time period show that, as First Vice President of Republic Bank, Fred was already being invited to speak at bankers' conventions throughout the country. Fred is also pictured with other prominent Dallas citizens welcoming important visitors to Dallas: for example, an April 28, 1927, clipping shows Fred as a member of the local reception committee for the New York Mexican Consul General when his special train stopped in Dallas en route to Mexico City.

In 1936, Texas celebrated the 100th anniversary of Statehood. The most important part of this year-long

181

celebration was the "Texas Centennial Exposition," held in Dallas on the Fair Grounds. It received world-wide acclaim and had a total attendance of 6,675,000 people. This was a remarkable feat in view of the fact that in 1936, Dallas' population was slightly less than 300,000 and the number of hotel rooms was very limited compared with what Dallas has today, and also because of the relatively short period that the Exposition was open—only June through October. Nathan Adams was Chairman of the Board of Directors, and R.L. Thornton, who would later be Mayor of Dallas, was Chairman of the Executive Committee—both men very much Fred's senior in years. The working job was given to Fred, who as President of the Exposition, and then only forty-five years old, was responsible for its success. There is little reward or glory in many of these mammoth undertakings except one's own personal satisfaction. In this case, however, it was a thrilling day for Fred when President Franklin D. Roosevelt was the Guest of Honor at a luncheon in Dallas on June 12, 1936. Fred introduced the President with the following words:

> Our guest, His Excellency, the Honorable Franklin Delano Roosevelt, President of the United States of America, to whom Texas and Dallas delight to give honor.
>
> A friendly man, a sympathetic man, a wise man and a political executive whose courage does not falter when confronted by obstacles which might terrify those less courageous.
>
> A bold man, whose boldness may be tempered by a native conservatism, but never by the promptings of a calculated expediency.
>
> A President who combines knowledge of the past with confidence in the future.
>
> Neither visionary nor reactionary, but rather an enlightened realist, Franklin Delano Roosevelt brings to his

powerful office an instinctive fealty to high principles and a sensitiveness to the needs of the mass. Never fervid, but always persuasive in speech, his influence is that of a thoughtful statesman who puts his dependence upon the logical reactions of a thinking people.

Dallas salutes him today, as Man and as President, and invokes upon him the choices blessings of health and happiness!

While Fred was entertaining the President at the Adolphus Hotel, Helen was entertaining the First Lady at a women's luncheon across the street at the Baker Hotel. Helen, only thirty years old at the time, was Chairman of the Women's Division of the Centennial. She presided at the luncheon and introduced the incomparable Eleanor and later received a warm thank-you letter on White House stationery.

The Florence archives contain a copy of the elaborate menu from the luncheon for President Roosevelt, with the President's great seal and his picture, under which he wrote, "For my friend Fred F. Florence from Franklin D. Roosevelt."

On August 5 of the same year, Helen arranged and presided at a luncheon honoring Mrs. John Nance Garner, wife of the Vice President. Later she received a three-page handwritten letter of thanks.

183

The penalty of being in public life is the exposure to criticism, which may be generated by honest difference of opinion, by jealousy or prejudice, or by someone's desire to further his own ambitions. As a prominent civic leader, Fred was subject to constant public scrutiny. From 1931 until 1958, he served as Treasurer for the City of Dallas. The city puts out specifications for bids for this office every two years. The bid includes the rate of interest to be paid on deposits of city funds, and the rate of interest to be charged on city overdrafts. Fred submitted his bid as an individual, although, of course, he could do this only because of his connection with the bank. The funds were deposited with him as City Treasurer, but actually they were deposited with Republic National Bank.* Even though this was not an elected office, the fact that Fred held this position, and was also so active and influential in civic affairs, inevitably involved him in city politics—and politics, as we all know, gives vent to the most violent of all criticisms and permits of the most untruths as well.

Prior to a City Council election on April 4, 1936, an organization calling themselves the "Citizens Non-Partisan Council" fought to elect their slate of candidates instead of the slate endorsed by the Citizens Charter Association, whose selections were invariably elected. The Citizens Charter Association consisted of prominent Dallas businessmen who acted as a nominating committee for candidates for Mayor and City Councilmen. This non-partisan organization selected a very qualifed and responsible slate.

During the heat of the 1936 campaign, the "Citizens Non-Partisan Council" put out a sheet blasting the Citizens Charter Association slate as "banker controlled" and alleging domination by Fred F. Florence. I ran across a copy of this flyer in the Florence archives. Across the top in bold red letters are the words, "Fred Florence Controls the Banker Charter Ticket," and across the bottom in similar type, "Shall Fred Florence or the People Rule?" There are 17 "news" items on the sheet, and a cartoon of an octopus

184

* Interestingly, there have only been four Treasurers from 1931 to 1979. Following Florence were James Aston, Nick Roberts, and Bill Hatfield, all officers of Republic National Bank. On July 8, 1979, James A. Brickley of the First National Bank became City Treasurer.

(Fred Florence's name and caricature in the center), its tentacles wrapped around City Hall, the City Treasurer, Karl Hoblitzelle, several candidates, and $10,000,000 of "hidden assets." There are a variety of charges against Fred and the Citizens Charter Association. One item is headed "$160,000 Judgment Against Florence Paid in Bond Deal" (this was the Crummer judgment referred to in the *Newsweek* article mentioned in an earlier chapter); another asserts that "Fred Florence Pays No City Taxes." (Fred lived in University Park, a city completely surrounded by Dallas, and therefore paid taxes to them.) Another article alleges that Fred Florence was given the job of city treasurer with a bid of ¾ of one percent interest on daily deposits, even though Jack D. Gillespie of J.D. Gillespie Bond Corporation had submitted a bid of one percent, ¼ of a percent higher than Fred's. This article concludes, "Thus Banker Fred Florence was again named City Treasurer at a cost to the taxpayers of approximately $30,000.00 annually."

I found these extreme charges against Fred rather amusing, and I took them with the proverbial "grain of salt," even though I did not know the full story or what the complete truth was. I was extremely interested later to find, in a scrapbook belonging to David Florence, a newspaper clipping (minus the date and name of the paper) with the headline, "Facts and Figures Refute Charges Against Banker." I assumed that this referred to the charges made during the 1936 election campaign until I noticed a reference in the article to the 1938 fiscal year. Apparently the same issues were being raised by the Non-Partisan Association two years later, because this article specifically answers the charge that Fred was improperly named City Treasurer. It quotes a man named Jack Burrows, the Chairman of the Non-Partisan Association, as saying on the radio that Fred Florence was paid "more than $50,000 per year from interest on the city overdrafts." The article refutes this as follows:

> City finances are perfectly regular and should not be made an issue in the city campaign, Stuart Bailey, city auditor, said Friday upon inquiry.
>
> He gave out a statement of interest paid on overdrafts by the city to the city treasurer, and of interest paid by the city treasurer on cash balances for the fiscal year ending Sept. 30, 1938.

> The record shows:
> Interest paid by the city to
> F.F. Florence, city treasurer $ 8,234.87
>
> Interest paid by F.F. Florence,
> city treasurer, to the city on
> cash balances   26,284.39
>
> Net amount received by the city
> in interest from F.F. Florence
> during the fiscal year $18,049.52

Thus, the article concludes,

> Instead of receiving large sums of interest from the city, Fred F. Florence paid out more in interest than he received, this statement shows.

Apparently Fred had won over Jack Gillespie again in 1938, because the article explains why Fred Florence was given the job even though, on the surface, it appeared that Mr. Gillespie had submitted a better bid both in terms of interest to be paid and interest to be charged:

> There was no controversy over the appointment of Fred F. Florence at the time. The bid of Jack Gillespie did

186

NOT meet specifications the city required. Gillespie agreed to put up a bond, but reserved the right to further use the securities on that bond in a manner the city attorney ruled did not meet city specifications. His bid was therefore rejected.

Over the years, Fred received much more acclaim than criticism. It was not receiving an honor, a degree, or an award or being elected to some office of esteem that Fred wanted or sought. He did receive recognition for his deeds, however, and his genuine modesty made the granting of each plaque or scroll or degree as much a pleasure for the one presenting it as for the one receiving it. The Florence family archives contain a large amount of material about Fred's civic and charitable activities and the many awards he received. I carefully plowed through the large metal boxes of archives that Fred's son David put at my disposal. David also had boxes of pictures and copies of speeches, as well as the actual citations, plaques, and letters of recognition. I would like to describe some of these awards, but there were so many that there may very well be some that I have missed.

In 1944, Fred was the 16th recipient of the coveted honor, the "Linz Award." Almost 60 years ago, one of Dallas' finest and probably oldest jewelry stores and the *Dallas Times Herald* instituted a plan to encourage citizens to be active in civic affairs. The guiding rules for the selection of the honoree for the annual Linz Award speak for themselves. These rules read as follows:

187

> The awardee is to be that citizen of Dallas County, man or woman, whose deed or deeds during the year 19--(current) has conferred, in the opinion of the committee, the greatest benefit upon the community of Dallas.

The deed or deeds upon which the decision will be based may be humanitarian or civic. The awardee must have received no salary or monetary compensation in the performance of such deeds.

Nominations sent to the *Times Herald* by the public, or nominations made by any member of this committee, will be eligible for consideration by the committee. Only one nomination is necessary, as this is not a contest. The awardee will be chosen solely by the plurality vote of this committee.

Twelve years after Fred received this award, I sat on the selection committee, and I know that the awardee is chosen only after very careful consideration. As of this writing there have been forty-nine who proudly possess this honor. During World War II there were a few years in which the project was suspended. In looking over the list, I can say with authority that selections were all meritorious.

Helen tells me that Fred was the first chairman for Dallas County of the National Foundation for Infantile Paralysis, and that he held this office until his death. Since the conquest of infantile paralysis, or polio, by vaccine, the funds raised by the March of Dimes now go for research and education concerning the causes and prevention of birth defects. One of the awards Fred received was a Certificate of Appreciation from this organization in recognition of his 15 years of "Devoted Effort and Outstanding Service on behalf of the men, women and children of the United States of America who have been stricken by infantile paralysis—and those others whose future will be free of fear from this disease because of this scientific knowledge you have helped make possible." This award was presented by Basil O'Connor, who at the time was president of the Foundation. Basil O'Connor was a law partner of F.D.R. and was also president of the National Red Cross during

188

World War II. We had become friends when he defended a client in a tort suit brought by my father. (Father lost!) When O'Connor visited Dallas during the war on behalf of the Red Cross, Jack O'Hara, who was chairman and president of the then small but fast-growing Dr. Pepper Company, asked me to be O'Connor's escort.

On the campus of Southern Methodist University stands a beautiful building used as part of their law school. On April 18, 1951, the pleasant task of presiding at the dedication was given to Fred's great friend, Karl Hoblitzelle, who contributed the money for the remodeling and refurbishing of the building and at whose request the S.M.U. Board of Governors named it "Florence Hall." According to Helen, this honor was one that Fred treasured most to that date. Mr. Hoblitzelle's words were short and are inscribed on a bronze plate in the Hall which reads in part as follows:

> The privilege of naming a building in the legal center for my friend, Fred F. Florence, affords me the greatest pleasure. He justly deserves this honor because of his manifold contributions to the financial and business world of the great Southwest, and for his unselfish and enthusiastic support of every worthwhile educational, constructive and charitable enterprise during the last thirty years.

189

Dr. Robert G. Storey, then Dean of the S.M.U. Law School, announced that the name "Florence Hall" had been approved by a unanimous vote of the S.M.U. Board of Trustees. Mr. Hoblitzelle had felt so strongly that Fred deserved this honor, and had such confidence that the Board would agree, that he had decided he would withdraw the offer if there was even one dissenting vote.

Each of us has experienced the joy of some award or even some sincere flattery and lavish praise. Only a few are favored with great honors, but these are not the things toward which one becomes blasé or bored. We all enjoy recognition, and sometimes a few words of thanks naively given by a small child at a school function can be as meaningful as a tribute from a dignitary at a black tie banquet. One relatively small honor which meant a lot to Fred was his selection as "Man of the Month" by the East Texas Chamber of Commerce, noted in the December, 1954 issue of their official publication, *East Texas*. This honor, while dwarfed by others herein described, touched Fred's heart, because it came so genuinely from his old friends who by this award indicated their pride in the man whose beginnings were with them. It is a measure of true greatness when a man who has forsaken the community of his youth to venture forth is still loved and admired as was Fred.

The mythical Kudos College was established by the Dallas Advertising League in 1948. Its purpose was to give an annual award to an outstanding Dallas citizen as public recognition for promoting the interests and achievements of Dallas, and for bringing favorable national publicity to the city. Each awardee received a plaque and was also elected President of the "College" for a year. The first recipient of the award in 1949 was Doak Walker, the S.M.U. football star. Fred was honored in 1955, the year he became President of the American Bankers Association. In 1979, Dallasite Bill Clements received the award for having become the first Republican Governor of Texas since 1870.

When Fred became President of the American Bankers Association, Jerome Crossman, himself a very prominent Dallas citizen and a close mutual friend of both Fred's and mine, created "The Citizens Committee to Honor Fred Florence." On February 14, 1956, at the Statler Hilton Hotel, this committee presented a scholarship fund in Fred's honor to the Southwestern Medical Foundation, to be used "for human advancement through the provision of scholarships and other forms of aid to deserving students, regardless of race, color, creed or sex, in the fields of medicine and health." These scholarships are still being given.

In a previous chapter, I mentioned that the Southwestern Medical Foundation was nearest to the heart of Karl Hoblitzelle. Evelyn Whitman, who has been its executive director since 1945, six years after its inception, has been kind enough to furnish me facts about the Foundation and its activities. Mrs. Whitman told me that Fred Florence, Karl Hoblitzelle, and Dr. Edward H. Carey, Sr., were the three principal founders, with the help of many other important Dallas leaders, including Herbert Marcus, Sr. Dr. Carey had built the Medical Arts building located in downtown Dallas. This building, recently demolished, had a small but very efficient hospital. Carey was the first president of the American Medical Association to be elected from Dallas. He was also one of the first specialists who ever came to Dallas to practice medicine. He had a large clinic in his beautiful building, and office space for the medical profession in all fields. With its laboratory, drugstore, special prescription pharmacy and flower shop, it was the first complete facility of its kind in the fast growing community.*

191

For the story of how Fred helped build the Southwestern Medical Foundation, I quote Mrs. Whitman:

In 1939, when the leaders of this community realized that we needed a vehicle to help take care of the health

---

* The demolition of the Medical Arts building was a major undertaking. I often watched it out of my 30th floor office window, as it was directly below me. The building was solid reinforced concrete and it took longer to raze it than it takes now to build one.

needs of our people, Dr. Carey, Mr. Hoblitzelle, and Mr. Florence sat down and decided that they would start to work on creating a foundation purely for the purpose of meeting the health needs of this community; that it would be broad in scope; that it would not be limited to a medical school, a nursing school, or a hospital. So in that year, the charter was granted for Southwestern Medical Foundation. They began putting money into it from the personal wealth of the Careys and the Hoblitzelles and the Florences, plus the banks and the utility companies, and they went to the community and said, "Look what we have here. Now you help us to put more money into it so that we can really do something."

From 1939 to 1943 were war years. The Foundation did its work through the Baylor Medical Center here in Dallas. But in 1943 it was evident that a lot more doctors had to be educated, and so the Foundation established and operated the Southwestern Medical School which is now the great University of Texas Health Science Center at Dallas. Mr. Florence stayed by the side of these two men, Mr. Hoblitzelle and Dr. Carey, and everything that he could possibly do to lead his people and to interest his financial friends, he did. He raised much money; he caused many wills to have a bequest to Southwestern Medical Foundation in them. Mr. Florence was active in the Foundation, being a Vice President and the Treasurer of it from the beginning until his death in 1960. And on that Christmas Day in 1960 when he died, Mr. Hoblitzelle came away saying, "What a contribution he's made to medicine." The family of Mr. Fred Florence asked that any money, or any memorials that anybody wanted to give, be to the Southwestern Medical Foundation. Needless to say, much money has been given and been raised for the Foundation in the name of Fred Florence. And to honor the memory of Fred Florence, those leaders who had worked with him and by his side chose to put together a building—not a building of bricks and mortar only, but a building where the most scientific minds could come together—and we now have in the Health Science Center this tremendous Fred Florence Bioinformation Center."

Mrs. Whitman said that with his busy schedule, Fred was never too busy to attend all meetings. She further said, "Now, many people will be on boards, but they never attend meetings or are active in the activities. But as the Treasurer, he actually put the funds together; he helped us devise a program that would take care of our funds."

The Southwestern Medical Foundation established Southwestern Medical School in 1943 and operated it until 1949 when it was given to the University of Texas. The operating budget now comes from the state, and the Foundation provides money for the "extras" that make it a great medical center. The Foundation supplies funds for special projects, supplements salaries, grants scholarships, and helps to support many other undertakings. Besides making annual grants to this medical school, the Foundation has made grants to the University of Texas Medical School at Galveston and the University of Texas Medical School at Houston. The Foundation also gives support to all hospitals in Dallas, including Baylor, Parkland, St. Paul, and Methodist.

On May 31, 1972, Helen was one of the first two women elected to the board of the Southwestern Medical Foundation; Mrs. J.B. O'Hara, now deceased, was also elected at the same time. Helen still serves on this board, which now has five women among the sixty-five trustees. The Foundation currently has an endowment of over twenty million dollars.

Mrs. Whitman reminded me of Fred's interest in St. Paul Hospital, and how well he always worked with the Sisters there, who loved him dearly. Sister Mary Helen, who

193

was in charge, sent Christmas cards to Helen for many years after Fred's death. The Sisters of Mt. Saint Michaels, who operated a school that was one of Fred's favorite charities, still cherish his memory by sending both Helen and me a gift at the holidays.

Mrs. Whitman told me that Fred was instrumental in getting Southwestern Medical Foundation to provide the land for the present St. Paul Hospital location. Fred and Mr. Hoblitzelle had acquired all the land that they could around the medical school and Parkland Hospital. Fred felt that the medical school needed another hospital near it, and St. Paul Hospital had decided to move from the old location on Bryan; so Fred persuaded the executive committee of the Southwestern Medical Foundation to donate the land for the new hospital.

Fred's work for St. Paul Hospital and for other Catholic charities led to his greatest glory and perhaps one of the finest expressions of esteem that can be presented to anyone. It is best described in the language of the award itself:

> His Holiness, Pope John XXIII, has deigned to decree and to bestow upon Mr. Fred Florence the Gold Medal established for one who merits especially well with regard to affairs of the church and gives to the same the faculty of adorning himself with this decoration.

194

Such is the citation on the occasion of the awarding of the Benemerenti Medal on the evening of September 15, 1959. The black tie dinner was held at the Sheraton Dallas Hotel. The Master of Ceremonies was the Right Reverend Monsignor William F. O'Brien, P.A., Vicar of the Dallas-Fort Worth Diocese. The Invocation was given by Reverend Luther Holcomb, Executive Director of the Greater Dallas Council of Churches; the Presentation was made by the

Most Reverend Thomas K. Gorman, D.D., D. Sc. History, Bishop of the Dallas-Fort Worth Diocese; and the Benediction was given by Rabbi Levi Olan of Temple Emanu-el.

The Benemerenti Medal is the highest decoration that can be awarded by the Roman Catholic Church to anyone not of the Catholic faith. It is an award of distinction and honor bestowed by the Holy See upon men and women who merit a public token of gratitude from the Pope for their services. The conferring takes place by means of a diploma issued from the Papal Secretariate of State.

The Medal is awarded in three grades, Gold, Silver, and Bronze; Fred received the Gold Medal. The front bears the effigy and the name of the reigning Pope, and on the reverse side is a crown of laurel and the word "Benemerenti," which means "one deserving well." The Medal, to be worn on the left chest, hangs from a yellow ribbon edged with white.

Pope Pius VIII instituted the Benemerenti award in 1830, and it has been used by most of the succeeding Popes to reward outstanding service, both civic and military.

The address delivered by the Most Reverend Thomas K. Gorman so ably states the reason for the Pope's selection of Fred:

Esteemed Honoree, Distinguished Guests: 195
A very happy purpose has summoned us to break bread together this evening. We are come to witness the bestowal of a decoration of merit upon an admired leader in our community, Fred Farrel Florence.

Pope John XXIII, in honoring one of our leaders in the person of Fred Florence, has recognized the stalwart character and effectiveness for good of the type of leadership with which the Community of Dallas is blessed

Many who have had a hand in creating this living, vital, human city, I see here before me tonight. They and their fellows in the work of forming the soul of Dallas, of making the community a good place in which to live and work and play and worship may well view with pride the honor that comes tonight to one of their fellow Dallas soul-builders, a co-worker in the magnificent program through the years to create the spirit that is Dallas.

What need for me to recall here for you the life-long services rendered by Fred Florence to this community in business and banking, in civic and charitable welfare.

What I do want especially emphasized here tonight, as giving point to this gathering and the presentation to follow, are the many years and understanding and generous cooperation with our Catholic educational, charitable and welfare activities by Fred Florence. Through the years his has been a warm friendship for Mother Clement and a helpful generous cooperation with Mount St. Michael and the program of the Sisters there for underprivileged girls.

Fred Florence serves as Chairman of the Lay Advisory Board of St. Paul Hospital. He it was who, in cooperation with Karl Hoblitzelle, a previous Dallas recipient of the Benemerenti Medal, laid the early foundation, stimulated the community interest and led an enthusiastic group of civic leaders to the successful completion of the campaign for funds to build the new St. Paul Hospital, one of the most effective and fruitful fund raising efforts in the history of this community.

Mr. Florence and his family visited Rome a little over a year ago. They were received in private audience by Pope Pius XII, just a few months before his death. It was to the late Holy Father that the civic and charitable merits of our honoree were pointed out. He died before he could act in the matter and thus there was delay while new medals were being designed and struck. Thus the citation comes from John XXIII and bears his friendly likeness rather than that of the inspiring Pius XII whom Fred had met.

It may be of interest to note that Fred Florence is surely among the first, if not the first, in the United States or anywhere to receive the Benemerenti Medal of the reign of the dynamic John XXIII.

The letters and telegrams of congratulations streamed in from far and wide. They would fill a huge scrap book, and although I have not read all, I can confidently say that they were far from the stereotype greetings that most people have for varying occasions. The names include Dwight D. Eisenhower, then President; Tom Clark, Associate Justice of the U.S. Supreme Court; Lyndon B. Johnson, then Democratic leader of the Senate; Ivy Baker Priest, Treasurer of the United States; and governors, mayors, clergy, and laymen from many places and of different religions.

Helen tells me that the three honorary doctorates that Fred received meant a great deal to him. Quite understandably, for a man who only finished high school in a small East Texas town, being the recipient of doctoral degrees from three fine universities must indeed have been great satisfaction, because institutions of learning, at least up until 1959, were very careful that their choices fully merited their selection.

In 1955, in Fulton, Missouri, Fred received his first LL.D. from Westminster College, which was founded in 1851 as Fulton College and two years later took its present name. It is a small liberal arts college for men, affiliated with the Presbyterian Church. On June 3, 1957, while serving on the Planning and Development Committee of the Westminster Development Program, Fred was chosen to deliver the commencement address to the seventy-eight graduating seniors.

On May 28, 1956, Fred received his second LL.D., from Oklahoma City University. Affiliated with the Methodist Church, coeducational, founded in 1904 as Epworth University, it was renamed several times until it

197

received its present name in 1924. During the commencement ceremony, Bishop W. Angie Smith gave the following citation, which is herewith quoted as it is interesting to note the reason that prompted the faculty to nominate Fred for this distinguished honor:

Upon the recommendation of the Council of Deans of the Faculty and by vote of the Board of Trustees of Oklahoma City University, I take pleasure in presenting to you, Fred Farrel Florence, the Honorary Degree of Doctor of Laws.

Mr. Florence was born in New York...Moved to Texas with his parents when six months old...Educated in the public schools of Rusk, Texas...When a fifteen year old newsboy in the piney woods of East Texas was offered a job sorting checks and sweeping out a small bank in Rusk, Texas.

He has risen from that $15-a-month bank sweeping job to the presidency of the Southwest's largest bank...Has been associated with practically every great movement in that entire state...In banking, oil, industry, philanthropy, and civic work.

He is a director on a dozen or more of the big industries and institutions of the South...Trustee of Southern Methodist University...Cited by the National Conference of Christians and Jews for his outstanding work for Brotherhood.

Served his country in the Aviation Corp of the United States Army in World War I...Holds the Honorary Doctor of Laws Degree from Westminster College...Former President of the Texas Banking Association...President of the Republic National Bank of Dallas...President of the American Banking Association, the highest office in the banking world.

After careful investigation of his life, education and distinguished achievements, I have the honor as President of the Board of Trustees of Oklahoma City University to present Fred Farrel Florence for the Honorary Degree of Doctor of Laws.

Bishop W. Angie Smith

Had Fred lived longer he might have received many more degrees. The last was awarded to him only six months before his death. Helen says that the Doctor of Laws Degree, *honoris causa*, from Texas Technological College of Lubbock, in his own beloved state, probably meant more to him than most previous honors. He was the only recipient of an honorary degree bestowed by "Texas Tech" as it is known, in 1959. The citation, beautifully bound in leather in the red and black colors of the college, begins with the following paragraph:

Other institutions of higher learning have recognized you, Fred Farrel Florence, by conferring honorary degrees upon you. Texas Technological College gains honor to itself by joining the list of these institutions.

On May 25, 1959, the President of the Council of Social Agencies of Dallas, awarded Fred a framed testimonial plaque which reads, "For brilliant Leadership in the Affairs of this Community as an expression of our admiration and appreciation for his vision, his dynamic energy, and his profound wisdom." Later the same year, the Dallas Hospital Council bestowed upon him the Award of Appreciation "for dedicated service in Dallas and the Southwest through outstanding leadership in hospital building fund campaigns." He was presented with a gorgeous bronze plaque with the skyline of Dallas engraved.

Posthumously, Fred received many honors. On November 17, 1963, the Dallas Independent School District dedicated the Fred F. Florence Junior High School,

199

containing 135,000 square feet and designed to accommodate 2,000 pupils.

Earlier in this chapter I mentioned a building at the University of Texas Health Science Center in Dallas that bears the name Fred Florence Bioinformation Center. This five-story 162,225 square foot building was dedicated on April 27, 1975. Located in the center of the campus that houses the Southwestern Medical School, the Graduate School of Biomedical Sciences, and the School of Allied Health Sciences (all part of the University of Texas system), it stands as a great memorial.

In addition to its library consisting of 135,000 books, journals, and serials, it maintains its own Learning Resources Center for the collection and dissemination of non-print media. In addition, the library serves as the headquarters for the Regional Medical Library Program which serves the five states of Texas, Arkansas, Louisiana, Oklahoma, and New Mexico.

Its Medical Computing Resource Center provides computing resources and expertise for the various needs of the medical community. Information systems, laboratory information, on-line data entry and retrieval, etc., are handled by the center's own computers and are linked with others to form the core of the most powerful medical computing facility for interactive computing available anywhere. Their systems are hosts on the TYMNET international computer distribution network. Dr. David Mishelevich, the director, explained the primary functions as being a place where currently 140 U.S. cities and twelve foreign countries are hooked together by phone into the Florence Bioinformation Center computer. For example, there are thousands of available kidneys and huge numbers of people needing a transplant. The computer in Dallas keeps a record of where the kidneys are and data about

200

them so that the best possible match can be made. The computer also serves as an important learning tool in the field of biochemistry. Dr. Mishelevich also spoke of the vast amount of research being done in this most modern equipped building—research in almost all fields of medicine. Their Biomedical communications Resources Center provides media development and production services, instructional support, and assistance in evaluation, curriculum design and instructional practice. Numerous awards have been won by films, video, photographs and illustrations produced by the department.

The above are only a part of the many services rendered to the medical profession by the facilities available in this unique complex. There is a bronze bust of Fred in the entrance. The dedication was made by Dr. Charles Lemaistre, Chancellor of the University of Texas, and by Dr. Charles Sprague, President of the Center. Governor Allan Shivers made the dedication speech, with many dignitaries, including Lady Bird Johnson, in attendance.

Several years after Fred's death The University of Texas Health Science Center at Dallas, Southwestern Medical School, and the Metropolitan Dallas Chapter of the National Foundation-March of Dimes joined together to sponsor the annual "Fred Florence Convocation for High School Students." The stated purposes of the convocation are:

201

> To recognize scientific scholarship and humanitarian achievements of students in the Metropolitan Dallas area; to make available to them outstanding speakers who have gained world-wide prominence in the life sciences; and to present to these students an opportunity to hear, learn and question these speakers—in that way to encourage them to pursue programs of study in the life sciences.

Participants in the "Fred Florence Convocation" are selected by the principal or headmaster of each Metropolitan Dallas Senior High School—public, parochial, or private. The sixth annual convocation held in December of 1979 determined to print the following in each year's program:

> Fred Farrel Florence was a man whose humanitarian instincts and influence touched those in need throughout his illustrious lifetime.
>
> He was a great benefactor of The National Foundation-March of Dimes and the Chairman of the Metropolitan Dallas Chapter of The National Foundation from its founding until his death in 1960, a period of over 20 years. A the time of his death, Mr. Florence was Chairman of the Executive Committee and Chief Executive Officer of the Republic National Bank of Dallas.
>
> The Fred Florence Convocation for High School Students has been established by all March of Dimes volunteers as a living memorial to Fred F. Florence.

What motivated Fred to become so involved in civic and charitable work? What prompted his interest, and was this interest strictly altruistic or was there another motive? I also wondered how he selected the organizations in which he became involved, and once he selected them, did he really work or did he just lend his name? In other words, what did he actually *do* to deserve all the praise, the thanks, and the acclaim that he received?

Dr. Lefkowitz was the first to inspire Fred's real interest in philanthropy. Dr. Lefkowitz was the type of religious leader that we compare with the great prophets and teachers of the past. His sermons were clear and easily understood, spoken in the language of the times, and reflected his own philosophy which was to bring succor to the oppressed and aid to those in need. There is no doubt that the Rabbi encouraged and even led his son-in-law into many charitable and educational fields that Fred might not otherwise have entered. He gave Fred a sense of mission and an optimistic outlook on life, and he taught him to look for the good in people.

I often wondered about the fact that with Fred's Jewish background, he seemed to show no personal preference for any one worthy religious organization, so long as their purpose suited his. One day when discussing Fred with Rabbi Levi Olan, he remarked that Fred was both "particular" and "universal": particular because he was always a Jew, universal because he reached out to everybody. Born to Jewish parents, Fred believed in the religion of his birth. He never denied his faith and was always loyal to it. He never indicated in words or actions that he would rather have been a Christian. He respected all religions, attempted to understand them, and worked as hard with one as with another. He was above prejudice—loyal to his own faith, but with compassion for the needs of all peoples of all other beliefs. Perhaps just to say that Fred had "social consciousness" and that he "cared" sums it up well.

Fred attended Friday night services at the Temple regularly, and for a great many years was their treasurer. When the members of the congregation began to move to North Dallas from South Dallas and the physical facilities of the Temple became inadequate, Fred served on the committee to find a new home. Helen and Fred bought twenty acres of land on the corner of Hillcrest and Northwest Highway. At that time it was obvious that the expanding residential section of Dallas in this area would make this an ideal location. Time has proven their wisdom and the land that they gave to the Temple as a gift is today worth well over $3 million. The building was completed in

203

1957, so Fred enjoyed it for three years. The misfortune was that Dr. Lefkowitz did not live to see it used. The Lefkowitz Chapel memorializes his name.

Germane to Rabbi Olan's remarks about Fred's universality is a story which I came upon quite by accident. I had heard that Fred was involved in something called "The Laymen's Movement." Helen told me that the late J.C. Penney was an enthusiastic supporter of this organization, and had encouraged Fred's interest in it. Having met Mr. Penney's widow, Caroline Penney, I phoned her in New York. She contacted Alfred D. Sunderwirth, Executive Director of Wainwright House, who was kind enough to write to me. Wainwright House, according to Mr. Sunderwirth, is the Center for Development and Human Resources, into which the Laymen's Movement has more or less been assimilated, and is located in Rye, New York. Mr. Sunderwirth described the Laymen's Movement as follows:

> The Laymen's Movement was an organization of Christian men who wanted to put into practice their deepest convictions about life. This meant gathering regularly for lunch or dinner or on retreats in order to be together and study and discuss ways of practicing their faith in business, the church, politics, family life, social engagements, and personal life in general. There were chapters of the Laymen's Movement in most of the major cities in the United States and some chapters overseas.

Mr. Sunderwirth went on to describe how Fred Florence became involved in the Laymen's Movement, giving credit to a man who is a life-long friend of mine:

> Ray Montgomery was one of the chapter leaders in Dallas, Texas. He was the principal contact with Fred Florence who then became involved in the breakfast type

prayer and discussion groups in Dallas along with other businessmen. In the late 50's and early 60's the Laymen's Movement had a program in which it presented annually a national award to that Christian layman whose social, ethical, and personal consciousness and leadership were exemplary for business principle and practice. Fred Florence received this award.

After receiving Mr. Sunderwirth's letter, I searched the archives for more on the subject and found a copy of a speech made by Mr. J.C. Penney at the presentation of a Laymen's Movement Citation to Fred Florence. Mr. Penney presented the award, which read:

The Laymen's Movement awards this Citation to Fred F. Florence for his concern and example set in the application of moral and spiritual values in business practice, and for his outstanding humanitarian service in community and national affairs.
Presented in New York, January 13th 1958
Harold S. Miner, Chairman

Mr. Sunderwirth made the comment in his letter that this citation recognized Fred as the "Christian Layman of the Year."

This distinguished honor; Fred's early participation 205 with the Methodist Church in Alto; his receiving the Benemerenti gold medal from the Pope; and the high esteem which Fred enjoyed with those of his own faith, are full proof of an unusual philosophy which went beyond mere tolerance. Perhaps we might say that Fred saw the good in all religions and therefore found no contradiction in being described as a "Christian layman," because he sought to live by the best precepts of the Christian faith as well as by the teachings of his own Jewish faith.

After Dr. Lefkowitz, Karl Hoblitzelle undoubtedly had a greater influence on Fred's charitable activities than any other person. The entertainment industry has always been famous for interest in caring for their own and supporting all worthwhile causes. The moving picture industry, through Variety Clubs, has sponsored "Boys Clubs" and "Boys Camps" nationwide. Mr. Hoblitzelle helped to make the Dallas Variety Club one of the nation's largest and most generous. He personally gave money to worthy institutions worldwide, and through the years was a major contributor to every capital fund drive in Dallas, as well as to annual needs.

In Mr. Hoblitzelle's civic and charitable activities, Fred was his delegate. In a way, this is also true of the building of the bank, but Fred was by no means just a "front man." He often actually implemented the visions of his close friend and partner. Fred often served on charitable institution boards, not only to represent himself, but also to represent Mr. Hoblitzelle. Mr. Hoblitzelle wanted the charities in which he had an interest to spend their money wisely, and he knew that if Fred was a part of the organization, he could have full confidence that this would be done.

I have some hesitancy in even wondering whether or not some of Fred's charitable and civic activities were 206 strictly altruistic. Fred was a modest man; no one can say with certainty that he did anything for his fellow man or for his community because it would bring him any personal glory or aggrandizement. His only selfishness may have been his constant awareness that as Dallas grew, so would his bank. Fred wanted a great bank and he knew, and often told his friends, that he needed a great city in which to build this great bank. He therefore set out to have both, and the results tell the story. In many instances, division between eleemosynary and civic advancements is impossible.

Libraries, adequate hospitals, substantial institutions of learning and the performing arts—all fall in the charitable category; but were it not for these and many other related facilities, industry would not have come to Dallas. In this respect, Dallas was most fortunate because there were many others along with Fred who unselfishly, and in spite of being business competitors, worked hard and as a team to build a great airport, to sponsor hotels and convention facilities, to have a great medical school and the great annual State Fair of Texas, the best attended state fair in the country.

Important people who have money or have access to it are deluged with requests to serve in every conceivable capacity, sometimes for causes foreign to their wildest imagination. Also, there is no question in my mind that the man or woman who does a good job for one organization is sought after by others. Word gets around, and once your reputation as a "doer" is known, and particularly when you are known to be as capable and experienced as Fred Florence, it is necessary to choose the organizations that best merit your participation.

To me, the man who gives for *any* cause and doesn't know what he is supporting is guilty of negligence, because there are untold places where the money could have done good. The Better Business Bureaus located in many large cities publish a list of the net proceeds that many charities enjoy after administrative and fund-raising expenses. This is a splendid guide for intelligent giving. Some drives net less than half the money contributed, and "benefits" are generally for the benefit of the promoter. In some cases, the charity gets as little as 10 percent of the contributions.

Fred was a cautious donor. He knew the purpose of the organization, the reason for their need, the past performance, and above all, the people behind it. Fred carefully

207

selected those to whom he could give both time and money, and those to whom only a monetary contribution fulfilled his requirements. If he permitted the use of his name, he did so only after knowing of the organization's purposes and its reputation for accomplishment. In the countless activities in which he was involved, the archives do not reveal a single one that could be questioned from the standpoint of respectability. Records show that Fred turned down many requests from many organizations. He was a master at the art of gracious refusal.

When Fred did accept an assignment, it was only in rare instances that his interest was passive. Some men have charity in their hearts, but feel that giving money and letting someone else do the work is enough. Some will contribute, but will not work either because they are so engrossed in making money or following their own pleasures that they refuse to accept any philanthropic or civic responsibility; and then there are some who accept every job offered them, yet do nothing. Unfortunately, there are also many people of means who have never been educated to give either of their time or their money. Fred's greatest gift was the gift of himself.

I think I understand why Fred became "great" and why his activities led to so much success. I use the word "great" because when his name was connected with any drive for funds or a civic undertaking, it was an endorsement and an assurance to the prospective giver or to the one debating the question of involvement that he was doing the right thing. Most experienced philanthropists judge an organization seeking funds by the list of the officers and directors. Certainly this is not the only criterion of the merits of the project, but the endorsement by prominent and dedicated people is tantamount to success. So it was that Fred was appointed to the major positions in the really important undertakings.

Valuable as Fred's endorsement was, it was an even greater advantage to an organization to have the backing and active participation of the *man* Fred Florence in addition to the use of his name. When Fred was at a meeting where a decision needed to be made, he had the ability to recognize a good plan or a good objective; he grasped the problem quickly and clearly understood it, and if he approved of a proposed solution, he was able to find the best way to implement it. If he was not entirely satisfied with a proposition, he was able to suggest sound ways to make the necessary changes. Fred was known to have walked away from many things that were impractical, unncessary, ill-conceived, or just plain wrong. His vision of the end result was of great relevancy in his own decisions. So it was his advice that was invaluable, as well as his judgment on which his conclusions were based. Fred was a great listener, a rather unusual quality for most men of importance, and perhaps his greatest forte was his understanding and evaluation of people. He was always willing and ready to take advice from experts, with a keen perception as to their ability and honesty. As a leader, he had the skill and dexterity to conduct a meeting, whether or not he sat in the chairman's chair. If he was dedicated to a project, it had to be successful, and there was no such word as "can't" if it could be done. He worked as hard at making a campaign in which he 209 had a major role a huge success as he did to close a deal for the bank. Perhaps I should mention a most important attribute, which not only applied to his civic and philanthropic work, but to everything he did, and especially to the bank. I refer to the rare and all-important willingness to accept risk and responsibility.

Every individual or group who decides to sponsor a charitable, educational, or civic project wants it to excel. Those joining an established one expect to bring it new life and to broaden its horizons. Fred was a visionary, with a sense of progress yet with common sense restraint. To Fred, the past was the past, and it was often said that "if he was just visiting with you, it was difficult to talk about last week, much less ten or twenty years ago." Many people have held high positions in industry, the professions, sciences, and the ministry without ever achieving prominence or even minor recognition outside their narrow field. The honors Fred earned were awarded not because he had built a great financial institution but because he used his remarkable talents unstintingly in a wide range of activities for the betterment of mankind.

CHAPTER XII
THE BUILDER

The real essence of Fred Florence's story is his role as one of the builders of Dallas. Like an architect, Fred envisioned a great metropolitan city in an area 300 miles from the sea, not on a navigable river, not in a climatic garden spot, not where the richest of our country's early landowners and business tycoons had settled. When Fred came to Dallas in 1920, its population was a mere 159,000. To the west, Fort Worth was trying to outdo Dallas with the slogan —"Fort Worth is where the West begins, Dallas where the East peters out." People living west of Fort Worth often went to Dallas to do their shopping because of Neiman-Marcus and a larger variety of stores. This so irked some of the Fort Worth merchants that salesmen using Dallas as headquarters while working North Texas were told to come back when they had a Fort Worth address. This is not just hearsay; it actually happened to me. During this period I felt that this jealousy was self-destructive.

Dallas had little to justify its existence. It had all the handicaps already mentioned plus the fact that Texas was a vast expanse with poor roads and mediocre train facilities. In 1923, it took me three days in the rain to drive from Houston to Dallas. My car slid off the dirt road twice driving through the Navasota bottoms, and was towed through the mud near Alvarado. I am convinced that the farmer watered the road so as to improve business with his team of mules. On the plus side, however, Dallas was then and still is the hub of the Southwest. Although Houston, the nation's oil center and a great port, is now larger than Dallas, Dallas is more centrally located. Geographically, Dallas is almost equidistant from the East and West coasts. Within a 500-mile radius are all of Texas, Oklahoma, Arkansas, and Louisiana, with large cities like Kansas City, St. Louis, Memphis, and New Orleans within its trade territory.

This central location has contributed enormously to its growth. In the early days of Dallas history, its leaders saw the possibility of its becoming a great distribution center. New industry began to eye Dallas. Insurance companies, who had been based mostly in the North and East, saw great possibiities. The Southwest, with its unlimited natural resources in agricultural and mineral products, needed transportation, processing plants, factories, and warehouses, and the people to man them.

The secret of Dallas' success may well be attributed to the large migration from the North and East—people who came to make their fortune and to work hard to accomplish it. To attract such people to Dallas, the city needed to offer comfortable and affordable living conditions, cultural and religious facilities, good educational institutions, and sound, honest local government. Dallas was very fortunate in that these requirements became a challenge as well as a problem to many dedicated and far-sighted men. They realized the necessity of meeting these needs, and they worked hard to provide such amenities as a good symphony orchestra, entertainment in all forms from ballet to burlesque, the largest State Fair in the country, and excellent news media.

By 1920, a few charities were helping the needy; the Dallas Advertising League, the city's first trade association, was in its embryonic stages; a university was budding; and streets were being paved. The vast neighboring resources lay waiting to be tapped; but many cities with the same advantages failed to blossom, while Dallas bloomed so rapidly that even its oldest citizens needed a street map. The spirit of progress prevailed. The stage was set—all that was needed were the leaders.

Before reporting further about Fred's important contribution to the history of Dallas, it might be well to mention that it is not my intention to detract from the contributions of its many other great leaders. Dallas had many men and women of vision who not only contributed money to such things as art museums and scientific research organizations, but who also gave liberally of their time to all kinds of civic activities. These leaders were like a family who will fight among themselves but stick firmly together against all who tend to disrupt their basic purposes and objectives. The leaders of Dallas were never satisfied with mediocrity. Their vision and determination in many instances outstrips the wildest imagination. Often against many deterrent odds, these men fearlessly undertook projects that seemed hopeless to most Dallasites. The availability of such dedicated leaders and their untiring efforts built this city.

The banks were in the mainstream of all endeavors. With the constantly increasing deposits that needed to be put to work, the various financial institutions had the funds to provide the necessary backing for any worthy project. The development of industry was a most important task. Dallas generously supported its Chamber of Commerce, which worked to bring new firms to Dallas. Public utilities needed to expand, homes needed to be built, and streets and roads needed extensions and improvements. It is quite understandable that all of this required money. The *Texas Oil Journal* in July, 1950, reported on a banking transaction that is a good example of how Fred and other Dallas bankers worked together over the years to finance the growth and expansion of the city and its industry:

213

The largest transaction ever handled by a Texas bank was completed at the Republic National when Lone Star Gas Company secured a loan of $85,000,000 to help finance a five-year expansion program. The final transaction took place in the Republic National board room. Checks for the $85,000,000 were deposited in the Republic Bank and payment of the sum will also be made through this bank. Republic participated to the largest extent with four other Dallas banks, with three Fort Worth banks, three Pittsburgh banks and the Prudential Life Insurance Company of America.

This transaction brought together again two of Texas' foremost leaders, Mr. Florence and D. A. Hulcy, president of Lone Star Gas, and demonstrated how Republic National is working hand-in-hand with Texas and Southwestern industry in the further development of a great empire.

An intelligent optimism, a continuing faith in the future of this great section, a thorough understanding of banking and finance, and a will to work have made Fred Florence a giant among men. His inspiration and leadership has enabled the Republic National Bank to marshal the resources of this rich land so as to build not only a tower for itself but also enable business and industry to finance projects of similar magnitude to provide better service to the people.

214 Just as important to the city's development as the availability of money was the prevailing mood of optimism, the disposition to look on the bright side, and a genuine conviction that everything was ordered for the best. Fred himself never envisioned defeat. Once his philosophy became known, he was included in all important plans for expansion and development.

Too often, a highway is built too narrow and without provisions for greater traffic; an auditorium is found to be too small by the day of its opening; or a contract let for a City Hall has been so diluted that the building is inadequate on the day of its dedication. Fred always wanted everything bigger and better. Often when a suggestion for a civic project was brought to him for his opinion, or when he was one of a group who were considering it, he would insist on its being made larger. He foresaw the needs of the years to come and, if an undertaking was basically sound, he knew it would be successful and that the money could be made available. Conversely, if he foresaw trouble or felt that a project was ill-advised and headed for failure, he could be firmly against it.

For years after Fred came to work in Dallas, there were only two first class downtown hotels - the Adolphus, built by Adolphus Busch, the beer baron, and the Baker, completed by Fenton Baker in 1925 to replace an older hotel, the Oriental. Fred knew Conrad Hilton, who had had his beginnings with a small hotel in Dallas. Hilton had already acquired the well-known Statler chain. Fred knew that Dallas could not grow without adequate accommodations for visitors. It was through his efforts, and his having made the financial arrangements, that the Statler Hilton (now the Dallas Hilton) with its 1000 rooms was built and opened in 1956. This gave Dallas many additional facilities to attract conventions and new businesses.

One day I had an informal meeting with Red Webster of the Lone Star Steel Co. Red had been a reporter for the *Dallas Dispatch* (a newspaper no longer published) and he knew everybody of any importance in Dallas as well as what was transpiring. He reflected on times gone by and said:

> You can hardly mention any one of the big three of those days—Fred Florence, Uncle Bob, or Mr. Nathan —without the others. They were just like one. All three of them had their hearts set on, of course, promoting their banks, but primarily on building Dallas.

And you stop and think about it—you look at the Republic building down there. That's not really what Fred Florence built. He built hundreds upon hundreds of homes and businesses and stores and factories, and everything else here, that contributed so much more than just that symbol down there, which is the big bank building. And the same thing applies to Bob and Nathan.

J. Richard Brown, a long-time Dallas advertising executive and another life-long friend of mine, recalled:

I used to see Nate Adams, Bob Thornton, and Fred Florence go into the Baker Hotel at noon for lunch. That evening and the next morning the Dallas citizens learned from the newspapers what was planned for the betterment of the city.

Today many would protest this procedure as being undemocratic; but like it or not, it got the job done, and to the benefit of Dallas.

One event that was a great turning point and accelerated the growth of Dallas was the Texas Centennial in 1936. In October, 1836, the Republic of Texas became a permanent government with Sam Houston, the hero of the battle of San Jacinto, as its president.* One hundred years later, a great centennial celebration was planned; and the logical location seemed to be the city of San Antonio, where the siege of the Alamo had proven the courage and determination of the early Texans to become independent of Mexico. However, the business leaders in Dallas saw this as a great opportunity to bring people and profits to their city and to establish it as THE city of Texas.

216

*Texas became a state of the U.S. in 1845.

The heads of the three banks enlisted the help of the business community to bring this great event to Dallas. This was an enormous undertaking, but Dallas had the necessary facilities, the money, and the leadership to get it accomplished. The group of leaders met often and worked hard, and the great Centennial Exposition, of which Fred was President, came to Dallas. It was because of this effort that Bob Thornton conceived the idea of a permanent group to work for all projects that would benefit the city, and it was with this in mind that the Dallas Citizens Council came into being.

Lester T. Potter, who for many years was Chief Executive Officer of Lone Star Gas Company (now Ensearch, N.Y.S.E.), wrote a book called *Glitter, Glitter* in 1975 which includes a chapter about the Dallas Citizens Council. Potter served as President of the Council in 1966 and for a few years after his retirement in 1971. The following quotation from Potter's book tells how the Council was formed:

> The Council was incorporated by Judge C. F. O'Donnell, Mr. R. L. Thornton and Mr. Ernest R. Tennant, an insurance man and two bankers. There is the story, now almost a legend, about Mr. Thornton who, having labored prodigiously raising $3,500,000 from Dallas business concerns to provide the Dallas financing for the 1936 Centennial, declared: 'I'm tired of running up and down Main Street raising money for this, that and the other. I want us to form an organization of business men where we can get them all together at once. I don't want any of "them proxy fellows," I want the men who can say "yes" or "no" for his business. I want the top men.' So the Dallas Citizens Council was formed...

217

The Citizens Council was incorporated under a Charter effective November 22, 1937. Twenty-two prominent business men including Messrs. Florence, Hoblitzelle, and Adams were the original directors. According to Potter, the purpose of the Council is stated in the first two sentences of the purpose clause of the Charter, which read as follows:

> The purposes for which the corporation is formed are wholly educational and civic; that is to say, this corporation is formed to study, confer and act upon any matter, which may be deemed to promote such welfare. The corporation shall be absolutely non-political in character.

The Dallas Citizens Council should not be confused with the Dallas City Council which is the governing body of the City.

Over the years the Citizens Council has been criticized by people who felt that it was too autonomous and dominated by big business. They further felt that, in spite of the provision of the Charter, it was very powerful politically.

The qualification for voting members in the Citizens Council reads:

> The individual must be the Chief Executive Officer or President or the top executive official of a business enterprise transacting business actively in the metropolitan area of Dallas County, Texas, and not more than one individual shall be eligible from each such business enterprise. (It is not intended that this specific wording will be interpreted to exclude from eligibility the top executive officer, located in the metropolitan area of Dallas, of a large national corporation doing substantial business in the Dallas area but whose main general office is located elsewhere.)

From this there can be no doubt that the accusation of the Council's being big business dominated is true, but what is

218

bad about *that*, if the results are good? It is also true that the Council has had political clout, but on a non-partisan basis. People need reliable information about candidates for public office. Voters are inclined to vote against projects that they feel will raise taxes, but bond issues are necessary if there is to be progress. Through its efforts, the Council has been able to bring to fruition many improvements for the growth of Dallas and Dallas County, and for the well-being of its citizens.

In his book Potter gives the following explanation for the controversy surrounding the Dallas Citizens Council:

> The Dallas Citizens Council has, since its beginning, refrained from publicizing its activities. This policy has disadvantages as well as advantages. One result has been the rather broad misunderstanding or lack of understanding about how the Council functions and a strong but erroneous suspicion on the part of some that the Council acts in self-interest and to the disadvantage of non-members. Then, too, the fact that the Council serves basically to shore up the efforts of other organizations, which do seek and encourage publicity of their work, causes the public generally to fail to perceive the important contribution of the Council to the success of the programs of other organizations.

I contend that the Citizens Council has done so much good that even its critics would acknowledge that it has been a powerful factor in the building of Dallas.

I was fortunate in having become a member of the Citizens Council in 1939 and am now, because of retirement, an advisory member. During those forty years of affiliation I have seen the Council's influence used many times. During World War II, the fund raising drive for the Dallas County Red Cross was far short of its goal only a week before the campaign was to end. As Chairman of Public Information I worked closely with the Chapter

219

Chairman, Jack O'Hara, who sought the help of the Council. Telegrams went to all members calling an emergency breakfast meeting to be held a few days later in the Texas room of the Baker Hotel. The members responded almost one hundred percent. O'Hara introduced the Red Cross campaign chairman, who made an appeal for action. Each member was given the figures showing the amount that his company and his employees had contributed and the amount that had been expected. He received a new company pledge card and the cards for his employees. Members who could not attend the breakfast received their cards by messenger later that day. The drive went over the top.

The above is just one example of the many accomplishments that have been achieved throughout the years. The Citizens Council works hand in glove with the Chamber of Commerce and other civic groups. Fred was a very important part of the Council. He was one of its policy makers, and whenever moral or financial support was necessary for its success, he was always ready and eager to help.

The results of Fred's efforts are manifest in the great progress Dallas has made in the almost twenty years since his death. We can only surmise whether the results would have been even better had he lived longer. But there is no doubt that Fred and the other dedicated leaders of his time laid the groundwork, and that those who lived on and those who joined their ranks have benefited from the pattern they set.

Of recent years, the jealousies between the neighboring cities has diminished. In Fred's day, it was unthinkable to even so much as mention a joint airport to serve the two cities, but in 1973 the Dallas-Fort Worth Regional Airport was dedicated. It is located almost equidistant from both cities, and occupies 17,800 acres of land, which is approximately the size of Manhattan island. Twelve major airlines, loading 63,000 passengers daily, use this facility. When the current expansion is completed, it will have 110 ramps for boarding passengers.

The counties of Tarrant and Dallas, with the many thriving cities and towns surrounding both Fort Worth and Dallas, are now known as the Metroplex. From a financial standpoint, this area has had a phenomenal growth. There are presently 97 corporations listed on the New York Stock Exchange that have their headquarters in these two counties (most of them in Dallas). Some of these are among the largest in the country, or in their particular field. The Metroplex is also home base for innumerable companies listed on the American Stock Exchange and Over-the-Counter Markets.

Fred would not be disappointed if he could see what has happened in the last twenty years. While the remarkable financial growth of Dallas would be of great interest to him as a banker, I daresay that the expansion of the city's facilities for sports, for the arts, and in the fields of medicine and education, would have pleased him even more.

CHAPTER XIII
HIS PEERS SPEAK

I have been delighted by the willingness—and in many cases eagerness—of Fred's friends and associates to help me with this book. Out of the dozens with whom I spoke, only one man said that he did not wish to be involved, which I never understood; and I played tag with one lady for an appointment for months and finally gave up. My great regret is that so many who could have (and *would* have) added much of interest, have already passed away. I particularly would have liked to get the story from Fred's competitors, Nate Adams and Bob Thornton. As I mentioned in the Introduction, the death of Harry Ransom, who was a good friend of Fred's and an experienced biographer, was a great loss to me. Fortunately there are still many men who knew Fred well and who wanted to tell me of their experiences. I have mentioned some of these in previous chapters, but four interviews deserve a separate report.

J. ERIK JONSSON

Since it was Erik Jonsson who gave me the thought of writing this book, and because he knew Fred as well or better than any businessman not connected with the bank, I welcomed the opportunity to interview him. Erik Jonsson ranks as a builder of Dallas at least equal in importance to R. L. Thornton, Nathan Adams, and Fred Florence.

Erik Jonsson, Cecil Green, and Eugene McDermott, with Dr. Clarence Karcher, were the founders of Texas Instruments, which today is one of the leading technologically-based industrial firms in our country, with revenues of over two and a half billion dollars. Cecil Green and the late Eugene McDermott, like Erik Jonsson, were not only successful businessmen, but each was also a great philanthropist and a beloved citizen of Dallas. This book could become volumes if I attempted to document the many worthwhile deeds of theirs and other friends and associates of Fred.

I have had a casual but long time acquaintance with Mr. Mayor, as I like to call Erik. I feel a special closeness because we have some similarities. He was born in Brooklyn, New York, less than three months before I was born across the river in Manhattan. We both graduated from high school at sixteen, both studied for a Bachelor of Science degree in mechanical engineering, and both graduated in 1922—he from Rensselaer Polytechnic Institute in Troy, New York, and I from Princeton University in Princeton, New Jersey. (Perhaps unfortunately, I switched from engineering to art and philosophy after my freshman year.) Erik's first hobby, which he began at the age of nine, was stamp collecting. He would walk for blocks and take a streetcar across the Brooklyn Bridge to visit and trade with stamp dealers, most of whom in those days were located around Nassau and Fulton Streets. I also collected a little when a boy, and beginning in 1937, pursued the hobby vigorously. The Wineburgh Philatelic Research Library at the University of Texas-Dallas is my pride and joy.

On a few occasions Erik has, unbeknown to him, made me very happy. Often when we are waiting for our cars in the Republic Bank garage he has asked me where I was going. When I have told him that it was to the Library, or to some other of my extracurricular activities, he would say, "You're in my business, the do-gooder business."

In November, 1978, Mark Shepherd, Jr., Chairman of the Board of Directors of Texas Instruments Incorporated, dedicated a book to Erik and his wife Margaret, to whom he gives full credit for "full partnership in all their endeavors—business, civic, cultural and humanitarian." Even this thirty-six page book only briefly tells of Erik's many deeds for mankind, the City of Dallas, the State of Texas, the nation, and for industry. I can only mention that in addition to serving 8 years as the Mayor of Dallas, 1964-1971, he has been the prime mover in almost every project of importance to the city for the last two decades. Through his and Margaret's generosity, educational institutions, hospitals, libraries, the arts, sciences, and his church have benefited to a degree beyond imagination. Their gifts have not been confined to Dallas or even to Texas. They have reached from Massachusetts to California and embrace all races and religions.

During the Jonsson mayoralty, Dallas embarked on "Goals for Dallas" (his personal dream), built one of the most modern Convention Centers, and the world's largest and finest airport. Many have given vast fortunes in similar directions, but few have also contributed of their wisdom, their talents, and particularly of their time to the degree given by J. Erik Jonsson.

Erik and Margaret have been fortunate in having as 225 dedicated and interested helpers their sons Philip and Kenneth, together with their daughter, Margaret, and her husband, George Charlton, to share in and carry on their undertakings and achievements. Nelle Johnston, longtime administrative assistant to Haggerty, Jonsson and McDermott, and then to Jonsson alone from 1967 to now, has capably helped to implement their goals and aspirations.

When I asked Erik to tell me something about his experiences with Fred, he was so clear and articulate that I could only do his reply an injustice if I attempted to paraphrase it, so I quote it verbatim:

I came to know Fred Florence very well over a period of quite a few years. I thought of him as a banker of unusual characteristics. One of these was that he stretched banking policy farther than would have been acceptable in Boston, Massachusetts, or in New York. He was perfectly willing to risk his banker's credibility as a top-rank president on his judgment of a person or a company or an institution, based on how he saw the individual or the company with respect to their intrinsic integrity, their ability to perform, their character in many other ways than just business. His experience dominated his decision to support or deny support to an individual or institution. Once he had made up his mind that a man or a company would perform as they said they would, he would lend them almost beyond what would be prudent in other parts of the country.

Of course, everybody knows that banks in Boston don't make loans on what might be thought of as a liberal basis, as opposed to a conservative one. I'm not saying that Fred Florence stretched credit beyond reasonable limits, not at all; but when he had made up his mind that performance was in accordance with reasonable banking standards as he saw them, he would stretch to the ultimate limit in trying to assist a business either to get going, or to grow, or to maintain its position competitively. Whatever that company wanted to do, if he felt they could make it, he'd help them in any way he could that was reasonable.

I remember in dealing with him that he always asked me just two questions about a company loan, and later on I suppose he probably said the same thing to me individually when I borrowed substantial amounts of money. First he'd say, 'Are you gonna make money on the deal?' And I said, 'Yes,' because I wouldn't borrow money without that! The second thing he said was, 'Have you a plan for repaying the loan?' And I'd say, 'Yessir.' He never would ask me what the plan was. He'd say, 'Come in and see (whoever was in charge of the Credit Department) on Monday morning (or whatever the day was that I wanted or that was convenient for him). I'll talk to him and the money will be ready for you.'

Now, in the past when I went to a bank for a loan of a few hundred dollars as an individual, I had been used to having them just wring me out to find out whether I was good for it. Not Fred! He found out about me some other way, I know, because he was nobody's fool, in any sense of the word.

But that was my relationship with him on any company or personal loan: Will you make money on it, and can you pay it back in an orderly way, according to plan? I could always get anything that made good sense from Fred Florence and his bank, provided I could answer those two questions and could back up what I said. So I never asked him for a loan for which I didn't have right in my hand the back-up arguments—but he never asked me for them because he'd found out already that when I said I would do something, that's what would happen. And so we had a marvelous relationship.

I want to tell you that he and I had a relationship that was a strong one. He would ask my advice a time or two about loans of other corporations or people, and I was completely and utterly frank with him in these matters—told him exactly what I thought—and this led him, having tried it a time or two, to ask me quite a few questions about people and companies because the end results were good.

Although I knew that Fred was a good listener and willing to learn from others, no one else had told me that Fred actively sought their advice. Until I talked to Erik, I had always thought of Fred as *giving* advice. Learning of him being on the receiving end added something new to the picture. Erik told me of one particular incident:

227

I went to Fred and said, 'Look, the man who's running one of your key departments is quite a bit beyond retirement age, and things aren't going to prosper in that department unless there is a recognition of a very straightforward, simple fact that I know you know: in that department, Republic's competition is not going to be with the banks in Dallas, Texas. If the bank does what it looks like it'll do, and the corporations in town develop and the town develops the way it looks to me, then the competition that you're going to have in that department is in New York, Chicago, Los Angeles, San Francisco; and you're going to have to set up that department the same way those big banks have set up theirs and you're going to have to have a department just as good and just as competitive as to be able to handle the competition from them.'

He answered it like this, he said, 'I believe you're absolutely right, and we'll begin.' And he made the changes that I suggested.

I think that he asked me numbers of times about other managements. I don't know whether he knew it or not, but in the fifties I was the counselor for a group of investment trusts in New York, and this group had a pretty substantial array of subsidiary investment companies that were under common management. My function was to tell them about corporate 'good managements' that I was familiar with, and express an opinion as to whether they were going to be outstanding in their growth or not, as I saw them, and also to tell them of any new discoveries of materials or scientific facts or engineering facts that might mean that a company was sitting on new products or services that might be unusually successful in a short time—in other words, a growth company could emerge from what was happening. Well, I therefore had contacts. Twice a year I'd go to New York and spend a solid day and on into the night with about twenty to twenty-five analysts who were very sharp and who simply asked questions all day and all evening, even through dinner. They were ruthless in their pursuit of what

228

was going to happen next in major industries and sometimes very minor ones that had a chance to become big in a hurry. So Fred used me, in a way, for that kind of insight, and I think I was helpful to him. But I was interested because, as I have said publicly so often, without Republic Bank's strong support in its early time, TI never would have been what it has become without more years of delay.

Fred was fortunate in having a man like Mayor Jonsson as a friend and advisor, not only because of his intelligence and sound principles, but because he possesses an additional quality—a keen sense of humor and a delightful twinkle in his eyes, which make all around him happy.

My saying that Fred was *fortunate* at least to some degree belies my own beliefs. I maintain that cultivating the right friends is a bit of an art, requiring diplomacy, careful observation, and the control not to be hasty. Perhaps Fred himself, rather than good fortune, deserves credit for surrounding himself with people whose judgment he could respect and in whose friendship he could take pride.

At the end of Erik Jonsson's biography is a quotation from an article titled "Erik Jonsson, Dreamer, Builder," by Lana Henderson, from the November 24, 1974 edition of the *Dallas Times Herald*, which says so much:

> But perhaps the spirit of Erik Jonsson is best summed up by a statement he once made to an associate at TI. 'Wouldn't it be fun,' he suggested, 'if we could give all this away and start all over again—just to see if we could do it?'

I wonder if Fred, who always thought ahead instead of backward, ever looked around at the great institution he had helped to build and asked himself the same question.

229

STANLEY MARCUS

On September 10, 1907, Herbert Marcus, Sr., with his sister Carrie and her husband, Al Neiman, opened the first Neiman-Marcus store in Dallas. It soon gained the enviable reputation that it still enjoys. Al Neiman left the company in 1928. Marcus, Sr., later with his four sons, brought it great success, in fact to a point where many Easterners and Northerners identified Dallas with Neiman's instead of Neiman's with Dallas. Often when I visited New York someone would say, "Oh, you come from Dallas. Isn't that the town where they have that great store Neiman-Marcus?" Sometimes they would say only "that great store." My knowing which one was to them a foregone conclusion.

The history of the store and the Marcus family is well documented in *Minding the Store*, written in 1974 by the oldest son Stanley. Over the years Stanley has become as well known as the store, with an international reputation as a gourmet, a connoisseur of art, and a splendid writer. He is also an articulate, amusing, and interesting speaker. He is a man of discriminating taste, with talents in many fields.

In the latter part of 1963, when Helen and I were seen together more than casually, it was rumored among our friends that an announcement of our intentions to marry was imminent. One evening in early January, Stanley and his charming late wife Billie invited Helen and me to their home for dinner. It was not too unusual in winter to dress formally, so we did not suspect that there was anything extraordinary about the occasion. My recollection after fifteen years is that it was a seated dinner for about twenty good friends. Helen and I had discussed marriage, but had never told anybody; so it came as quite a surprise, while we were having coffee after dinner, when Stanley rose and, in his gracious and eloquent way, announced our forth-

230

coming marriage. It was then official, and within two months we were wed (needless to say, happily).

Stanley headed Neiman-Marcus for twenty-five years and can be credited with much of its success and expansion. With the opening of the Dallas Prestonwood store in August, 1979, there are now twelve Neiman-Marcus stores. Stanley is now an Honorary Director of Carter Hawley Hale Stores, Inc., with which Neiman-Marcus merged in 1971. He makes his office a few floors above mine in the Republic Bank Tower.

The young lady who has helped me with the book, Freddie Goff, went with me when I visited Stanley's interesting and tastefully decorated office. After a few amenities, Freddie asked him to comment on a statement of his that had been quoted in a *Time* magazine article in 1958 about Fred Florence: "At Republic nobody thinks they're doing you a favor by lending you money. They look on banking as a commodity to sell, not a privilege." His reply was as follows:

> During the period of the forties and prior to that time, banks were operated in a fairly stodgy sort of way, where the spirit was one of privilege when they loaned you money; and I think Fred Florence was the first one of the new wave of bankers who regarded this as a highly competitive business, where he had a service to sell, and he wasn't doing anybody a favor, they were doing *him* a favor. His approach to all problems, all banking problems that confronted him, was always a very positive one. He always said, 'Well, now, how can we do it? How can we get it done?' Not, 'Here are the obstacles, here are the reasons we can't do it.' His approach was always positive, and as a result he found positive answers. When you look for negatives, you can find all the negative answers in the world. There's a little quotation I have here: it says, 'Nothing will ever be attempted if all

231

possible objections must be first overcome.' It's a very good statement, and I think it characterized Fred. His attitude was positive; he was dynamic, aggressive; he wanted to deal if it could be done, and he usually found a way to do it. And many, many people still alive today say they owe their success in business to Fred Florence who approached their project which looked shaky and found a way to do it and made them successful.

Fred also had a wonderful computer-like mind: as you fed the problem into him, the answer was coming out at the other end. He didn't have to sit down and study something, but he digested very quickly what you were telling him, and he came up with almost instantaneous decisions. He and Clint Murchison* were very much alike in that regard.

I asked Stanley about Fred's activities, if any, with Neiman-Marcus, which was a successful business before Fred came into the picture. Stanley replied:

> My father was on the board of the Republic, and a great admirer of Fred, so the Republic was the bank of Neiman-Marcus from the time that Fred Florence came in. Prior to that time they'd done business with the First National. So they switched to Republic, because of Fred and because my father was on the board of the bank.

Stanley told us the following story he remembers hearing about his father and Fred:

> Down at the old bank, when they had just brought Fred up, he was being paid fifteen or twenty thousand dollars a year, I think - something like that. My father told the board

*One of Dallas' most successful businessmen. His son, Clint, Jr., owns the Dallas Cowboys football team along with many other huge investments.

that he thought Fred was being underpaid, and recommended an increase of ten thousand dollars a year. The board didn't agree with him. And Dad said, 'Well, you gentlemen are just wrong. If you don't do it, I'll pay for it out of my own pocket.' So the board reconsidered and decided to increase Fred's salary.

Dad had a tremendous respect for Fred, and he could see what Fred was doing: that he was doing an aggressive job of merchandising money, which was the only way to come into this town that was sewed up by the First National Bank.

Fred eventually came on our board—the Neiman-Marcus board. He was very much opposed to our expansion. He said that Dallas had very few unique things, and one of them was Neiman-Marcus. He didn't want to see it passed around to Houston and to Fort Worth and other places around the country. I remember asking him at the time, 'Fred, would you feel the same way about the Republic Bank branching out if you had branch banking?' And he said, 'Oh, that'd be *different!*'

But Fred was always very helpful. We were never in the position of requiring any dramatic assistance like the oil boys were; but we had demands of a growing business, and Fred always met them constructively with suggestions of term loans or various other devices to help us weather the financial demands of business.

I digress a moment to comment that after Fred's death, 233 and particularly after I married Helen, people would say to me, "The bank isn't the same with Fred gone." They also told this to Helen. I am sure they felt that this flattery would please us. But nothing is the same today as it was yesterday, nor will it be tomorrow. Stanley made the following comment on this subject:

> With his quickness of mind and the size of the bank, Fred was able to do a lot of things purely on his own deci-

sion—things that you can't do in a larger bank, because ramifications are too great. You have to depend on other people to execute. And I think that Fred was very much a man of my father's time rather than a man of this time. Fred would have been successful in *any* time, but it would have been more difficult in the current conditions where he would have to delegate rather than making decisions of his own. I think that's one of the reasons that, when he died, he didn't leave the strongest type banking organization at the Republic; and I think one of the things Jimmy Aston* had to do over the years was to build an organization of specialists in real estate, oil, international banking, and so forth, that Fred never found necessary to do.

When I asked Stanley if there were any little personal things or experiences that he could tell me that might be of some interest, he replied:

Well, Fred was a very generous man, philanthropically, and generous with his friends; he was a big spender. He knew how to do things with a beau geste; he was never small, never niggardly. If he gave a man a gift, that man knew he'd gotten a *gift!* He never tried to satisfy him with peanuts—it took chocolates! Fred knew how to entertain; he'd learned that very quickly, because he didn't learn that in Rusk, Texas. He was a quick study. He saw how the big bankers acted, and how they entertained, and he took that on himself and he entertained munificently.

Fred had meticulously good taste, which he developed, and he was very interested in everything that Helen bought. He sat in while she fitted clothes, and helped select them—I don't think she ever bought a thing that he didn't personally approve of, that was over ten cents! He'd come in on Saturday afternoon, and I guess he spent a good portion of his Saturday afternoons in the fitting rooms at the store.

234

*James W. Aston became Chief Executive Officer after Fred died.

I told Stanley that Helen told me that Fred even liked a few things modeled for him. He replied:

He always appreciated beauty, and beautiful merchandise. I think all of this comes back to his being a quick study. He learned...he'd been rich and he'd been poor, and he liked being rich better!

Stanley was quick to say that this was not an original thought. We both searched our memory for the source. He thought it was a singer who was responsible; I came up with Sophie Tucker. Some reader may set us straight!

ARTHUR TEMPLE

It was Stanley Marcus who suggested that I talk to Arthur Temple about how Fred helped develop Temple Industries, and I am very pleased that he did because the result was a warmly human story that clearly illustrates Fred's special qualities. I had never met Arthur Temple, but when I contacted him he readily agreed to an interview during his next trip to Dallas. That appointment and several others had to be postponed because of conflicts in his schedule (and on one occasion, a fogged-in airport). There was obviously no reluctance to see me: Arthur Temple is just a very busy man. Besides being a Director of the Republic of Texas Corporation, he serves as Vice Chairman of Time, Inc., which publishes *Time, Sports Illustrated, Fortune, Money, People,* and *Life* magazines. This company also owns the *Washington Star* newspaper, the Book-of-the-Month Club, and the Inland Container Corporation, plus cable TV systems and the biggest "pay cable" network. In addition, because of its acquisition of Temple Industries in August, 1973, it is one of the largest integrated forest pro-

235

ducts producers in the country. Mr. Temple flies to New York from his home in southeast Texas approximately once a week to attend to his responsibilities with Time, Inc., and I understand that he and his family are the largest stockholders of the company.

We were finally able to get together one afternoon in the office of James Berry, Chairman of the Republic of Texas Corporation. Freddie Goff went with me, as she has for most interviews. Mr. Temple immediately put both of us completely at ease, and granted us the privilege of using our tape recorder. His friendly, gracious manner actually reminded me of Fred Florence. I did not mention this to Freddie (who never met Fred), so I thought it was very interesting when, back in my office after the meeting, she asked me if Fred Florence's personality and manner had been anything like Arthur Temple's. She had made the same comparison based on what she has learned about Fred from our research. I trust that Mr. Temple will take this as the great compliment it is intended to be!

I could not possibly tell this story as well as Mr. Temple told it, so with a few deletions for the sake of brevity and some parenthetical additions for clarity, I quote what he said:

236

Our company, which was then Southern Pine Lumber Company, a fairly large lumber company as they went in East Texas, went through a period of borrowing and growth which on the scale of that time was considerable. You have to remember, I'm going back to the '26-'28 period, which was before my time. We were headquartered in Texarkana at that time, and we had mills down through East Texas. In order to buy land and build mills and so forth, they (Southern Pine Lumber Company) borrowed two or three million dollars, which at that time was a lot of money. You know, it doesn't sound like much now, but it was a lot then. Incidentally, my grandfather was the founder of the business—T. L. L. Temple.

Well, anyway, they had gotten in a condition that by any standards would have been over-extended at that time, considering that the Depression hit when it did. Of course, when the Depression hit, we had several hundred thousand acres of timber land. Everybody knew it had value, and probably tremendous value, but you couldn't sell it. In fact, the only purchaser was the federal government during the thirties, and it put together the National Forest in Texas by going around to people like us who needed the money just to stay afloat, and they bought up several hundred thousand acres of timber land from various owners. Well, we found ourselves, when the Depression hit, with what my father thought was a tremendous debt—we'll say it was three million, I forget the number. The loan was held by a group of banks which included the Republic National Bank; the old South Texas National Bank of Houston, which Mr. Gossett, now dead, was head of; Boatman's National Bank of New Orleans, which was run by Mr. Wagonfeuer at that time; and the Texarkana National Bank, and I forget who was head of that at that time. Anyway, we were just up against it! We found that we were going to have a creditors' meeting, and there was absolutely no question in the world that we would have been thrown into bankruptcy, even though we had all these assets; we would have gone straight into bankruptcy and couldn't have kept out of it, if it hadn't been for Mr. Fred Florence and Mr. Gossett.

I was very close to my father, who had just taken over the operation of the business as a young man, or a relatively young man, and I used to sleep out on the sleeping porch with him; and he didn't sleep at all during the night because he just worried about this: how are we going to pay this money? So as the day for the creditors' meeting approached, well, Dad, of course, was just terribly restless. And they had the meeting down at the old Texarkana National Bank, I believe, and Dad went through the whole story and told them about all the assets and all the land we owned and so forth, and the retail lumber yards we had throughout Texas,

237

and the mills; and Mr. Wagonfeuer was insistent on putting us into bankruptcy. And Mr. Florence and Mr. Gossett calmed him down and said, 'Now let me tell you something, we don't know a damn thing about running a lumber company,' and said, 'We know Arthur'—that was my father—'we know he's honest, and we know if anybody can do it, he's capable, if anybody can do it he will, and we're a lot better off to just ride with Arthur and Southern Pine Lumber Company.' And they gave him the time it took, and within two years Dad had paid them off, which was remarkable in those days. You lived through the Depression; I remember it; and there wasn't any such thing as cash. And with great sacrifice, within a couple of years he paid them off.

Arthur Temple was still a child when Fred Florence helped save the family business, but it obviously made a lasting impression on him. It was nearly twenty years later before he actually met Fred. He says of that meeting:

> In 1948, I believe it was—I was twenty-eight years old, so it was 1948—I was at a cocktail party being given by George Brown with Brown and Root, down in Austin. And one of the guests was Fred Florence. I went over and introduced myself to him, and I told him the story (about Southern Pine Lumber Company). And he remembered it, about Dad. And I said, 'I just want to tell you something, Mr. Florence. I know, in my brief business career, that most people don't remember very long after they become prosperous. But I want you to know how much what you did meant to my father.' And I said, 'I just want you to know you'll never ever have to worry about *me*, because I will always remember.'
>
> I guess the next thing that happened was that I did bank with Republic; they became our lead bank. Then in 1955, I think it was—about then—I decided that it was time for us to

238

take a major step, cease being just a sawmill. I wanted to get into something, and my choice was fiberboard, which would require a pretty big expenditure of several million dollars—I think it was six million. And I had never borrowed six million dollars! But I had gotten to know Oran Kite (Fred's right-hand man who did his investigative work), and so I said, 'Oran, I want to come up and talk to you about borrowing six million dollars.' He said, 'Arthur, how long do you want it?' And I said, 'Oh, about seven years.' I knew damn well that was as long as a bank would talk to you about borrowing money in those days; that was a long-term loan for a bank in 1955. So he said, 'Well, Arthur, you come up here and bring all your presentation, get together all your facts and come up here, and I'll have Fred go over it with me.'

Well, I'm really just getting to the thing that was so great about Fred Florence. I went in, and we went in this little room down on the third floor, and I started this presentation. And I'd worked hard on it! I'd been going about 40 minutes, and Fred had a meeting coming up. So he turned to Oran, and he—bear in mind, now, I was 34 years old, and I guess in business circles that was a little younger then than it is now—but anyway, he turned to Oran and he says, 'Oran, let this boy have the money.' He says, 'Let him have it at the prime rate'—which incidentally at that time must have been about 3%! He says, 'Let him have it at the fixed prime rate, seven years okay; if he'd rather, let him have it to move with the prime rate, up and down.' And then he got up and started out and smiled, and he says, 'Hell, Oran, this boy is going to be real important to this bank.' He says, 'Arthur, you go make the deals; I'll get the money.' Those were his words.

Now, if you've ever borrowed any money, you know that if you've got a good loan and can prove it, and have the stuff to back it up, any bank's going to lend you the money. The difference in Fred Florence—and this is what's good for your story—the difference in Fred Florence was that the

239

other bankers would always sit down and tell you what a great thing they were doing for you, and how good they were being to you, and how they were worried but they were going to stick their neck out for you, young fellow! I'd borrowed a good bit of money from other banks before that, and they always made you listen to that speech.

What did Fred Florence do? He turned to his chief lieutenant and said, 'Oran, this boy's going to be important to this bank.' 'You make the deals and I'll get the money, Arthur.' Now, I was smart enough to know what he was doing. I knew he was pumping me up. But at the same time, think how flattered a young fellow from East Texas was, that Fred Florence would take the trouble, and to think that I was important enough to be pumped up, you see? That was the greatness. I've had others tell me the same story, that he did this. And what do you think I've done the rest of my life, and I'm now 59? I've worked my *tail* off to prove that Fred Florence was right!''

I would say that Arthur Temple has done just that—in spades.

JAMES W. ASTON

Jim Aston knew Fred better from a business standpoint than anyone else. I unhesitatingly make this statement because from December 1, 1945, when Jim joined the bank, until Fred's death fifteen years later, he worked closely with Fred and was his "heir apparent." Jim became President of Republic Bank on January 15, 1957, when Fred became Chairman of the Executive Committee and Chief Executive Officer (Karl Hoblitzelle remained Chairman of the Board). After Fred's death on December 25, 1960, Jim became President and Chief Executive Officer, and later Chairman of the Board. When the Republic of Texas Cor-

240

poration, a bank holding company, came into being, Aston served as its chairman from June 11, 1974, until he retired on June 1, 1977. He was then succeeded by James D. Berry. At the same time, James W. Keay became Chairman of the Board of the Republic Bank, and Charles H. Pistor, Jr., became its President. Republic is the holding company's largest wholly owned bank.

Jim Aston has been extremely helpful with this book, checking portions of the manuscript for accuracy and making himself readily available for interviews. I had known that Jim was once City Manager of Dallas, but had never heard the full story of his career until he told it to me on one of my visits to his office to talk about the book. How Jim Aston became a banker is a fascinating story, and one in which Fred Florence played a crucial part.

James William Aston was born October 6, 1911, in Farmersville, Texas, a small community about thirty-five miles northeast of Dallas. After graduating from the local high school, he went to Texas A & M College in College Station. This military school (now Texas A & M University) has a strong tradition of enthusiastic school spirit, unquestionably has the most loyal alumni of any school in Texas, and enjoys an enviable academic reputation as well. Jim graduated in June of 1933 with a B.S. degree in Civil Engineering, after gaining fame by becoming Cadet Colonel of the Corps and captain and fullback of the A & M football team in his senior year, 1932. In December, 1957, Jim was named to the Silver Anniversary All-American Football Team by *Sports Illustrated* magazine. On November 16, 1968, he was inducted into the Texas A & M Athletic Hall of Fame.

Jim's ambition was to become a city manager. He wrote to Mr. John N. Edy, who was then City Manager of Dallas, telling him of his wish to be an apprentice city

241

manager. He received a reply stating, "I'm sorry, I haven't a job for you. We don't have the money in the budget."

Jim was not the kind of person who takes no for an answer just once! One day during his Senior Week vacation from A & M, he recalled in our interview, he was on his way from Farmersville to Fort Worth to see Sarah Orth* at Texas Christian University. "I was very much in love," Jim told me. En route to Fort Worth, he stopped in Dallas and went to Mr. Edy's office, hoping to be able to get in to see him. He used the often-successful device of telling Edy's secretary, Mrs. Beulah McCallon (who later became Jim's secretary), that he was merely seeking some advice. Mr. Edy knew of Jim because he had read about him in the sports news, as captain of the A & M football team; so Jim got in. Jim says Mr. Edy told him that he had always wanted an apprentice, because he felt that that was the way to train city managers. He also told Jim that he had the proper background as a civil engineer. However—and he expressed his genuine regret—he said he simply did not have the money in his budget to permit him to give Jim the job.

Jim told me that because he had worked his way through college, his father had told him that if he wanted to do some graduate work, he would stake him. Jim also told me that he and his brother had had a little farm, so that he had saved some money. Therefore, between his father's generosity and his own savings, he was in a position to make Mr. Edy the following interesting proposition:

> If you will let me go to work as an apprentice, and let me work at least a month in every department of the city—police, fire, assessor and collector of taxes, public

242

*Jim subsequently married Sarah Camilla Orth of College Station, Texas, on June 29, 1935. They have one son, James William Aston, Jr., M.D.

health, sanitation, water filtration plant, sewage disposal, garbage collection, etc.—and if you will give me one hour a week for an interview, and give me whatever tests you want to give me—I want to do everything, I want to fill out every form, I want to do everything that the city does, so that I will know precisely what goes on and what makes this thing tick. If you'll do that, I'll work a year, or until I've completed the apprenticeship course to your satisfaction, without any compensation.

Mr. Edy replied, "That's a hard proposition to turn down," and after discussing the matter with Mr. Stuart Bailey, who was the city Finance Director, he told Jim that he would take his proposition, except that the city insisted upon paying him $50.00 a month because, as he said, "If you're not on the payroll, I can't fire you." Jim's reply was, "That's a better deal than I offered you, so I'll take it." On June 4, 1933, Jim started work for the city, and his first job was laying brick on Commerce Street right in front of the Baker Hotel. When Mr. Edy put Jim into training, he became the first apprentice city manager in the United States. At the end of the year, he had taken every test that was given in Civil Service—police captain, police lieutenant, police sergeant, fireman, fire captain, senior clerk, general clerk—and had learned everything he needed to become Assistant City Manager. Five years later Jim was named City Manager of the City of Dallas. (Just prior to this he had been City Manager of Bryan, Texas, for six months, in order, as he puts it, to try his own wings.) In his own words, Jim says, "By becoming City Manager of Dallas at the ripe old age of twenty-seven, I was vaulted into a generation ahead of myself." It was as the City Manager that he met with the members of the Dallas Citizens Council, which I have described elsewhere as being composed of the leaders of Dallas, men much older than Jim, including

243

Fred Florence and Karl Hoblitzelle, who later became his close associates.

In April of 1941, Jim was called to active duty with the armed forces. He reported to General Brehan Sommerville in Washington, who was in charge of post camps and stations throughout the United States. This job to which Jim was assigned, and in which he was an expert, was to build facilities to train people. These camps, located all over the United States, were really small cities, and had to have security, water, sewage disposal, housing, streets, maintenance, garbage disposal, etc.—all the things which were a part of Jim's training. After serving for seven months, he was assigned on special request by the Bureau of the Budget to temporary duty with that bureau, and later was transferred to Army Headquarters, Army Air Forces, as Director of Organizational Planning. He was appointed Deputy Assistant Chief of the Air Staff for Management Control in 1942; later became Assistant Chief of Staff, Supply and Service, Air Transport Command; and then in November, 1945, as a colonel, became Chief of Staff, Air Transport Command. Jim was awarded American Defense Service bronze stars, Legion of Merit and Distinguished Service Medal.

244 After the war was over, Jim was on duty in Honolulu when out of the blue he received a letter from Fred Florence saying, "I want to make a banker out of you," and asking Jim to come and talk to him when he got back from the Pacific. When Jim returned to Dallas and went to see Fred, he offered him a Vice Presidency and mentioned the salary. Jim tells me he had other job offers at the time that were three times as much. Fred told him, "If you had the training in banking that you have in other areas, we could offer you more. However, if you'll come to work for me, I'll promise you you'll never regret it."

Years before, Jim says, Bob Thornton had offered him a job at the Mercantile National Bank and Jim had turned it down. He wanted to be a City Manager, not a banker. But he says he had done a lot of thinking from the time he received Fred's letter, and he had decided that it would be an honor and a privilege to be associated with a man like Fred Florence. If Fred made the statement that Jim would never regret it, he felt that he could depend on this. Apparently he had such great respect and admiration for Fred—for his wisdom as well as his integrity—that if Fred said he should be a banker, then he should be a banker! The fact is that in spite of better offers in other fields, Jim took the job, and on December 1, 1945, he joined Republic. The records show that Jim and the bank have been good for one another. Jim went on to become the first Executive Vice President, having been elevated over others with longer seniority. This was Fred's way of letting it be known that Jim was being groomed to succeed him.

It is people that make a business a success or a failure. Investors are as much impressed and influenced by good management as by financial statistics. Good management is always seeking the best man or woman for the job. When Fred interviewed Jim Aston and told him that he would never regret having joined Republic, I would bet my bottom dollar that he had watched Jim for many years and knew that Jim had what he wanted. 245

Jim's record shows that he was and is a leader. In the Armed Service he rose to great heights, as I have previously described. In the civilian world Jim is a member of the Board of Directors of eighteen institutions, all prestigious. He is past President or Chairman Emeritus of many. He is currently a member of the Executive Committee of American Airlines, Chairman of the Directors' Executive Committee of the Republic of Texas Corporation,

Treasurer of the Southwestern Legal Foundation, and President of the Southwestern Medical Foundation, to mention a few. Fred can only be given credit for selecting wisely. Jim Aston is the perfect example of Fred's expertise in evaluating people.

It made me very happy to hear Jim say of the man whom I personally have admired so much and now have studied so closely, "Fred was really like a father to me."

CHAPTER XIV
VIGNETTES

A picture is supposedly worth a thousand words; similarly, I would say, a good story is worth, maybe not a *thousand* facts, but at least ten or fifteen! The most sophisticated reader among us, I suspect, would prefer a good story to a factual exposition on the same subject. There are many good stories about Fred which my assistant biographers were eager to tell me, and I have added a few stories of my own. Perhaps these will show Fred in a slightly different light and in a brighter vein.

* * * * * *

In a short history of the Republic National Bank (a historical research project of Republic National Bank), the bank's historian, George F. Gibbons, relates the following story about Fred:

> During his early employment with the Rusk bank, when he was about 17 or 18, Mr. Florence was sent to Houston to a group meeting. Already the outgoing aggressiveness which was so much of his character, had proved successful in his own community both in selling newspapers and in his banking career, paying off in new business and friends for himself, and the bank. In the company of his experienced and respected associates of Texas bankers, he had no hesitancy in introducing himself to the representatives of prominent New York banks with his card, 'Fred F. Florence, Teller, First National Bank, Rusk, Texas.'

He, himself, dismissed his reception with, 'I guess my brashness was refreshing,' but such men as W. L. Jones of the National Park Bank, later a part of Chase Manhattan, seemed to recognize more than just a brash, out-of-place young East Texan, and took him around, introducing him to the other leading bankers at the convention.

* * * * * *

On February 17, 1975, A. Frank Smith, Jr., whose father I have mentioned several times, wrote the following letter to Fred's nephew, Mike E. Florence, Jr.:

I deeply appreciate your courtesy in sending to me the Jacksonville Daily Progress article which is as factual as anything I have seen in the newspapers in a long time. I have heard this story from my father who valued, until the time of his death, the friendship of Fred Florence as much as he valued the friendship of any man. In fact, once I asked him who he considered to be his closest friend and he thought a few moments and then said, 'I guess Fred Florence.'

The article he refers to appeared in the January 11, 1974 edition of the Jacksonville (Texas) *Daily Progress*. The story, entitled "The Preacher and the Banker," was taken from *It Really Happened in East Texas*, by Robert M. Hayes of Tyler, and reads as follows:

The two men were close friends—a young Methodist preacher, just out of seminary, and a young banker, also a newcomer to his chosen field.

They were not of the same faith but the banker frequently went to Alto Methodist Church. Each cherished the other's friendship.

Vignettes

The preacher was drawing $100 a month. At the same time, more than 40 years ago, it was a pretty fair salary. He and his wife were in good health and they had a modest bank account. The banker told him, 'Any time you need a loan come into my office and I'll fix you up.'

The preacher thanked his friend but said he was getting along nicely.

The banker repeated the invitation every time the two met.

'Don't you need some new clothes?' he asked. 'Does your wife need a new dress? What about repairs to your home?'

No, the preacher informed him, the home was in shipshape and no new clothes were needed. Even the horse and buggy were paid for.

Finally, however, the banker found a weak spot.

'Do you own a typewriter?' he asked.

The preacher admitted he wrote all his sermons with a stub pencil.

'That will never do,' said the banker in mock surprise. 'You can't succeed unless you own a typewriter. And you might as well get a good one.'

The preacher capitulated, signed a note for $100 and was soon practicing 'now is the time for all good men' on his new machine.

Success came to the young preacher; but not even the banker felt that the typewriter had anything to do with it. For the Rev. A. Frank Smith's ability was quickly recognized throughout the state and his advancement was rapid.

249

Bishop A. Frank Smith of Houston, whose jurisdiction took in the Houston-San Antonio area, became one of the top figures in Southern Methodism.

The banker didn't do too bad, either. Fred Florence, who began a spectacular career in Cherokee County, became executive head of the Republic National Bank in Dallas, largest in Texas and one of the largest in the nation. He also served as president of the American Bankers Association.

A. Frank Smith, Jr., ends his letter to Mike Florence, Jr., with the following explanation:

In telling the story he (Smith, Sr.) indicated that Mr. Florence insisted that it was necessary for him to establish credit and the typewriter was the means finally of doing so.

* * * * * *

Eldridge Gregg in Rusk told me a story about how even in his very early days as a banker, Fred would not allow himself to be pulled in on a bad deal. He seemed to be able to detect a bad odor even if it was a mild one. During the period when he was making plans to move to Dallas from Alto, he sold all his stock in the Alto Bank for cash to James H. Kerr, who lived in Rusk. Apparently, the money had come from a loan from the First National Bank of Jacksonville, Texas, of which Mr. M. C. (Clyde) Parrish was President. Parrish also had an interest in the Alto Bank, which, in 1924, failed. The bank examiners began breathing heavily on Kerr because his loan was getting larger instead of smaller. The whole problem was very complicated, because relatives were involved. Hoping to alleviate the unfortunate situation, Clyde Parrish called Fred in and said, ''You are associated with a big bank in Dallas, the Republic Bank; you can take this loan,'' to which Fred replied, 'Yes, Clyde, but you *have* it!''

250

* * * * * *

I first met Fred early in November, 1923, shortly after my father had bought a Dallas-based outdoor advertising (billboard) business. I came to Dallas from New York City to learn the business and remained that year until just before Christmas. I had been given an introduction to Fred from

the former owner of our new company, who told me that the bank was a customer of ours and that we were a customer of the bank. With my letter of introduction, I presented myself to Fred, whose desk was in the very front area of the bank, just inside the entrance door and protected only by a low wooden partition and gate so that he could see everybody who entered and practically everything that was happening on the banking floor. Mr. Connor sat just behind the gate, to the left of Fred, and he likewise could see what was going on. There was not the customary rigorous or ceremonious adherence to established rules of banks, but instead an informality designed to make each visitor feel at ease. When a guard observed, upon my inquiry, that no one was at Fred's desk, he simply told me to approach him. Fred got up and shook hands, and we were both seated. His cordiality immediately made me feel at home. He was interested in me, welcomed me to Dallas, inquired what he might do to help me, and then took me to meet Mr.Connor. When I left, I felt that I had made a friend, which was very important for a twenty-one year old man in a totally unfamiliar part of the country, with a great challenge ahead, and with only the employees of his new company as friends. I tell this story because Fred never changed, and even when I went to his beautiful office in later years before he died, he got up out of his chair, walked   251
around his desk, shook hands, and made me feel the warmth and interest he extended to every visitor.

* * * * * *

Another personal story, from this same time period, illustrates how this young bank helped a business and, with Fred's guidance, built the bank on the success of its customers. Within a few weeks after I met Fred for the first time, the General Manager of our company, Milburn Hobson, sent me out to buy a small competitive business. Since I had been in the business world myself for only six months, and this mature man had been with our company for six years before I showed up, I have long been convinced that he thought that my failing to make a good deal, or to make any deal at all, would keep me from advancing too quickly. The son of a new owner could be dangerous. My assignment was to buy an electric sign manufacturing company that had only six or seven employees including the manager, John Pickett. Pickett had a reputation of being a superb salesman of both signs and outdoor advertising and would be a great asset to our business. He was the son-in-law of the owner, Mr. P. T. Borich, whose company operated under the name of Texlite Electric Sign Company and was the outgrowth of Mr. Borich's sign-painting activities that had begun in a small shop in 1879 in the very heart of Dallas. The purpose of the purchase was to acquire Pickett, then discontinue the sign business and incorporate their twenty or thirty painted bulletins into our company, United Advertising Corporation of Texas.

Borich was a man in his late seventies, a hot-tempered Italian immigrant, and although he wanted to sell, his idea of the worth of the business was greatly exaggerated. On my first call, he quoted me $22,500 cash, and made it clear that this was "take it or leave it." The next day and the day after, I tried to get a better price, and he finally came down to $20,000. When I knew that I was making progress, I got an idea I hoped might work. I called on Fred to seek his advice and to get eleven $1,000 bills. Fred was amused at my proposition; but being adventurous and, I am sure, hoping that my success would add an account, he loaned me the money on my I.O.U. I agreed that by the end of banking hours I would either return the money or sign a check for

$1,000 and a note for the balance. Armed with ten bills in my right pocket and one in the left pocket, I called on Mr. Borich. I carefully and *slowly* started laying these G notes from my right pocket on the table until all ten were there. Borich sat without emotion until they stopped coming and then said, "What do you have in the other pocket?" I produced the ace in the hole and told him that that was all, at which point he ordered me out of his shop. As I turned around, he delivered a good swift kick on my behind—and his cowboy boots were *not* soft toed. I returned the money to Fred and told him of my failure. He laughed, tore up the I.O.U., and suggested that I let things simmer for a few days.

Soon thereafter I got a phone call from John Pickett, the manager-salesman, telling me that he had received a large order from the Magnolia Petroleum Company, now Mobil, which he figured would make a profit of $7,500, and that he had talked the old man into accepting $18,500, so that with my original offer of $11,000, the deal should suit both parties. I phoned my father in New York, who gave me permission to make the deal, provided that I agreed to close Texlite when the Magnolia order was completed and to transfer Pickett to the advertising company. Father's terms agreed upon, I rushed to the bank, borrowed $10,000 on a note, and gave Borich a check for $8,500 on a New York bank, which my father made good. Because Fred was so helpful in the closing of this deal, Republic gained a very substantial customer. I operated Texlite until I sold it somewhat over thirty-six years later. Pickett, although in his early thirties, died of a heart attack within six months of our purchase; so I didn't really renege on my agreement with my father. From the original six employees, Texlite grew far beyond my expectations and had 660 employees when purchased by a Californian in 1959.

253

Magnolia, Texlite's largest customer at the time I purchased the company in 1923, was then owned by the Socony Vacuum Oil Company, later to become Mobil. During the thirty-six years of my ownership, this company was a continual customer, except for a few years during World War II when steel was not available for signs. In 1934 Texlite built the first large neon revolving sign for Magnolia and erected it on their building in downtown Dallas less than 100 yards from Fred's office. Magnolia had acquired the "Pegasus" as a trademark from Socony. The sign is constructed so that there are actually two red horses attached to a structural frame. Dallasites liked to say that the reason for this was so that visitors could not call Dallas a one-horse town. Recently Mobil gave this building to the city, and the sign was designated as an "historical landmark." The city has sold the building with the provision that the sign must be preserved. Sitting at my desk, I can see it through my office window.

* * * * * *

254

Two clippings from the *Dallas Morning News* during June, 1927, gave me a lead on an interesting story that none of the people I interviewed had mentioned. Fred played a relatively small part in this story, but it does illustrate his eagerness to participate in any activity that might bring acclaim to Dallas. During the summer of 1927, shortly after Lindbergh's historic flight from New York to Paris, Fred was one of twelve sponsors who contributed $1,000 each to help buy a plane in which Captain Bill Erwin, a World War I ace, would attempt to fly from Dallas to Hong Kong, by way of Hawaii. A widely publicized contest was held to name the plane, and Fred was one of the judges. The winning name, selected from about 10,000 names submitted by

3,000 people from all over the United States, was "The Dallas Spirit." Everyone connected with this project hoped that it would bring the same kind of fame to Dallas that Lindbergh had brought to the city of St. Louis with his successful flight in "The Spirit of St. Louis." Erwin's planned undertaking made front-page news in the Dallas papers throughout the summer. When the plane was finally ready, the unveiling ceremony took place at Love Field, with Fred as Master of Ceremonies. It was a big event, with Dallas' Mayor R. E. Burt and Governor Dan Moody of Texas as speakers.

Ted Dealey, the late publisher of the *Dallas Morning News*, has written the full story of Captain Erwin's attempt in an article entitled "The Dallas Spirit: The Last Fool Flight," which was published in the *Southwestern Historical Quarterly*, July, 1959. This is a fascinating and very dramatic story, which unfortunately ended in tragedy. Since this really has little to do with Fred, I will summarize it only briefly here.

In the aftermath of Lindbergh's flight, what Dealey has called "a virtual orgy of trans-oceanic projects" sprang into being. Prizes were offered for flights that were quite outlandish at the time. To coin a word, 'aeromania" was in the air (pun intended). One such project was the Dole Air Derby, a race from San Francisco to Honolulu, with a first 255 prize of $25,000 offered by James Dole of Hawaii. Captain Erwin planned to enter this Dole race and then, after reaching Hawaii, to continue on to Hong Kong in an attempt to win another $25,000 prize offered for a Dallas-to-Hong Kong flight by Col. William E. Easterwood, Jr., of Dallas.

According to Dealey's article, Captain Erwin had so much difficulty getting from Dallas to California that he declared at that point, "The worst part of the trip to

Honolulu is over. I would rather take a trip across the water anytime than make it across the mountains to California from Texas." The Dallas Spirit was one of only six planes that succeeded in taking off from San Francisco in the Dole race. Two had crashed on their way to California, one had crashed into San Francisco Bay during testing, and two crashed on the runway while attempting to take off. Less than an hour after their successful takeoff, Erwin and his navigator, Alvin Eichwaldt, were forced to return when a trap door in the plane was torn open by the force of wind in flight, and the resulting air tunnel stripped the fabric covering off the plane, leaving the bare framework exposed. Spectators considered it a miracle that Erwin was able to land the damaged plane without being killed. It took three days to repair the plane, and by that time both the $25,000 first prize and the $10,000 second prize had been claimed by the only two pilots to reach Hawaii at all. But in spite of the fact that the race was over, the Dallas Spirit took off again as soon as it was repaired, on what Ted Dealey called "a mission of love." Two of the planes in the race were down in the Pacific, and Erwin and Eichwaldt insisted on going back out to help search for survivors. This time the Dallas Spirit also crashed into the Pacific, and no trace was ever found of any of the planes that were lost in the race. A total of ten lives were lost. The entire venture was foolhardy: Lloyds of London, in spite of their reputation for insuring almost anything, had considered the flight so dangerous that they had refused to have anything to do with it, and Dealey has said that none of the planes had even the simplest safety devices that we would deem necessary for making a flight from Dallas to Fort Worth.

After reading about Captain Erwin and the Dallas Spirit, I talked to Florence and Monty Irion, close friends of Helen's and mine, who knew Captain Erwin and his wife,

256

Connie. Monty told me that he was present at the inspection of the plane, which was really a mess. The inspectors found over thirty changes or improvements to be necessary. Mrs. Irion told me that Fred had pleaded with Captain Erwin to cancel the attempt when these problems with the plane became evident before he even left Dallas for San Francisco. She also said that after Captain Erwin's death, Fred offered Mrs. Erwin the use of his car and chauffeur and showed his heartfelt sympathy in every possible way. This sad ending must have been a terrible shock for Fred and for all of Captain Erwin's Dallas friends and sponsors.

* * * * * *

Erik Jonsson likes to tell a story about Fred and Ben Ball, who used to be in charge of Republic's Correspondent Banks Department. During one particular year, Ben had been on the road 276 days. The year ended very successfully for his department, and Ben, thinking that he had earned a rest from so much traveling, was looking forward to spending more time at home. Fred called him in to congratulate him on his department's excellent record and said, "Good work, Ben, but maybe you can spend a little more time in the field next year."

257

* * * * * *

Jesse James, Treasurer of the State of Texas, telephoned Fred one time for an appointment to discuss the finances of the state. Fred inquired as to the trouble and was told that in the prior year the state had incurred a substantial deficit and that it was going to be worse that year. Fred told him that Republic would take all or any part of the loan required, and that James would not even have to come to Dallas. Mr. James called other Texas banks, many of which showed no interest until he told them what Fred had said. Invariably, the quick reply was, "You can't give Republic all that business! What can *we* do for you?"

* * * * * *

In 1948, twenty-five years after I had first met Fred, I sold the Texas portion of the advertising business to a large Cleveland, Ohio, company. The head of this company, Jack Zimmer, came to Dallas to meet with his new associates and his largest customers. It was incumbent upon me to be his guide, and it was important that he meet our banking connections, our suppliers, and some landlords from whom we leased multiple sites for our billboards and painted bulletins. The three major banks were all very good customers, and we kept substantial accounts in each bank. Republic was then already the second largest bank in Dallas. I can recall no particular reason for the order of the visits, but I first took Zimmer, who had been a banker himself, to meet the President of the smallest bank of the three, the Mercantile National Bank. Mr. R. L. Thornton, who was later affectionately called "Mr. Dallas" and who also later became the Mayor of Dallas, greeted us with genuine hospitality. His bank had just recently built the tallest building in Dallas, with a delightful reception room on the top floor where one got the best view of the city. He invited us to join him there for a cup of coffee and was most friendly.

Nathan Adams, the President of the First National Bank, was next on our visiting list. Unfortunately, Mr. Adams was away from the city, so I took Mr. Zimmer to a Vice President, with whom I did my routine banking. When we approached his desk, he remained seated, shook

258

hands with us when we offered ours, and leaning back in his swivel chair, inquired as to what he might do for us. We explained that we had "dropped by" to get acquainted; but since no one had anything to say, our meeting was brief. The Republic was next door, so we called on Fred. We had made no appointment, yet our wait to see him was very short. As always, he came out from behind his desk, acknowledged the introduction, and in our short conversation, inquired about Zimmer's business, his plans, and, in praising me, let it be known that he knew at first hand about our business and about our account. The interview ended by Fred's offering to help Zimmer in any way he could, particularly with train reservations, which at that time were extremely hard to get. Fred never passed up the opportunity to further the interests of people or organizations with whom he had an affiliation. At this time, Fred was a director of the Katy Railroad, and could simultaneously do his new customer a big favor and possibly get some freight business for the railroad in the future.

When we got back to the office, Zimmer discussed our three visits. He was very impressed and complimentary about Bob Thornton; and even now, I can remember his comment about Fred: "I have met many bankers, but that Florence man really knows his business. As head of an enormous bank, he knew you and knew your business, and that's the kind of flattery that instills confidence and the desire to favor his bank. Let's review our bank balances tomorrow!" I continued with Zimmer's company for several months, and I don't know that any policy change was ever made. Undoubtedly, though, there were many business men who were similarly impressed with Fred who did follow up on their intention to give him more of their business.

259

* * * * * *

Once each year for a number of years, Randall Gilbert, President of the Federal Reserve Bank in Dallas, invited business leaders to a luncheon after the annual meeting of its Board of Directors. Fred sat on the dais; I was one of the many invited guests. The luncheon speaker (I guess there must always be one) was a topflight investment man. I had always thought I knew a fair amount about the workings of the money and banking world; but although the speaker was quite eloquent during his allotted time, and in spite of my having listened to every word, I came away very unhappy with my inability to understand what he said. The luncheon was on the Hotel Baker roof, and after adjournment I happened to get into the same down elevator with Fred. I learned years ago never to discuss anything except the weather in an elevator, but I did ask Fred if I might walk back to the bank with him. On the street, I confessed my ignorance in not understanding the speaker. I was greatly relieved when Fred told me not to worry, that he, too, had no idea what the address was all about. Not only was my faith in myself renewed, but it was refreshing to find a man who didn't pose as a "know it all."

* * * * * *

260   Texlite, where I spent many years and added many grey hairs, had enjoyed several very profitable years during the Korean War. Expansion into new but related fields was in vogue. Either I talked too much or someone read my mind. One day a man who had a large, modern plant in Garland, a Dallas suburb, offered to sell me his business for $2,000,000. The owner, a man I knew only slightly, gave me a great deal of information verbally, but said that he would not furnish a financial statement, as he did not want anyone to know that the business was for sale or anything

else about his affairs. He took me through the plant and did a lot of fast talking. This, of course, made me suspicious. I told him that I would need to borrow some money, and therefore would have to show his business statement to Mr. Fred Florence, my banker. Actually, at that time we were banking more actively elsewhere, but Fred's judgment was what I wanted. The seller and his lawyer wife, a brilliant, attractive woman, very reluctantly agreed to let me show the statement to Fred, but I had to promise complete confidentiality. I gave Fred the statement, and he agreed to honor my promise. I felt privileged when he agreed to conduct a thorough but discreet investigation. About ten days elapsed before Fred's secretary, Thelda Barnett (now Mrs. Dunlop) called and asked me to come to his office. The interview took about three minutes, most of which was consumed by the greeting and farewell. In his straightforward manner Fred said, "Harold, if these people were to offer you this business for nothing, I advise you not to take it. Shall I tell you why?" I said, "No, thanks a lot, that's good enough for me." A short time later, the company that had been for sale for two million dollars cash had serious financial troubles, discontinued their business, and sold the physical plant to some other manufacturer. Fred's excellent advice, given freely, probably saved me a fortune. He never knew it, but after that I made it a point to give the Republic Bank the greater share of our business. 261

* * * * * *

On one of our visits to New York in the early 1950s, my first wife and I stayed at the magnificent Ambassador Hotel where we had been married twenty-five years before in one of their dining rooms. At the time of this story it was one of the most prestigious addresses in New York. Later this hotel became the Ambassador East and after a few more years was razed to make room for an enormous office building. One day in the lobby, we found Miss Evelyn Barnes, whose brother was one of Texlite's executives. Greetings included some chitchat about Texas, and we learned that Barnsey, as she was called by everyone who knew her, was a trained nurse and at the time attending a patient, a Britisher visiting the United States. Some weeks later, Barnsey's brother, Ernest, told me that his sister's patient was the fabulously wealthy Sir Victor Sassoon. Sir Victor was a bachelor and had become sufficiently interested in his attractive nurse to journey off to Texas to meet her family. Sir Victor and his family had amassed their wealth from the four corners of the world, particularly China and other parts of the Orient. He had offices on every continent and was engaged in enormous worldwide trade. He was a real sophisticate, and his visit to Texas created a bit of a problem for the Barnes family, who wanted to be sure that they entertained their guest in a fitting manner. Ernest knew that Horty and I were well traveled, so they sought our help. In the week or so that Sir Victor was in Dallas, we became quite enamored of him and of Barnsey. He was easy to please and was excellent company.

During Sir Victor's visit, there was a large public luncheon; there was something going on in Dallas every week, so my memory as to the sponsor of this one escapes me. Fred attended virtually all of these public "do-good" affairs and nearly always sat at the long head table with the dignitaries. It occurred to me that Fred should meet Sir Victor for business reasons, particularly since Sir Victor had indicated great interest in Dallas, its future growth, and its potential as a good place to invest money. Before the luncheon, to which I had invited Sir Victor and Ernest, I phoned Fred and told him I had a very important guest whom I thought he should meet. Fred, in a hurry, said, "Sure, Harold, right after lunch." I never got a chance to mention Sir Victor's name. During the meal, I went over to the head table, caught Fred's eye, pointed to where we were sitting, got an affirmative nod, and returned to my table. After lunch we waited—but no Fred, so we departed. A few days later, I ran into Fred, and told him how sorry I was that he had missed Sir Victor Sassoon. "Who did you say?" Almost before I had the chance to repeat the name, Fred said, "Invite him for lunch—any day." That very morning, Sir Victor had left for New York. Sometime later, he and Barnsey married. This man of great charm died a few years later in his eighties, leaving Barnsey, among other things, a home in Dallas, one in London, an enormous estate in Nassau, and one of the world's greatest and most successful racing stables. Fred never met Sir Victor, which only proves that even the best of us make mistakes.

* * * * * *

Olin Lancaster, an Assistant Vice President of Republic Bank, told me an amusing story he remembers about Fred. One time in the late 1950s Jack Bailey brought his "Queen for a Day" radio show to Dallas where it was broadcast from Fair Park auditorium. As you may recall, this was the show (also on television for a number of years) on which several ladies told about their personal or family difficulties—usually genuinely heartrending stories. Then the audience voted with their applause for the one to be proclaimed "Queen for a Day." The winner received whatever material assistance she had requested to help solve her problems, plus an assortment of other prizes. The prizes were given by various companies in exchange for the advertising value of having them presented on the air.

Fred was in the audience because Republic National Bank was donating a $500 savings account as one of the prizes. During the preliminary audience warm-up, Bailey announced the prizes, including the Republic savings account, and Fred smiled proudly. But when the program actually went on the air (and this was live radio in those days) the announcer became confused and said, "a $500 savings account donated by the *First National Bank*." This was more than Fred could take: at this point he got up and walked out. The error was later retracted, but somehow I doubt that this really made Fred feel any better!

* * * * * *

This story was given to me by Texas Lieutenant Governor Bill Hobby over the phone from Austin. Although William Clements, a Republican, beat his democratic opponent, John Hill, for Governor of Texas in 1978, Bill Hobby, a Democrat, won handily over his Republican opponent. Clements was the first Republican to be elected Governor of Texas in over 100 years. Bill Hobby's late father, William P. Hobby, a former governor of Texas, and his mother, Oveta, were very close friends of the Florences.

Many years ago, the *Houston Post*, owned by the Hobbys, was seeking a large loan from the Houston banks, but had been unsuccessful. Bill's father, Governor Hobby, phoned Fred, told him the details, and Fred approved the loan. The Governor thereupon told his local bank that Republic in Dallas was willing to handle the deal. Not surprisingly they told him, "If Fred Florence will take the loan, we will." Bill Hobby gave Fred credit for saving this great newspaper.

264

* * * * * *

A few weeks before Fred's death while confined in Baylor Hospital he asked Neiman-Marcus to send some men's house robes so that he might select some for Christmas gifts. Helen says the store sent a dozen or so dressy ones on a rack. She can remember the names of only a few of those who were to receive one. The list included some of his associates at the bank. One, however, was Dr. Luther Holcomb, who for many years was Chairman of the Dallas Council of Churches and at that time was Vice Chairman of the Equal Employment Opportunity Commission. Dr. Holcomb, knowing of this biography, wrote me the following in 1972 from his office in Washington:

> When I first met Fred Florence, I was an unknown Baptist pastor, serving an unknown residential congregation. In a visit with him, we began talking about Dallas. In a matter of minutes, I realized that I was in the presence of truly a great citizen. His capabilities for humanitarian interests were just as great as his genius as a financier.
>
> He began inviting me to serve on various boards and committees. As time moved on, we shared some personal and political friendships. He was highly regarded by the late speaker, Sam Rayburn, and former President Lyndon B. Johnson. It was through Fred Florence that I became acquainted with the late Karl Hoblitzelle.
>
> The story that I wanted to tell relates to the time after Fred Florence developed a critical illness. I am certain that he was aware that he was not going to recover. On his own initiative, he requested his nurse to get a particular clerk on the telephone at Neiman-Marcus. Mr. Florence asked the clerk to bring to his hospital room five or six of the most colorful, impressive, and expensive lounging robes. Needless to say, the clerk thought the robes were for Mr.

265

Florence. Within a matter of hours, they appeared at the hospital with the robes. Mr. Florence selected an Italian red silk lounging robe. He then smiled and said, "Please send this robe to Luther Holcomb." He placed a card in the robe which read, "may you have joy in the wearing of this robe," signed Fred Florence.

I shall never forget the day that I received the robe. It gives some insight into the nature of this great man.

Helen says that those who received these gifts, which they opened on Christmas, the day Fred died, said that it touched them more than they could express. All said that they would treasure this gift from a dear friend who, even on his death bed, was thinking first of others.

* * * * * *

Fred and Dr. W. A. Criswell, pastor of the First Baptist Church of Dallas, were good friends. The First Baptist Church has the largest membership of any Baptist church in the world. In the Florence family archives I found the following letter from Dr. Criswell to Fred, apparently written to thank him for a gift or for something he had done, and dated March 22, 1958:

266

To the incomparable friend, Mr. Florence:
I shall not try to thank you; words cannot contain the gratitude I feel in my heart.
Beyond any way you could ever know I am humbled by the love and friendship of so great and so good a man as you. You deserve the marvelous world-wide reputation you possess. As the Queen of Sheba said of kingly Solomon: "The half hath not been told." You excel even the praise of your dearest friends.
God bless you forever.

Your other pastor,
W. A. Criswell

Vignettes

The following is an excerpt from a sermon given by Dr. Criswell on the occasion of his 25th anniversary with the First Baptist Church of Dallas, on Sunday, October 5, 1969, in which he speaks about his friendship with Fred:

Fred Florence, the President of the Republic National Bank, a Jew, was one of the dearest, sweetest friends I have ever had in my life. Every year he would give us all a great deal of money, and he would give it to us for things we wanted to do on a vacation or going on a trip to buy something. Well, we took that money that Mr. Fred Florence gave us, and in order to have something to show for it, we bought the beautiful things out there in our home. One day while he was still alive I sat down and figured up how much Fred Florence had given us, and at that time it was more than $20,000, and he kept on giving. I just was overwhelmed by the friendship of Fred Florence.

Upon a day he called me to his office in the bank and I sat down by his side, and he said, "Young pastor, let's do something." And he called me "Pastor." He said, "Let's do something." He said, "Let's build the most beautiful Baptist Church in the world. Let's do it." And he said, "I will help you get the money; we'll do it!" Well, he had access to many, many foundations and he had access in friendship to many rich men. He said, "Let's astonish the world with the beauty and the glory of that cathedral. Let's build the most beautiful Baptist Church in the world." He said, "Now, of course, I am interested in the Church and I am interested in you, but I am also interested in Dallas and to have a Church house like that in the City of Dallas would be a glory to our city. Let's do it." What Mr. Florence wanted to do was to go out somewhere in a large acreage where we could have lawns and yards and all kinds of shrubbery and landscaping, and there in the center of it build this glorious and spacious cathedral, the greatest Baptist Church in the world. "Well," I said, "Mr. Florence, I don't know how to reply because we've been downtown and we've committed ourselves to this ministry downtown."

In his sermon, Dr. Criswell goes on to say that he made the prayerful decision to keep the church downtown. Fred's offer, although not accepted, is illustrative of his desire to build a better city for people of all faiths. In the ten years since this sermon, the First Baptist Church, with Dr. Criswell still the pastor, has continued to expand its services to its parishioners.

* * * * * *

Jake L. Hamon, Jr., independent Oilman and outstanding Dallas citizen, was another good friend of Fred's. Jake is the only independent oilman ever elected president of the American Petroleum Institute. I visited him in his spacious and beautiful office in the Republic Bank tower, where we discussed Fred's role in oil financing, and also some of Jake's personal recollections of their friendship. He told me the following story which vividly portrays Fred's character and independence. Although ever conscious of pleasing the customer, Fred did what he knew was right regardless of the consequences. Taking some liberties for brevity, I quote Jake:

268

> I was a big wheel at that time in the Republican Party. Eisenhower was running for office for the first time and was coming to Dallas. I was delegated the task of getting some prominent people to sit on the platform. Fred, and Ben Wooten, who was head of the First National Bank, agreed. General Eisenhower was a world-renowned figure. Of course, it was incidental that he was running for office. But when the Democrats at some of the correspondent banks got wind of this, they started calling Ben and telling him to

decline. So Ben called me and said, "Well, Jake, I've got to get off this whole thing, because I'm being criticized. I'm ostensibly a Democrat, and I'm being criticized." "Well," I said, "that's fine." So then I got hold of Fred and I said, "Now, in all fairness, I got Ben Wooten but he got off on account of the fact that he didn't want to be in the posture of supporting a Republican." Fred said, "Well, I told you I'd be on the platform, and it doesn't make any difference to me if *everybody* gets off, I think the General is deserving of recognition, and if I lose a few million dollars in deposits, why, I'll still stay on the platform."

* * * * * *

While reviewing Fred's file in the bank's public relations department, I found a typewritten copy of a biographical sketch of Fred, with a signature at the end, "Sincerely, Anderson M. Baten," and dated May 18, 1936. I found the abundance of adjectives rather amusing, and concluded that Mr. Baten must have had access to a Thesaurus and, furthermore, that he really admired Fred. Even though I was unable at the time to find out anything at all about Anderson Baten, why this article had been written, or whether it had ever been published, I was planning to quote this sketch in the book. In spite of his exaggeration and the adjective-laden style, Baten actually characterized Fred extremely well.

Some time later, one of my assistants who knew about the "Baten biography," as we called it, brought me a slim volume entitled *Slang from Shakespeare*, by Anderson M. Baten, that she had found in a box of old books in her attic. So Anderson M. Baten was a published author! This knowledge prompted a further search, which met with success at the McDermott Library at the University of Texas-Dallas. Here I found a book entitled *The Philosophy*

269

of Success, published in 1936, which contains the biographical sketch of Fred. The book is autographed by Anderson M. Baten to Waverly Briggs with the insciption, "A man with a prodigious vocabulary, a brilliant mind—a vigorous American." Waverly Briggs was the head of the Trust Department of the First National Bank for many years and a very good friend of Fred.

The dust jacket of *The philosophy of Success* includes a history of the author written by Hilton R. Greer of *The Dallas Journal*, one of the Dallas newspapers at the time. Anderson M. Baten was born in Brenham, Texas, on January 14, 1888, and was the great-grandson of Ephraim Williams, who endowed Williams College. Greer says that Anderson Baten was unique, and that in some respects his record and achievements were unrivaled. In the year 1926 Baten accomplished the incredible task of reading through the *Encyclopedia Britannica* from the first word in the first volume to the last word in the last. It is estimated that there were 55 million words on 55,000 pages. Baten also wrote a complete *Dictionary of Shakespeare*, the only complete lexicon of the sort ever attempted, containing 100,000 articles, definitions, and references, 1,500,000 words, and representing six years of research and recording. Apparently my original conclusion that Baten had access to a Thesaurus was not too far astray—he probably had read every single word of it!

270

The front cover of *The Philosophy of Success* asserts that it contains "the inside life story of 725 human beings who struggled through prodigious labors, gigantic handicaps, abject poverty, and sore affliction to success." Of course, one might argue the point of whether Fred actually struggled through 'gigantic handicaps" or "sore affliction"—but be that as it may, Fred is certainly in good company in this book. Included among the "725 human beings" are the likes of Napoleon, William Shakespeare, Louis Pasteur, Henry Ford, Helen Keller, Abraham Lincoln, and Joan of Arc. There are also several other Dallasites, including Fred's father-in-law, David Lefkowitz. The following is a portion of what Anderson Baten wrote about Fred:

> Everything about him is speed, spurt, spirit and rush—one thing remarkable about Fred's speeches: they are short, fast, logical and to the point, they are bubbling over with faith, confidence and enthusiasm. Everything about him is brevity, terseness, directness, simplicity. His enthusiasm is transmittable, contagious and catching.
>
> His life story is as thrilling as the Arabian nights. The story is almost unbelievable. It is even sensational.

Baten continues to accelerate, leaving little uncovered:

> He is cordial, sincere, hearty, friendly, warm, courteous and obliging, a doer and a performer. What he says is keen, piercing and pointed. In his thoughts he is ahead, in advance, and all the time going forward. He makes the first move. In his life there is no blemish, taint, flaw, deformity or scar. He does not boast, brag or vaunt. He is not an egoist, braggart, or pretender, not cold-blooded, ruthless, heartless, or merciless. He has breadth, width, and spaciousness. Caution, discretion, forethought, calculation, deliberation and foresight guide him through life.
>
> He never loses his calmness, self-possession or presence of mind. There is a briskness, liveliness and bouyancy about his personality. He has color, glow, flush, and luminosity, is a gentleman of courtesy, politeness, refinement, and breeding. Gallantry, chivalry and good manners are part of his genuineness.
>
> He is at home when a transaction becomes perplexity, intricacy, entanglement, quandary, dilemma or a Gordian Knot!

271

The Texas Banker

I have seen him rushing down the street—everything about him radiating power, strength, intensity, life, and animation. He carries with him fire, punch, backbone, vim, and mettle.

He is a living, and driving force, and a human dynamo, working for the interest of humanity.

His briskness, hustle, alertness and quickness stimulate, invigorate, activate, excite, pep up, magnetize and electrify those with whom he comes in contact.

He has an immediate apprehension of what is going on.

His direct perception, his innate knowledge, his insight, his intuitiveness has been the marvel of the banking world.

He keeps up with the pulse beat the throb of the world.

Florence has no pomp, veneer of tinsel about his personality. He knows nothing of haughtiness or vain-glory.

He has a certain assurance and precision. He is a man sometimes of abrupt decision, demanding sure results. His life has always been a picture of optimism when all about him was despair. A sort of clairvoyant instinct seems to dictate his decisions. He is the epitome of enthusiasm, aggressiveness and dynamic activity. He is a man with a world of self-confidence. He meets you with agreeable frankness.

Fred Florence has the agility of a tiger in his movements. His judgment is comprehensive and accurate. In what he says he is decided and definite. He comes to conclusions quickly. His directness and his simplicity in describing business matters is well known.

Energy is stamped on every feature of his face, and his eloquence is most convincing. He has an enthusiastic admiration for all that is good. He has an extraordinary rapidity for working out complicated business entanglements. He is as far-sighted as the eagle. He has a fierce ambition, and determination to serve mankind. Generosity is deep seated in him. He is a giant of action. He carries his ship by dead reckoning and sea instinct.

Florence carries the KEY of action. He will cling to his resolve with all the tenacity of a bull dog.

272

Florence exudes *SELF CONFIDENCE!*
He has fought through insurmountable obstacles to success. He has a raven's instinct for scenting out happenings. He has an invincible determination, and an inexhaustible energy. He has an immense endurance and beaver-like driving power. He has an unbreakable will power; yet he is a friend to everybody.

Florence is a light-ray of *GENEROSITY!*
He is action itself! He has made his way by dint of sternest self-denial. He moves with bewildering rapidity. He never feels fatigue. He is utterly courageous in planning, and carrying out his objective. His energies are stimulated by opposition. His driving power is abnormal.

One of his greatest virtues is *COMMON SENSE!*
Florence's mind lays fierce hold upon whatever interests him. His name is synonymous with energy, ambition, faith, labor and enthusiasm. His personality radiates an electrifying influence. His thoughts flash like lightning. His whole being gives forth a fine perfume of health and strength, and intelligence. There seems to be no limit to this man's inexhaustible power. He has a certain intense sureness about everything. He has intense vigor, and eager intelligence. He is familiar with all the intricacies of banking and business.

Florence is the very picture of *ENTHUSIASM!*
He is another name for *OPPORTUNITY!*
In his walk he is lively, vivacious, vigorous and forcible. He has a magnetic personality. This man is of mathematical exactness and precision.

273

He has a refreshing and invigorating handshake that carries evidence of sincere friendship. He has that indefinable charm of mixing with all classes of humanity.

In the banking world he has a certain self-assured supernatural knowledge.

When the occasion is piled high with difficulties Florence rises with the occasion. The resources of his power are boundless.

He is the very symbol of invincibility. There is something rare, and boundless in his bearing.

He has two-fold vigor, uncanny precision and an intuition that functions perfectly.

Fred Farrel Florence has the *COMMON TOUCH!*

If this is what Anderson Baten thought of Fred in 1936, I wonder what he would have written based on the full history of Fred's activities 25 years later.

CHAPTER XV
THE WORLD TRIP

In 1960, nearly forty years had slipped by, during which time Fred had served three masters: his family, his stockholders and employees; and, perhaps most important, humanity. Approaching his sixty-ninth birthday, in the best of health and with the same drive and vigor described in the preceding pages, he was persuaded by his close friends Joe C. and Peggy Thompson, with insistence from Helen, to take a real vacation. This was not the first vacation the Florences had taken, of course - over the years they had taken vacations with the children and had even been to Europe - but this trip was to be much longer and more extensive, a real chance to "get away from it all." Mr. Thompson was known as "Jodie" to his close friends and associates. Jovial and big-hearted, he was liked and admired by the elite and the not-so-elite wherever his path took him. Jodie, like Fred, had developed a highly successful business enterprise from its infancy. His vast food company, the Southland Corporation, today is the largest chain of retail stores (in number) of any company in the world. In 1978, they had over 5,000 company-owned outlets and over 2,000 franchised; and they are still growing. Jodie and Peggy, who was fun to be with and very compatible with Helen, were a perfect team to go around the world with the Florences.

The story of the Florence-Thompson trip taxed Helen's memory somewhat, but my research was easy because Jodie enjoyed letter writing and, as I have done on numerous trips, wrote one letter home which his secretary typed and mailed to family and close friends. During their ten-week trip, which began on March 21, 1960, Jodie wrote twenty-nine letters, all by hand. On their return, it was decided to put these letters into book form so that he could enjoy his memorable trip again and again, simply by reading the descriptive letters he wrote as he toured many fascinating, far-away lands. The three Thompson sons, knowing how their parents had enjoyed this trip, arranged to have it documented by having a few copies of an unusual book prepared. This large (18" x 13") beautiful scrapbook containing 46 pages plus 14 full-page silk screen illustrations is entitled *Around the World with the Thompsons*. The pages were specially printed, and the art work, or what I have called illustrations, is so unusual that it warrants further description. The artist, Jose Amador, Jr., who was 31 years old and lived in Miami, Florida, had already earned a fine reputation for portraits of famous people in Cuba and also famous Americans who had visited Cuba before the Castro regime. Amador painted fourteen characteristic scenes to introduce the letters. The pictures illustrate a Hawaiian beach with the island's colorful red ginger plants, a Japanese pagoda, the junks of Hong Kong, the dancing 276 girls in Thailand, and continue with appropriate illustrations for most of the countries the Florences and Thompsons visited. After Thailand, they went on to Ceylon, India, Lebanon, and Egypt. At this point, the Florences flew to Athens, Greece, before going to Israel, because in 1960 Jews could not go from an Arab country into Israel. The Thompsons went from Egypt to Syria and then to Israel because, being Catholic, this restriction did not apply to them. The couples were reunited in Jerusalem and continued on to Turkey, Switzerland, Germany, and France, ending in London before flying home.

Robert G. Storey, who had recently retired as Dean of the S.M.U. Law School and was a close friend of both couples, made many of the special arrangements that made this trip such a once-in-a-lifetime experience. Storey had been Executive Trial Counsel at the Nuremberg trials under Robert Jackson, Justice of the U. S. Supreme Court. Dean Storey was also the founder of the Southwestern Legal Foundation, of which Fred was a trustee and the treasurer from its beginning. When the Dean heard of the proposed trip, he encouraged Fred to make it so that he could get a firsthand picture of international affairs, because as we all know, they very materially affect our domestic economy. When the trip was finally set, the Dean saw it as an excellent opportunity for him to repay Fred for many favors; so with the help of the American Bar Association, he arranged for the foursome to meet many people of importance in diplomatic circles and saw to it that they received special treatment not available for the average tourist.

Throughout the trip, the Thompsons and Florences were entertained by many of our government representatives. Flowers were sent to their rooms in virtually every hotel. In Japan, they were entertained by Ambassador Douglas MacArthur and Mrs. MacArthur, and in Hong Kong they were received at the United States Consulate. In Ceylon, they were first invited for cocktails at noon by the Consul for Finance. Apparently, the tourists passed muster, because they were then asked for dinner at the Consulate that same evening. The Ambassador was out of the country, but his charming wife was hostess. Going on to India, they had lunch with Mrs. Ellsworth Bunker (Mr. Bunker, the Ambassador, was in Washington). Later that same day, they had dinner with a Mr. Brown who was the Charge D'Affairs. In Egypt, they visited the very personable Ambassador G. Frederick Reinhardt and his attractive wife, and had

277

cocktails with the Lonegraves, a couple from the Embassy. To further give my readers an idea of making a trip around the world with so many people to see, as well as the wish to have an enjoyable vacation, I quote from one of Jodie's letters regarding their visit to Israel:

> Because of Fred's prominence, the Secretary of Treasury, the Head of the Hebrew University, the head of this and that—were waiting in line for a visit with him. Poor fellow, he must be perfectly exhausted. There are now four nights past 2:30, plus last evening at the American Embassy, that we have been up. The young and personable Ambassador, Ogden Reed, whose family owned for generations the New York Herald Tribune, invited us for a place-card dinner...fun—interesting—grand people with such interesting pasts.

One Sunday evening while writing this story, Helen and I watched the Mike Wallace *60 Minutes* program on television. Twenty minutes of this telecast was about Teddy Kolleck, the Mayor of Jerusalem. At the conclusion of the program, Helen remarked that Teddy had put on some weight since she had met him in 1960. Naturally, I wanted details about this.

278   At the time Fred and Helen were in Jerusalem, Teddy Kolleck was an aide to Prime Minister Ben-Gurion. Israel was then, and still is, very much interested in selling bonds and receiving contributions. The Prime Minister, knowing that Fred was not only one of our country's few important Jewish bankers but also very influential in Jewish philanthropies, assigned Teddy Kolleck to take care of the Florences while they were in Israel. Teddy arranged for Helen to have a tour of the city and kept Fred busy meeting all the bigwigs of the country. In addition, Teddy took them to his very modest home for cocktails. Coincident-

ally, Mike Wallace was also there. Helen was fascinated with Teddy's artifacts, priceless gems from excavations in Canaan, displayed in a large bookcase against one wall.

One afternoon when Fred and Teddy were doing something without her, Helen visited a shop near the hotel. She said that the proprietor showed very little interest in her. The next morning, a messenger brought her a gift from Teddy—a cruet two and one-eighth inches high, very beautiful, in perfect condition, and over 2,500 years old. It is now in our bookcase. Later that morning, when Helen visited the same shop, the owner bowed and scraped. He knew (how, she will never know) that she had received this gift from Kolleck.

The Thompsons, who had been to Damascus and had spent several days visiting religious landmarks and shrines, rejoined the Florences on their last day in Jerusalem. Teddy Kolleck had recommended a fine restaurant for the four of them for their last evening before going on to Tel Aviv the next day. Apparently, while they were having dinner in the restaurant, Teddy Kolleck was attending a dinner honoring American Ambassador Ogden Reed, and Teddy told Reed of Fred's presence in Israel. Helen recalls that while they were sitting at the table in the little restaurant Teddy had recommended, Fred was called to the telephone. The caller was an aide to Ogden Reed, who invited them to dinner at the Ambassador's home in Tel Aviv the next evening. Fred explained that they had traveling companions who would be with them in Tel Aviv, and that they would not accept without them. The aide, with apologies, said that it was a seated dinner, and that it would not be possible to have more than the planned number of guests; so Fred declined the invitation. The next morning—very, very early, Helen says—Ogden Reed personally called Fred and said that he would be delighted if all four of them would come. Fred

279

had sat on the board of MGM with the Ambassador, and they had become good friends.

Helen recalls that the dinner at the Ogden Reeds' was at individual tables for eight. The guests numbered about 35, and after dinner, there was entertainment and dancing. Helen sat next to Dr. Sapir, who was the Secretary of Commerce and Transportation. He asked her if she had been out to the Weitzman Institute (Fred was the Chairman of the Danciger Foundation in Fort Worth, Texas, which had given a great deal of money to the Weitzman Institute in Israel). Helen told Dr. Sapir that she really hadn't had time to see much of anything because in Jerusalem the various officials had kept Fred so terribly busy. When Dr. Sapir learned that Fred had not been to the Weitzman Institute, he immediately said that this must be remedied. Helen replied that she was afraid this would be out of the question because the four of them were leaving the next morning at seven o'clock for Istanbul. She recalls that he said, "Think nothing of it. I am Minister of Commerce and Transportation, and that plane will not take off until I am ready for it to do so." He then got up and went over to Fred, and arranged to pick him up at five o'clock the next morning, and to drive him to Haifa or somewhere near Haifa where the Weitzman Institute is located. Although the invitation included Helen, she had developed a high temperature and felt very ill, and therefore could not go. Fred made apologies for her and went with Dr. Sapir, while Helen and the Thompsons went to the airport later to get a bite of breakfast before the seven o'clock flight. As the time grew closer and closer to seven, Helen began rather anxiously to look around for Fred, and finally found him and Dr. Sapir in a private area having a leisurely breakfast. Dr. Sapir made his promise good and held the plane.

Jodie wrote from Istanbul, Turkey, about the advantages of having connections in high places:

280

The World Trip

How wonderful it is to be an American. The telephone rang, a Miss Carp stated the Ambassador had sent her to do what she could about our stay in Istanbul. The Ambassador is out of town. I hurriedly descended and found her. I was informed there is no whisky during the Martial Law, but the Ambassador had, at his disposal, the American P.X. No money can change hands in public, so to the washroom—in a secret envelope I put the money. I felt like I was passing the Hope Diamond around—such secrecy. The Ambassador, or Consul General, has offered us the launch of our Government for a trip up the Bosphorus...

My observation is that these two couples met more people whom they knew from Dallas and other parts of our country, than anyone else ever has on a trip around the world. I know from my own experiences that one does meet friends from time to time; but from reading the Thompson diary, it appears that on this trip people showed up practically everywhere, and they seemed to have had a remarkably good time with everyone they met.

In fact, there is no doubt that both couples had a marvelous time throughout the trip. Probably the most refreshing thing I learned from reading Jodie's letters was that Fred could and did shed his banker's image and often, as the saying goes, "let down his hair." Jodie was a good—or if you wish, a bad—influence on Fred, or maybe he just enjoyed loosening him up. In Japan the two men had a delightful time going to the baths where, Jodie reports, they had a massage by attractive Japanese girls about eighteen to twenty-two years old; and of course, they were fascinated by being bathed by young girls, which, Jodie, reports apologetically, is the *custom* in Japan. After lunch one day in Kyoto, Japan, Jodie and Fred each had a manicure administered by *three* girls. That evening the foursome took in two night clubs.

You should see them (the clubs)—music wonderful and continuous—marvelous floor show. The Geisha and Maiko girls working. It was most fun. To bed at 1 A.M., even though Fred wasn't ready.

Later in the trip, in Cairo, Jodie wrote similarly about taking in the town, visiting several night clubs:

...even at 2:30 A.M. Fred wanted to go to another. Belly dancing was under study that evening—so much more interesting than the mosques we visited this morning.

It seems as if Fred was almost like a different person on a trip like this. Helen has told me that some years earlier on a trip with the Fenton Bakers (he owned the Baker Hotel in Dallas), Fred and Lou (Mrs. Baker), one morning at 5 A.M. in Havana, decided to take a walk and got their kicks from turning over garbage cans. Rum has always been an effective drink!

Scotch works well, too, as Jodie wrote from the Kawana Hotel in Izu, Japan:

We have just had dinner Japanese style—take off your shoes—sit on your feet. Our dinner was Sukiyaki (meat). It was eaten entirely with chopsticks—fun—I was like a 16 year old girl—laughed until my face hurt. Fred, after two stiff scotches, would get so excited with a successful bite and then would go completely to pieces and would have to have another complete lesson from the attractive and beautiful Japanese girl.

282

Apparently both Fred and Jodie were delighted by the beauty of the Oriental girls. Helen tells me that in Hong Kong they would ride back and forth between the two portions of the city on the ferries, and that there were always very attractive girls on these ferries who were "available" to any men who desired their services. I could not find out from her if, by any chance, these services were used by either. I must assume that they at least had a good time *looking*, or they would not have continued to spend their money (the fare was ten cents first class, five cents second class) to ride the ferry!

When they arrived in Hong Kong, the Thompsons were greeted with a package from their sons which contained at least a dozen cans of chili, one of the favorite dishes for all Texans. Jodie was particularly fond of this, and was very pleased to receive this fine shipment, including a large can filled with his favorite crackers. It came at an opportune time, because it so happened that at the Peninsula Hotel, they had a kitchenette with a stove.

I might report here that Jodie had been having some back trouble, so when they left Hong Kong, he persuaded Fred to carry the carton with the remaining chili and crackers. In Bangkok and Ceylon, the hotel chefs readily agreed to let Jodie cook a can or two of the chili for his own consumption. When they got to India, however, he had difficulty because the Indian religion does not permit them to eat beef, and the chefs in the hotel did not want to let Jodie cook something which they would not cook themselves. Helen believes that Jodie told them it was 283 something totally different, so that they would let him go ahead and make his favorite dish.

Remember that all this time, from Hong Kong to Bangkok to Ceylon to India, Fred was carrying the carton of chili and crackers. The story goes that when they finally got to Rome, Fred issued an ultimatum: they would either eat what was left, he said, or they would throw it away, because he had no intention of carrying chili any further!

Even the most delightful vacation has its share of difficulties, both minor and major, and this trip was no exception. Some of them were rather amusing. It appears that by the time they got to the Miyako Hotel in Kyoto, they were quite acclimated to sitting on the floor for a meal; but here, when they were shown a room with only a comforter to make *sleeping* on the floor a luxury (and the only bath three floors below), Jodie reports that he "shouted for Fred." (Jodie and Fred took turns being "manager" and this was Fred's week.) After some negotiating, they finally were assigned rooms with all the modern conveniences—like beds.

In one letter from India, Jodie wrote that

> The main purpose (of the letter) is to describe the dilemma of Fred. Upon arrival in Colombo, I happened to be the banker for the week. You already know that we trade each Monday A.M. and put up $100.00 at a time. Well, when I went to the bank window in the hotel to get some rupees, I was told that upon leaving I could not cash them in for American money. This immediately threw the challenge to me that I must come out even, and that's *hard* to do with the tipping that must take place upon leaving. But, Fred, in the meantime, had run out of American dollars, had only $100.00 travelers checks and was busted—absolutely no rupees, no dollars in his pocket, sweating plane delays, broke and no telephone—a nervous wreck. Helen, Peggy and I had a lot of fun laughing about his nervousness. It all passed quickly upon arrival here, for he got a travelers check cashed and was lending me 100 rupees out of sympathy. We continue to giggle, laugh until it hurts.

284

One experience they had was *not* so amusing. It happened on March 31 at the Grand Hotel in Osaka, Japan. Jodie's letter describing it was mailed from Istanbul on May

11 with this explanation: "I did not mail you the attached letter from Osaka on purpose, but now that we're almost home and everything is alright, I did want you to know what happened."

With Helen's help, I am paraphrasing the report. Peggy was in bed with a very bad cold. Jodie left their room on the twelfth floor, which was about six rooms down the hall from Fred and Helen, whom he was supposed to meet in the bar for cocktails with a couple from Memphis. Not surprisingly, the man represented a good Republic account. As Jodie left his room he encountered two Japanese girls, yelling—and the smoke told that the hotel was on fire. The Florences had, at that moment, stepped into the hall. The girls pointed to the end of the hall, the Florences ran there, and Jodie went back to his room to get Peggy up. At the end of the hall the Florences found an enclosed fire stairs which they descended in record time. Imagine their panic when, having run down twelve flights of stairs, they found the door locked. They were trapped in a burning building. Hoping that one of the doors on another floor might be open, they ran most of the way back up, but all doors opened only from the outside. Exhausted, scared to death, they again ran to the bottom level where they each removed a shoe and, while screaming "Help," banged on the door and tried to push it open. Fortunately, someone heard them and opened the door. Eureka! the fire was out; but the hotel was completely filled with smoke. Worried about Peggy and Jodie, Fred quickly recovered his equilibrium and rushed to phone their room.

The Thompsons had an even more hair raising (if possible) experience. I quote it in Jodie's own words:

> We—poor us—Babe's (Peggy's) illness found her without clothes and somewhat under dope. We were too

285

frightened to think. Finally, we did get out to the steps—the smoke ran us back—so we closed the door to our room—smoke from the underfloors coming by our window outside. No chance from the 12th floor, so we decided again to try it, but with towels. This is what almost got us—four floors down, couldn't go further—to get back—please only to get back to the 12th—stumbling, praying, we did, but the call was close. There were moments when I thought we were gone. Then the minutes seemed like hours—crying, praying, looking agonizingly out the window at the safe and well people. Finally, Fred was able to get to us.

The elevators were running and the fire was out, but the smoke was still so intense that everyone breathed through wet towels. Fortunately, the further experiences of these globe-trotters were not as harrowing as the fire in Osaka.

The Florences and Thompsons included in their travels some very interesting, out-of-the-way places that most people miss. For example, in Ceylon (now Sri Lanka), many world travelers stop only at the capitol and principal city, Colombo. The Florences and Thompsons also journeyed to Nuwara Eliya, a town of about 32,000 population, 72 miles inland and 6,000 feet up in the mountains. It was cold, whereas Colombo was hot. Portions of Jodie's voluminous report are typical of the way the two couples enjoyed their travels and describe a little about this interesting side trip:

> We saw for the first time rubber trees—miles and miles of them being tapped for the raw fluid. Then tapioca trees—always loved it as a child. Saw gum trees, coconuts by the thousands, but this trip mainly is through the tea country which made Ceylon. There are a million or more acres of tea shrubs. They grow 4' high. Only 30-50 leaves are taken from each plant each week—thousands of workers.

On the way up we saw a logging area—the use of elephants to load the trucks with large 20' - 40' logs—quite an art the elephant does have, and mechanical in shoving it forward on the truck.

Walked around, through the town, through the early morning market place. The rhythm of the chants of those selling their goods—the noise of the crows and birds all strange sounds.

Fred and I rode on an elephant after lunch near Kandy. They only work at the logging camp until noon and come to the river to bathe and rest—was fun. Went through a tea factory—do you want to know anything about Pekoe Tea? We are authorities. Then we saw the most beautiful park in the world—it should be with 200 inches of rain a year. Saw many, many kinds of flowers—trees—has more than any place in the world.

No matter how much fun they were having, Jodie never forgot that he was the head of his company, and Fred certainly did not forget about the bank. In one letter, Jodie wrote, "Fred and I talk enough business to keep each others's mind from growing rusty," and added, "Fred also assured me that there would be plenty of money for the Southland Company." In a way, it seems to me that Jodie never really left his office. He had an almost unbelievable volume of correspondence, and in his letters home, he gave many instructions and also made many suggestions that he thought might be helpful to his management. Both he and Fred made numerous phone calls from all over the world, and apparently Fred made even more calls than Jodie. In one place, Jodie refers to a call Fred made from Beirut which cost $160.00. They ran into a problem in Hong Kong, where the telephone exchange was closed during business hours in Dallas because of the time difference, and Jodie wrote:

> Fred is so upset—he was so glad that Leland Dupree was in the bank at 7:00 a.m. yesterday.

Another time Jodie reported:

> Fred is calling the bank at 11:30 tonight—8:30 a.m. Dallas time. Yes, he wants to be sure everyone is on time, so he calls early.

Helen has told me that the phone calls from these far-off lands were usually appointment calls, and that there were some times when the operator called Leland Dupree to be at the bank at some ungodly hour, such as 3:00 a.m., and he was there to receive the call.

Apparently when Jodie got to Hong Kong, where he knew things were inexpensive and where he knew that goods came from all over the world on a tax-free basis, he went wild. Jodie was an extremely generous man, and decided that he would like to bring some of the beautiful things that he saw in Hong Kong back to his family, some friends, and particularly to those people who had worked hard for him and were continuing to make his company a success. Under these circumstances, he wrote that he had bought material for 100 suits, and he also purchased eighteen vicuna and cashmere topcoats. In one letter he wrote: "Never was I more impractical, but it's such divine material, it's a job to keep up with my purchases," and in another letter: "How fine it is to have such good smart sons who make their Dad a lot of money." The bargains he found amazed him, and he wrote: I continue to feel we are saving money when I write a check."

Jodie was also pleased whenever they found a bargain in accommodations or meals. When they were in Tokyo at the prodigious Imperial Hotel, he sent a bill home with this comment:

288

The bill I am enclosing is for dinner last evening—8492 yen. At .003 cents each, it was only $25.00 for six people including drinks for Evelyn Lambert's party of five.*

Those were the good old days—this year friends returning from Tokyo have reported coffee as high as $2.50 a cup! Throughout the trip, shopping was as important as sightseeing—for all of them, but especially for Jodie—and from the time they were in Hong Kong until the last day in London, the search never ceased. From London, Jodie wrote:

> We bought like mad—ties—perfumes—ranch pants (our ranch foreman). Babe an exciting raincoat and loads of wonderful things from Switzerland. Our Istanbul whiskey is about to run out, at $2.50 a litre (about 1½ quarts). Really makes you think you should drink twice as much—you are saving so much money.

There seems to be nothing in Jodie's notes about any purchases which were made by Fred, but Helen tells me that Fred did make numerous purchases, although on a much smaller scale than Jodie. Helen tells me that Fred got a tremendous kick out of attempting to buy at the very best price. Everyone knows that in the Orient, and in the Near East, it is customary to pay a price considerably below that which was first asked; and judging from my own experiences, I know that Fred had lots of fun beating the merchants down to the price they would accept. No one ever knows whether they have reached the bottom price, but at least they have the satisfaction of knowing they did not pay the ridiculous price that was first asked.

289

*Evelyn Lambert is the widow of Joe Lambert, who established one of the largest and best known landscape firms in the Southwest.

All travelers remember one or two occurrences or experiences about a trip more vividly than anything else. Helen got a real kick out of telling me the following story which starts in Ceylon and ends in Switzerland. Our tourists, like most, visited hotel shops. In Colombo they visited the hotel jewelry store, about which Jodie wrote:

> Fred still looks for more jewels for that sweet Helen. While I'm certainly not the enthusiast, I have a feeling that something kinda big and on the down side is about to happen to my bank account. My love has never had much, however, so if we find something real good looking she'll have it. Saw a $5,000 star sapphire. Man wanted us to take it, have it appraised, and if it wasn't worth $10,000 in United States to return it, no money down—kinda tempting.

In addition to the sapphire, there was a catseye which intrigued Helen. She wanted Fred to buy it for a ring for himself. No purchase was made at that time because Fred just didn't want the catseye and Jodie did not want to buy the sapphire without expert advice.

Helen says that from the time they left Ceylon, Fred bugged Jodie about passing up a real bargain. Jodie wrote:

> When we had been away four or five days from Ceylon, Peggy and Fred kept wishing they had those stones—the dark blue sapphire for Peggy and the catseye for Helen.* The suggesting of cabling an offer met with immediate acceptance, and the price and date of meeting in Rome made firm. How was he to get the stones to Rome if he accepted the lower price? His reply to our cable was vague. But, upon arrival in Rome, we knew pretty well the stones had left

*Probably meant "for Helen to give to Fred."

Ceylon and were in Italy. We missed connections with Mr. Savage at the Excelsior in Rome. He was the courier. We received five cables and sent five cables before fixing and agreeing upon the date and place of passing the jewels. It sounds—it is a story worthy of an Alfred Hitchcock TV show.

Helen says they finally made connections in Zurich, where Jodie bought the sapphire. Peggy still has it and it is worth many times its cost. The catseye was 43 karat and the selling price was $3,000. Fred decided not to buy. Helen says that the catseye was a magnificent stone—worth a fortune today. This story pleased me immensely because I found it refreshing to know that even Fred Florence showed a little poor judgment at least *once* and missed out on a good deal.

After the two couples left Switzerland, they went to Munich, Germany, for the specific purpose of seeing the Passion Play at Oberammergau. For people like the Thompsons, who were very religious, this Passion Play is one of the great sights that one can see. I know this at first hand because I was fortunate enough to see it in 1922. The Passion Play, as I recall, at that time, at least, was only given each ten years; but since 1920 was such a short time after the war, I believe it was postponed until 1922.

When they left Munich, they visited Paris and then London, doing the same things that all tourists do in Paris and London. All of them had visited both cities before, and apparently they did very little this time other than to visit the shops where they bought many things. They also continued to meet people, as Jodie wrote from London:

291

> Our luncheon with the directors of the largest bank in Europe, Barclay's, was most interesting. Every place we have met important business men, bankers, embassy men. As a result, with a predetermined plan of asking many ques-

tions, we probably are about as well informed on the feelings of the people of Europe as the usual foreign correspondent.

Jodie's entire diary of the trip is well worth reading. It comments on customs, political problems, interesting sights, and things to buy; and although the trip lasted ten weeks, their activity in this comparatively short time is fantastic. How Jodie had time to write all that he did is miraculous. It was refreshing to find four people who were so compatible, and a pleasure to enjoy the doings of travelers who were not limited in their expenses. In numerous letters Jodie writes endearing words about his friends such as, 'Helen and Fred are so much fun to be with." The whole story clearly shows that Fred could and did relax and that he really could enjoy the fun things in life.

CHAPTER XVI
THE END OF THE STORY

1960 brought great happiness and great sorrow. Fred came back to Dallas with a light heart, revitalized, rested, and gratified with the knowledge that his staff had capably and successfully run the bank in his absence. The welcomes were warm. One often finds as much joy in the anticipation of a trip, and then telling about it, as afforded by the trip itself. Helen had taken some pretty poor pictures, but they enjoyed them. Neither Jodie nor Fred took any. The family, the faithful servants, and even Pepe the poodle participated in the glad reunion. Evelyn Whitman, Executive Director of the Southwestern Medical Foundation, told me that Dr. W. A. Criswell invited Fred to meet with his congregation at the First Baptist Church to tell about his visit to Israel. Mrs. Whitman recalled that before Fred spoke, the song "Around the World" from the movie, *Around the World in Eighty Days*, was played.

Apparently Fred never had any serious thought about retirement. One summer about twenty years before his death the family were enjoying a vacation in Santa Barbara, California. At that time he told Helen that when he retired he would like to own a small bank in a beautiful resort city so that he could continue his banking interest, enjoy more time with the family, and relieve the pressure, which, while its existence was never acknowledged, nevertheless was always present. Helen says that they even selected a bank and kidded about it someday being theirs. The purchase of a bank was just family talk, as that is where it started and ended.

Henry Wade, Dallas' highly respected veteran District Attorney, told me that one Sunday morning in late October on the seventeenth hole of the Lakewood Country Club, Fred told his fellow players that he didn't feel well. Henry suggested that he go back to the club house and relax. When the group finished the round, they found Fred quite miserable, so Morris Freedman, one of the foursome, and his cousin, with whom he rode to and from the club, took him home. Helen's story is that he rested that night and the next day went to the bank as usual. Fred did not consult his physician, Dr. W. Erwin Crow, because he never even wanted to admit fatigue.

However, a week or so later, Fred came home at his usual time and told Helen that he was just too tired to climb the steps upstairs. Later that evening Dr. Crow was summoned. He suspected hepatitis, so to be sure sent Fred to St. Paul Hospital for verification and then sought an additional opinion. Dr. Alfred W. Harris, who was considered a top diagnostician, also identified the disease as hepatitis, which is rarely fatal. Hepatitis is inflammation of the liver characterized by jaundice. Fred had never had any indication of a liver condition; in fact, he was always in excellent health and in sound physical condition. A few days later Fred was moved to Dallas' largest hospital, Baylor University Medical Center, where at that time isolation facilities were more adequate. Also, Dr. Harris' office was close by and he was on their staff.

294

Nineteen years is a long time to remember every detail, but Helen thinks that about ten days later Fred's condition worsened. They decided to summon a specialist from the Mayo Clinic in Rochester, Minnesota. The day he arrived Fred went into a hepatic coma which Helen says was the most horrifying experience in her life. Fred had to be constrained, and she was the only one who could quiet him. At this point, Dr. Boone Powell, the hospital administrator, gave Helen a room next to Fred's suite. Friends kept her busy on the telephone. Calls came from everywhere —Homer Livingston from Chicago, Governor Hobby from Houston, and others wanted to know his condition every day. The reports were discouraging and from Fred's remarks she gathered that her voice could be heard by him so she moved across the hall.

Everything known to medical science was tried. The Mayo doctor had upset Helen by referring to Fred as an "old man," a thought which had never occurred to her. Dr. Harris came to see Fred several times a day, often after midnight, and made himself available for a call at any time, but in spite of all efforts the comas came more often and December 25, on Christmas Day, the end came; it had claimed a wonderful man only seven weeks after his 69th birthday. Coincidentally, a few months later, his dear friend Jodie Thompson succumbed to cancer at the early age of 59.

Looking back, it is hard to believe that such a short time before, they were enjoying their trip and Jodie had written the following from Zurich:

Our golf game of yesterday afternoon was wonderful except Fred had to carry my clubs.* We couldn't play because of no caddies—he insisted. What a man—up and down hill. He's exactly ten years older than I. He always wants to go a bit more—never ready for a siesta—hates the bed. I'm always exhausted—take a siesta every chance I get. Some men are old at 50, some at 60. He won't be at 90! Never have I seen such energy—always ahead of us and walking.

295

* Jodie had a bad back.

It seems so ironic that less than a year after Jodie wrote this, both men were gone.

The funeral was held in the sanctuary of Temple Emanu-el where Fred had served continually as Treasurer and as a member of the temple board from before his marriage. This beautiful house of worship built on the land donated to the temple by Fred and Helen and now somewhat expanded is one of the most modern in the country and has a membership of 2,200 families. Fred was very proud of Temple Emanu-el. The temple holds approximately 2,000 people when they use it to capacity, only on the high holidays. That day, not only was every seat occupied, but people stood against the walls and some just waited outside. The solemn ceremony was conducted by his two long time friends, Rabbi Levi Olan and Bishop A. Frank Smith of the Methodist Church, and by his esteemed brother-in-law, Rabbi David Lefkowitz, Jr. Although my late wife Hortense and I attended, I can remember only vaguely the beautiful words that were said in eulogy. When in grief, one listens, but makes no effort to remember. Everyone knew that the high praise and commendation were inadequate and that his deeds and his spirit would live after him. He left a heritage that will live to eternity.

The thousands of mourners who attended Fred's final rites were only a handful of the multitude of his friends throughout the world who paid homage to this man, who had done so much for all humanity. Men and women in all walks of life, from every ethnic group, black, brown, and white, gentile and Jew, competitors as well as associates alike, made obeisance for this very unusual human being, whose life was snuffed out at a time when his plans and his acts still could have served so many so well.

It was not only the business community and Fred's personal friends who came to mourn. Those who served with him in his charities, those who waited on him at a club or in the bank, and many who never knew him except as a name, came to pay homage and last respects. Helen tells of a Dallas policeman who was proud of having sat on Fred's lap when he was a small boy in Rusk. His daddy knew Fred and at one time had taken him to the bank. When Fred died, he asked to be in the police procession.

Helen's nephew, Lewis Lefkowitz, Jr., was doing his residency at the Dallas V.A. Hospital when Fred died. Lewis Lefkowitz is now a successful research doctor at Vanderbilt. The morning of the funeral, Lewis asked another young doctor in residency to take over, as he was leaving to go to a funeral. The other said he would also like to get off to go to Fred Florence's funeral. Lewis asked him how he knew Fred Florence and learned that Fred had paid for his medical education. The young man had heard that Fred had on occasion paid tuition for deserving students. He had made an appointment with Fred, and after talking to him, Fred had agreed to provide the funds.

At the Temple the family sat away from the other mourners but where they could see them and the altar. Helen has often mentioned how impressed she was when she saw the multitude of nuns crying bitterly during the funeral rites. Fred had told Helen when he was dying that she should always take care of the "Angels of Mercy." 297

So often the widow of the departed receives gifts and telegrams after the funeral and is visited by her close friends and relatives, and then come the sad lonely hours and days. The flowers have wilted, the telegrams and condolence notes have been stored away, never again to see the light of day, or have been destroyed. Fred's friends were genuine and they loved Helen. In addition to the usual attentions bestowed upon a widow, there were many remembrances of an unusual nature. The boards of the various charitable, educational, civic, and business institutions with which he was associated passed memorial resolutions of sympathy, reviewing his activities and accomplishments. These memorials were written to be a permanent reminder for Helen, and to become a part of each institution's records. The words are sincere and are encased in beautiful leather binders, with Fred's name in gold letters. Many are exquisitely printed or are lettered in vivid colors. There were also many articles of praise and of sympathy in newspapers and magazines.

Helen has often told me how Fred never believed he was going to die when he lay stricken in the hospital. Very few were permitted to see Fred in the hospital during the last days of his illness. His faithful friend and capable associate, Leland Dupree, said that Fred told him a week or so before he died, "Leland, I've had a lot of time to think up here, and I've figured out a way we can double the bank in half the time I had planned." Leland told me that was the last thing Fred ever said to him.

299

300

301